D0586648

SEEING RED

SEEING
RED

TWELVE TUMULTUOUS YEARS IN WELSH RUGBY

ALUN CARTER
WITH
NICK BISHOP

MAINSTREAM
PUBLISHING

EDINBURGH AND LONDON

First published in Great Britain in 2008 by
MAINSTREAM PUBLISHING COMPANY
(EDINBURGH) LTD
7 Albany Street
Edinburgh EH1 3UG

ISBN 9781845964245

A catalogue record for this book is available
from the British Library

Typeset in Caslon and Franklin Gothic

Printed in Great Britain by
CPI Mackays of Chatham Ltd, Chatham, ME5 8TD

ACKNOWLEDGEMENTS

The professional life I have led over the last ten years would have been impossible without the love and support of Catherine. I would like to thank her for the fantastic job she does, continually helping both me and the little people, whilst acquiring a new role herself as English coordinator at Ysgol Erw'r Delyn special school in Penarth. I would like to thank Emma, Henry and Isabelle, who are a constant source of fun and an inspiration to all who know them.

To my parents, Brian and Gwyneth Carter, for their love. Standing in all sorts of weather next to Mel Picton, Derek Cleverley and Bill Gunter, making countless 'taxi' journeys to and from venues both near and far, and in general cheering from the sidelines, you have ignited a passion within me for Welsh rugby that burns deeply.

This adventure started five years ago after a conversation with Nick Bishop about Pontypool and the impact this rugby fraternity had on not only Welsh rugby, but rugby worldwide. More recent events provided the catalyst to bring it to fruition.

I would like to take the opportunity to thank many people for their help and time during this adventure and for their contribution no matter what.

First, to you, Nick. You have had to endure close to a hundred voice recordings, many of which have been dreary in tone; they have been 'magically' brought alive through the written word. In compiling this opus, you have shown the patience of Job. To both you and Mike Wadsworth – your support and friendship have been uplifting.

A big thank you to Mike Ruddock – your friendship has been and is highly valued. The commitment to voice your own thoughts and reflect on what was such a haunting time for you is remarkable. Hopefully, we can all move on now stronger and wiser for it, knowing the full detail of this explosive chapter in Welsh rugby.

Thank you to Cecil Duckworth and the opportunity to start anew at Worcester Warriors RFC. It is a vibrant club with a great future, and it is exciting to be part of it, along with some very professional people and fantastic supporters.

Second, to a group of people whose occupation is all-consuming and whose value and intellectual property have been lost to Welsh rugby at a high level: Kevin Bowring, Clive Griffiths, Allan Lewis, Lynn Howells and Chris Davey. And on the managerial front, Wayne Hall. Your contributions have been highly valued and eye-opening.

Thank you to both Steve Black and Iestyn Harris.

To Olivia and Graham Selby, whose love of local sporting history is infectious, Steve and Sinead Jackson, and Dave and Janet Hobby, whose attention to local knowledge is unwavering. To Glyn and Monica Jenkins, who cheer from afar. To Deb and Ian Carter, Clem and Bram. Ian, you helped give a sense of perspective with your humorous outlook on life.

On the Penarth front, to Ann and Glyn Davies, Margaret Hole, Mike Hole and Helen Wilkins, Jeff Hole, Paul Mumford, Jo Skilton, Walter and Shona Gear, the Phillips family, Rod, Pam, Danny and Joel, and Gordon and Abi Whyte.

To Peter Corrigan for helping to drag me into a whole new world whilst giving such sound advice. To Corris and Joan Thomas, Steve and Catherine Maggs, Sam and Olly Maggs, Simon Knott, Terry McCusker of Kilsby & Williams, Steve Williams (the 'Silver Fox'), Hugh Copping from Sportstat and Mike McNamee. To Trevor and Peggy James.

Thanks to Pat Kiely from Acorn for giving me the confidence to stand up to my former employers, and all for a pint of Guinness.

To Gareth and Clare Potter, Mikel Mellick, Esther Laugharne, Jason Williams, Lisa Saw, Keith and Sue Lyons, John Stanhope, Andrew Lewis, Mike Hughes and Sean Power.

Jason Smith, your support on the legal front is much appreciated, as is your friendship. To Alastair Milburn and 8 Total Management.

Thanks to Huw Evans of Huw Evans Picture Agency.

To those who still fight the good fight: Rhodri Bown, Huw Wiltshire, Caroline Morgan, Andrew Hughes, Neil Jenkins and John Rowlands.

Thanks to those people in the media world who have shown me that there is life after analysis, whilst realising that Gwyn Jones & Co. have very little to worry about from this direction: Geraint Rowlands, Huw Eirug, Aled Llyr and Lynn Davies. A big thank you to Robin Davey and the *South Wales Argus*.

To close critics and rugby intellects, Ian Matthews, Alun Cleverley, Alan Rees, Selwyn, Robbo, J.M. and Neil Robbins.

To the educationalists, Peter and Anne Williams from Kelly College, Graham Swift from Newcastle High School, Alan Hodge from Jones' West Monmouth, Huw Powell from Aberystwyth and Phil Jones of Pontypool Tertiary College.

To the Pontypool contingent, including Graham Price, Neil Waite, Mark Brown, Kevin Moseley, Roger Bidgood and Ian 'Buffy' Jones. To the Newport contingent, including Gerry Jones, Roly Mason, Roger Powell, Glenn George, Kevin Withey and Paul Turner.

To Eric and Jean Ward, Clive, Matt and Kate. To Satch and Silverdale Cricket Club.

Finally, thank you to Carol Harrington, Peter Harrington and Cath Harrington. The number-one Bargoed RFC supporter, Alan Wadley. To Sara Myers, Elizabeth Harrington, Rachel Harrington and Hannah Stephens.

During the writing of this book, in memory: Betty Mumford, Margaret Davies, Audrey Gray, Joan Jones and Stephen 'Junna' Jones.

Nick Bishop would like to thank Graham Henry for his contribution and continued friendship, and Debbie and Catherine for their constant support and encouragement. I would like to thank Elisa Terren for reigniting my passion for writing. My parents, without whom nothing else would have been possible. And, finally, thank you to Alun, a highly valued friend and colleague for the past ten years. This project has been a great ride.

Both Alun and Nick would like to thank all at Mainstream Publishing for their patience and professionalism, especially Graeme Blaikie, Iain MacGregor, Paul Murphy and, of course, Bill Campbell.

CONTENTS

1

ROOTS IN THE VALLEY

'It is not the critic who counts: not the man who points out how the strong man stumbles or where the doer of deeds could have done better. The credit belongs to the man who is actually in the arena, whose face is marred by dust and sweat and blood, who strives valiantly, who errs and comes up short again and again, because there is no effort without error or shortcoming, but who knows the great enthusiasms, the great devotions, who spends himself for a worthy cause; who, at the best, knows, in the end, the triumph of high achievement, and who, at the worst, if he fails, at least he fails while daring greatly, so that his place shall never be with those cold and timid souls who knew neither victory nor defeat.'

Franklin Roosevelt, 'Citizenship in a Republic'
speech at the Sorbonne, Paris, 23 April 1910

It is 19 September 2007. I am driving with Dad, who is in the passenger seat of my car, and we are looking up at the slate grey sky looming indifferently above St Hilda's Church, Griffithstown. It is morning, no more than 9.15 a.m., an hour before the funeral service for Steve 'Junna' Jones is due to begin. People are spilling out of the church onto the adjoining paths, unable to get in. They are anything but indifferent to the death of one of their own. Junna was only 55 years old, and there is a silent realisation that in death he sits closer to the heartbeat of the community than many of those still living and present in the church that morning.

I squeeze up to a Pooler and Newport contemporary of mine, Kevin Moseley, as we stand at the back of the church. A good friend, we went through the ranks at Pontypool together and left for Newport at the same time. Our coach, Ray Prosser, nicknamed him 'Boris', mainly because he could never remember anyone's name. I look along the line. There is Chris Jones, or 'Bighead', who gestures in turn to Martin Jones. 'I wonder why Pross called him "Horse"?' whispers Chris as we gaze at Martin's outstandingly long, chiselled features. He could indeed have just come in from his morning run in the paddock.

Everyone physically able to come is here: Mike Crowley ('the Bear'), Mostyn Davies ('Upside-down Head'), Mark Brown ('Shaft') and many others; the 'Bish' and the 'Perk' – David Bishop and John Perkins, two of Pontypool's greatest sons.

Graham Price ('Sheepshead') gives one of the eulogies, describing how Junna and his mates from Twmpath School used to wait for him as he emerged from West Monmouth Grammar. They'd pick on Pricey, sending his cap tumbling all the way down the railway embankment and on to the line, time and again. Pricey was a strapping lad, so there'd be a fight. When they joined Pontypool RFC as teenagers, they ended up fighting just as regularly. Grinning, Junna would offer his hand afterwards, as quickly and as forthrightly as his fist minutes before. The wicked sense of mischief, the wholesome set of double standards, never left him.

Steve's sense of humour was as biting as the wind that whips across the valley tops but entirely democratic. It didn't matter whether you were white, black or any colour in between. When Junna started nodding and you appeared on his radar and caught his eye, watch out. Our flanker, Mark Brown, was black, and he was subjected to some memorable verbal batterings from Junna, but it was acceptable and a positive within the Pontypool environment. Steve was perceptive about people and knew how to hit on their weak points, but if anyone outside the Pooler environment was to try and knock Shaft down in the same way, Steve would be the first to sort them out.

That dichotomy in Steve Jones was the essence of Pontypool RFC. He was everything that was good about the club. Perhaps, as Kevin Moseley said to me on the way to the crematorium, he distilled the spirit of the club as clearly as our revered coach, Ray Prosser. Even when he became one of the highest-qualified coaches in Welsh rugby and was sought after by other larger and more fashionable clubs towards the end of his life, Junna obstinately stayed with the red, black and white right through to the very end.

He was bloody-minded, opinionated and belligerent – very belligerent. I remember my very first derby game for Pooler as a callow 18 year old. It was against Newport at Pontypool Park. I was apprehensive, wondering how I'd come to be sitting under this peg with a number 8's jersey hanging from it. Then, suddenly, Junna was in my face, picking me up by the chin, spitting out instructions: 'Son, you make a man of yourself today. Never take a backward step. Never let them see they've hurt you.' I looked into his glazed eyes and saw that he'd already 'gone'. Mentally, he was out of it.

Out on the pitch, the first scrum unsurprisingly erupted in fisticuffs. I knew that Junna was at the heart of it, and I kept my head down while swinging my arms blindly in the direction of my opposite number, Wayne Rendle, hoping, one way or another, that it would all be over quickly. Thankfully, I heard a few urgent, shrill blasts on the whistle of the referee, Les Peard, and a crooked finger beckoning Junna towards him. Les was an imposing ex-policeman who once famously told Wayne Shelford, the All Blacks captain, to mind his own business when Shelford was going through his usual routine of trying to referee the game by proxy: 'You play. I fucking ref. Got it?'

'Penalty against you, Steve Jones,' said Les, 'for punching Spike Watkins. Another penalty against you for coming back in and hitting Rhys Morgan. And a third one for running ten yards over there to punch Wayne Rendle.' He might have been borderline psychotic, but at that moment I loved Steve more than anything for his loyalty and the need to protect his own at all costs.

The incident at Newport was one example of how Junna would unfailingly help out a member of his extended family. He was an incredibly selfless individual. When I first started at Pontypool, Junna, along with David Leighfield and Neil Waite, would take a group of the eager ones training at Pontypool Leisure Centre or for a run by the banks of the canal. He introduced me to a disabled athlete called John Harris, who helped Boris and me develop physically through weight training. Junna also worked with special needs youngsters in the community and fostered no less than 17 young boys and girls in his own home.

He was the vital glue in the environment Ray Prosser created, and if he could see that a young player was honest and had the right basic values already in place, he'd take them under his wing and foster growth in their talent and character alike, as if they were indeed one of his own children. He left such an impression on the Canadian international prop Rod Snow down at Newport, that Rod even wore a black armband with 'Junna' on it in a match at the World Cup in 2007. 'Nobody opened his heart or home to me more than he did,' Snow said. 'He had some great antics, and we were very close. I'll miss him. I loved the guy.'

The funeral ends with a thank you from Steve Jones's brother-in-law and a reminder of Mr Hyde: 'Thank you to all those who made it possible for Steve to finish building his house for only £80. Thank you to Terry Howells Timberyard, B&Q, Price builders' merchants, RAF Glascoed and Pontypool College. You probably don't realise that you've been sponsoring Junna all this time, but you have. Thank you.' The old Kenny Rogers classic 'Ruby, Don't Take Your Love to Town' strikes up as Junna's coffin is borne down the aisle.

'Work hard, play hard' was Junna's credo and Pontypool's mission statement. Although amateur, Pontypool RFC was an extremely disciplined environment in which to learn your trade. Training was always well attended by supporters of the club. There was a group of diehards who knew that something special was going to happen every Wednesday night. The session before the 1983 cup final was attended by more than 1,000 supporters.

Men such as Chris Huish would do a full day's work and find time to train in the evening and even during their lunch breaks. Staff

Jones worked at the colliery on top, and he once walked the 13 miles from Ynysybwl to get to training. If Brandon Cripps got a late call from Ray Prosser to fill in in the front row, he'd leave his work as a builder immediately – there would never be any question. Once, he returned from a game to find his shovel still standing up, hardened and immoveable in the concrete where he'd left it. It was a pressurised environment that bred mental toughness.

During training, time was never wasted, and we practised in the manner and at the speed we were expected to play. 'Train in an orderly fashion, play in an orderly fashion,' Pross used to say. If we practised lineouts, for example, they would be related to positions on the field: inside our own twenty-two, drive off 'two ball' and box-kick from halfback (there would always be a halfback there as part of the group); in between the ten-metre lines, off-the-top ball from the middle and two set phases; inside the opposition twenty-two, peel off 'back ball' and drive into midfield.

Scrums were contested and often fractious, with men in the B front row not far short of starting quality and encouraged by Pross to have a go at the 'stars' in front of them. A fight would almost inevitably break out, and then Pross would intervene, quietly laughing to himself. When you saw Graham Price taking the Phil Orrs and Colin Smarts of this world in hand on a Saturday afternoon in front of 60,000 screaming Welshmen, what you didn't see was how he had been driven to his limit and beyond by Mike Othen or Mike Crowley on the Wednesday night earlier in the week, or scrummaging as part of a tight five against as many as eight or nine opponents. In squelching mud and driving rain, and watched by nobody in particular, except maybe Pross and Ivor Taylor.

If you wanted to stick around at Pooler, you had to brace yourself for some very painful, frequent and public verbal humiliations. Eddie Butler had to endure countless barrages after he returned from three years of study at Cambridge University as 'Educated Edward', but he took it all and became a true Pontypool stalwart, earning the respect of men such as Pricey. I've no doubt that it helped him to become a regular Wales international and ultimately captain of the national side. Together with Chris Huish and Mark Brown in the back row, they formed a perfect unit: 'Madman', 'Shaft' and the 'Cambridge Blue'.

It was part of Pontypool culture that you were harsh on your own in order to look after your own. If you had a delicate or sensitive nature, it forced you to come out of yourself; it brought the man out of you. It certainly dragged the man out of me – kicking and screaming. Junna in particular pushed me to my limits, and I never felt comfortable with him. But I trusted him implicitly, because I knew that he always had my best interests at heart, both as a person and as a rugby player. Even when I left to go to Newport and he was still coaching up at Pooler, he kept pushing me and giving me advice. He never let politics interfere with true friendship.

The Pontypool ethos left a powerful mark on the opposition teams that played there. The ex-Gloucester flanker Andrew Stanley told me that Gloucester would come down determined to match fire with fire, and they'd amp up the noise and adrenalin in the pre-match warm-up. 'The unnerving thing was this deathly silence coming from the changing-room opposite,' he said. 'Sometimes I didn't even know whether there was a team in there, it was so quiet. It was eerie, and it used to bother us no end.'

On the inside of that silence, there'd be the backs on one side of the room, forwards on the other. As captain, John Perkins would circle slowly between the two lines, slightly bent over and with his left index finger curled, wagging out instructions just as it would warn opponents on the pitch later on. There was complete quiet, with just the occasional growl that seemed to emanate all the way up from Perk's gut. When we heard the noise from the other changing-room, Perk would stop: 'Hark at them in there, pissing in the wind . . .'

Pross would have been encouraging us to think about our immediate opponent all week: 'Get a picture in your mind's eye of what you are going to do to your opposite number. Think how you can hurt him. Think of all the little ways you can get an edge on him. Do whatever it fuckin' takes.' There was nothing left but focus and attention. Our mentality was always that we would do our talking on the pitch, and it belonged to our outlook as a club, especially on our own *blood-twmp* (home patch).

I meet Pross for a cup of tea the day after Junna's funeral at the Drop-In Café – or, as his daughter Beverley jokingly renames it, the

'Drop-Out Café'. He's 78 years old, and his left knee has just been replaced. He's upset a lot of the staff down at the Royal Gwent Hospital and left a trail of wreckage in his wake. We get talking about Gareth Jenkins, the incumbent Wales coach. 'The problem with him, Alun, is that he just can't stop talking. He's like the talking horse. He talks too much. He must have been vaccinated with a gramophone needle.' Pure Pross. He talks about the Wales pack, lamenting the overall lack of 'dog', while complimenting the play of individuals such as Alun Wyn-Jones, Chris Horsman and Gethin Jenkins. I sense that, knee allowing, Pross would like to be back on that training field with the whistle between his lips, moulding some of those players, screaming obscenities at them, building in them that great intangible – a hard, unyielding edge in mind and body.

He is surprised that so many people attended Junna's funeral: 'It was a good turnout. I didn't know so many people liked the bugger . . . But I hope only two people come to my funeral . . .' A few eyebrows are raised around the table. Pross looks up suddenly with a glint in his eye. 'Then I'll know I've outlived all the bastards.'

I leave with a strong sense of renewal inside me, remembering the best and worst years of my rugby life between 1983 and 1989. The foundation of my rugby philosophy was set in those years at Pontypool Park, and attending Junna's funeral, meeting Boris and Pricey and Pross again, has brought the wellspring of my feeling about the game of rugby football back to life. As my mind drifts, I recall how Pontypool values were at the heart of Wales's rugby success during the golden era of the 1970s. Yes, there was a gifted generation of backs, but the pieces didn't truly click into place until the Pontypool ethos was grafted on to our forward play – or, to put it in a nutshell, when they stopped picking the likes of Glyn Shaw at loose-head and started selecting Charlie Faulkner, even well into his 40s.

Pross never liked the backs much, except for Dai Bish, and he made him an honorary forward. On tour to Argentina in 1998, I had the pleasure of a long chat late into the night with Bob Templeton and Syd Millar. 'Tempo' recalled sitting down with Pross and Ivor Taylor, the backs coach, at the Pontypool Leisure Centre the day before the Australia versus Pontypool match in 1984. There was a little bit of sparring, with neither wanting to give much away on the eve of such a big match. Then Tempo asked Pross, 'What are your backs like, then? Who have you picked for tomorrow?'

Pross thought for a moment, then replied in a blasé fashion, 'Aw, I don't deal with the backs. That's Ivor's job . . . I don't know who's playing tomorrow.'

The Pontypool front row and the likes of Terry Cobner and Jeff Squire brought an edge to Wales in the '70s; later, it would be Staff Jones, John Perkins, Steve Sutton and Eddie Butler. The presence of the Pontypool front row, and Squire and Cobs, gave a balance to the team that allowed Gareth and J.P.R. and Phil Bennett to flourish and do their stuff. An English front-rower of the time once told me over a pint, 'Wales won fundamentally because they beat everyone else up for ten years or so – except France for a couple of seasons. It was organised thuggery.'

As I walk slowly away from my meeting with Ray Prosser in the Drop-In Café, I begin to understand that the two most successful Wales coaches I've worked for over the past ten years, Graham Henry and Mike Ruddock, have had that same Pooler edge to their mentality and a similar set of values embedded in them, even though they come from vastly different backgrounds. When I watch Warren Gatland and Shaun Edwards being interviewed on TV and read their comments in newspapers now, I get the same smell in my nostrils. There's the same blue-collar emphasis on a disciplined approach, an unbreakable team ethic and a rock-hard foundation in the tight-forward play. And there's that same merciless desire to prune the branch right back to its root by whatever means possible to get a stronger growth – 'I might even have to break a few of them', as Gatland put it.

Even when I moved to Newport and earned the first of my caps for Wales, I found myself surrounded by men of similar stock. I was disenchanted and felt that I'd come to the end of the road at Pontypool before the beginning of the 1990 season. I'd missed out on the big games the previous season and didn't reckon I featured prominently in the plans for the coming year. Junna, who was the club captain by then, kindly dropped off a Chinese takeaway for me one evening while I was working as a policeman in the Newport area to persuade me that I was still wanted, but the die was already cast. I played a couple of games early in the season, but still lost out in selection for the big games, and that was that.

Paul Turner, who only lived a short distance from me in Griffiths-town, approached me about playing for Newport. We had a common bond as a result of our love for the history and detail of the game of rugby. We both hoarded programmes and cherished little-known statistics. And even if Paul had mixed feelings about the way Pontypool went about the process of winning games, he still maintained a distant respect for both our practices and achievements. When I went to see Gareth Evans, the Newport coach, on Paul's advice, he told me that Port had just been demoted as a result of the newly revised league structure. It struck a chord, and I knew that I'd found exactly the challenge I needed.

I was a driven man, having given up my childhood dream to play for, and captain, Pontypool. A mixture of anger and determination to prove myself sent me hurtling forward on a path I'd never before contemplated in my wildest imagination. I would've laughed in your face if you'd told me I'd be a Black and Amber player even a couple of years before.

My renewed enthusiasm was immediately enlisted by two knowledgeable back-rowers, Roger Powell and Glenn George. I'd played with and against Glenn ever since our early teenage years in the rival Pontypool and Newport school sides, and Roger had given me one of the most memorable lessons in openside-flanker play I'd ever received during one particular Pontypool–Newport match. He really bossed me around all afternoon. By the end of that match, if he'd said it was in fact Sunday, I wouldn't have argued. He was one of the great secrets embedded in the very sediment of Welsh forward play in that era – one of the men who, although never quite good enough for international rugby, added real substance and depth to both the Gwent rugby scene and the Welsh game as a whole.

When I moved to Rodney Parade on the understanding that I would be playing openside, there was a secondary understanding that Glenn would inherit the number 7 jersey that Roger had worn with such distinction. It was a sign of the respect that Roger commanded. I ended up playing openside but wore the number 6 jersey, which I was happy to do.

Roger Powell's coaching of the forwards, in typical Gwent fashion, was excellent. He was a lecturer at Pontypool Tertiary College but was as down to earth as they come. He made a tremendous impact and taught me everything about openside-flanker play, giving me the springboard I needed to prove myself at the highest level. As flankers and as personalities, Glenn and I were opposite and complementary. While I could blow hot and cold, he was Mr Consistent and never seemed to have a bad game. While I often played with emotion, he offered stability, an even keel.

It gave me particular pleasure to travel up the valley to Pontypool and help Newport beat them for the first time in 14 years on their own patch the following season. Typically, Junna was waiting to congratulate me after the game. We followed that by beating Neath just after Christmas, ending their record-breaking string of 51 successive victories over Welsh opposition. That was all I needed to get and hold the attention of the national coach, Ron Waldron, especially as one of my main rivals, Martyn Morris, had been sent off in the same match and was subsequently suspended. Once I got a foothold in the squad, I was determined to make the most of my chance and impressed sufficiently for the 'Possibles' at the trial to be selected for the 1991 Five Nations game against England. Even though I didn't remain in the Wales squad for long, I remember feeling that it was the values I'd learned up at Pontypool from the likes of Ray Prosser and down at Newport from Roger Powell that had gotten me there. A child grows up to be a man quickest in a healthy environment, and my background in the twin Gwent hotspots enabled me to grow up in rugby terms and fulfil my potential.

Mike Ruddock was a Blaina boy who went to Nantyglo Comprehensive. His dad used to take him to watch Blaina play every Saturday, where he saw men such as back-rower Terry Maggs and Barry Davies in the centre, who were also good enough to represent Monmouthshire against Australia. Alan Tucker, another back-rower, played against New Zealand for the region, so Blaina were a tough outfit who didn't give second best to anyone at the time.

From Blaina, Mike moved up to Tredegar: 'I had a couple of seasons with Blaina before joining Tredegar, and one incident stands out in my mind. I remember watching the 1977 Lions tour of New Zealand, during which the All Blacks became so desperate at their helplessness in the scrummage that they even resorted to three-man scrums. When we went up to Pontypool the next season, we had a plan to emulate the All Blacks, as we knew Pontypool would have Graham Price, Charlie Faulkner and Bobby Windsor in their front row. The plan was for me to stand behind the three-man front row and play halfback, but, unfortunately, as I went to pick the ball up at the first scrum, all the forwards drove right over the top of me, and I was buried at the bottom of a very painful ruck. No more three-man scrums after that. It showed me the physical and psychological effect a good scrum could have on the opposition. Pontypool left their mark on me that afternoon, more than they knew.

'My first senior coach was Denis Wright, who had played number 8 for Pontypool. His first bit of advice for me as a wing forward was to stop the opposing scrum-half coming round and disrupting our heel by treading on his foot. So I looked across eagerly towards the touchline before the first scrum, and Denis was nodding animatedly and making a stamping motion with his foot. I trod on the bloke's foot as I'd been told, but sadly hadn't accounted for the other leg as it swung around and caught me squarely in the 'crown jewels'. I went down hard, like I'd been poleaxed.

'Tredegar really had an imposing pack when I joined. One of the props, Sid Wharton, was a Monmouthshire regular. On the other side there was "Mad" Mel Bevan – I can still hear Mel growling at the front of the lineout now, just as I could hear him clearly on the pitch when I was standing ten yards away at the tail. Glad he was on our side. Steve Duke and John "the Pop" Williams packed behind those props . . . There were three or four players who played regularly in a strong Monmouthshire pack.

'My real break into first-class rugby occurred when I moved to Swansea. They had a fantastic team back then, with the likes of Malcolm Dacey, Dai Richards and Bleddyn Bowen in the backs and some tough nuts, such as Barry Clegg and Richard Moriarty, up front.

But an accident while I was working as a linesman for the Electricity Board cut short my career. My back and skull were fractured. It was 1985, and I had just turned 26. That was that.

'A guy called Steve "Snickers" Jones was coaching Blaina at that time. After the accident, I would pop down there to see how things were going, and I remember one day Steve saw me standing on the touchline and walked over, a huge "Zapata" moustache framing his big grin. Well, within a few minutes he'd asked me to help out coaching the forwards . . . I was more than willing and felt committed enough to attend WRU [Welsh Rugby Union] coaching courses the following year, in 1986. When Steve moved to Cross Keys, I was left alone as the head coach at Blaina. We lost our first four games, and there were rumblings in the committee, but then we turned it around and won every league game for the rest of the season to end up as Monmouthshire Premier Division champions. After coaching spells at Cross Keys and Bective Rangers, I returned to Swansea as head coach, and we won the league twice (in 1992 and 1994), beat the touring Australians in 1992 and won the Welsh Challenge Cup in 1995.

'So, my basic rugby values were hewn out of that dark Monmouthshire coalface. They were based around the forwards physically imposing themselves on the opposition. I didn't believe anything was possible without that. But then, as a player and a coach, I kept on finding myself in West Wales, at Swansea, in the land of the expansive free-flowing passers and runners.

'One of my biggest influences there was undoubtedly Stan Addicott, a great servant of Welsh rugby at Swansea University. Stan believed in the 15-man game, and I took a lot from that. I saw the possibilities. Another guy there was Ian Hall, the former Wales centre who also used to coach at Swansea. The keys for Ian were attitude and fitness. Fitness and defence became important to me as a measure of a side's character. Those areas tend to show a team's basic attitude more clearly than anything else. The really good teams show pride in their defence and an ability to last the whole 80 minutes.'

I began working under Keith Lyons for the Wales national squad in 1996, and over the course of the next 12 years I naturally felt most attuned to those coaches whose rugby values coincided with my own. Those coaches turned out to be Kevin Bowring (initially), Graham Henry and Mike Ruddock. I felt that Graham and Mike had a complete vision of how rugby could be played, but they were very pragmatic in terms of putting the basic foundations in place. They turned out to be the most successful coaches for Wales since the high watermark of the 1970s, winning over 60 per cent of their matches. Kevin Bowring, while not quite as successful as the other two (he had a 52 per cent win record), did, however, have a very strong grasp of what needed to happen in Welsh rugby for it to succeed consistently at international level. I didn't think that Steve Hansen, Scott Johnson or Gareth Jenkins had such a complete feeling for the big picture when they coached Wales – how an international rugby squad should be run, how it could be developed into a unit with a winning mentality. Gareth and Steve achieved only a 30 per cent win record over the course of their Wales coaching careers, and Scott didn't win any of his three games in charge. The results speak for themselves.

How did Graham and Mike come to be in possession of the 'big picture' when they took over the reins? In Mike's case, the short version is that he was willing and able to travel to either end of the M4. He began in humble Blaina, but there was never any danger that his rugby education was going to end there. His playing and coaching careers swung him to and fro from Gwent to Swansea and back again. After serving a tough apprenticeship as a young player among the hard heads at Tredegar and Blaina, he flourished within a Swansea side intent on playing fast, attacking rugby. He received the Stan Addicott vitamin supplement to his rugby thinking as eagerly as he'd learned from that first three-man scrum against Pontypool, in which he'd been first bowled over and then crushed. As a coach, the pattern was very similar, and Mike never allowed himself to get trapped by geography, by East Wales–West Wales thinking. He took the best of both worlds, added some spice from an extended coaching sabbatical in Ireland and applied what he'd learned to a primed Welsh squad that couldn't win Test matches – at least until he took over in 2004.

It is no accident that many of Mike's successes as a coach have been achieved working in tandem with Clive Griffiths. Clive is an avowed

West Walian himself and learned his trade under Carwyn James, who took him down to Stradey Park from Penclawdd at 17 years of age and taught him that flair can never, must never, be stifled. Other older contemporaries in the Llanelli or Wales squads, such as Phil Bennett and J.P.R. Williams, reinforced the lesson. Later in his career, Clive moved up north to play, and ultimately coach, rugby league. He still remains the only Welshman to have coached the Great Britain Lions, the pinnacle of the sport. Clive's presence is, and always has been, a reminder to Mike of the need to include the West Wales mentality in his coaching style and encouraged him to think outside the box by cross-referencing with other sports that were far better developed in professional terms than rugby union.

With such a rich mixture of influences, Mike Ruddock proved equally comfortable with high-tempo fluidity and the forward slog. He could see that Wales needed more of the latter than the former, so he concentrated on selecting and coaching the forwards correctly, while simply refining the all-court game that we already had within us after the 2003 World Cup. He shifted Gethin Jenkins back to his natural position on the loose-head and gave Adam Jones twice as much game-time as Steve Hansen, which solidified the scrum. He looked for complementary attributes in the back two rows of the scrum and made an out-and-out footballer, Michael Owen, the main man at number 8. Michael's confidence expanded so quickly that he was actually the captain who lifted the Six Nations trophy in 2005.

Total game fitness and resilient defence defined the 2004–05 team's character. Mike continued to give Andrew Hore, the single biggest positive of the Steve Hansen era, his head on conditioning programmes until he left to go back to New Zealand in the autumn of 2005. I instantly recognised Horey's methods from my Pooler days, and he would have dovetailed very neatly with Pross and Ivor Taylor. He was always in players' faces and never allowed them to get away with anything.

Mike also gave a retread to Clive Griffiths, who had been marginalised by Hansen. He returned with a vengeance, coaching a niggardly defence that allowed only eight tries and eighty-four points in five games – and five of those tries occurred against Ireland and Scotland with the games already in the bag. Meanwhile, I was given the budget and the freedom to recruit a brains trust – including Rhodri Bown, Nick Bishop and Corris Thomas – that generated superior analysis and game planning, and ensured that no one out-thought or out-planned us during the 2004–05 season.

Graham Henry came from a vastly different background to Mike, but he managed a similar fusion of influences in pretty short order after taking over from Kevin Bowring as Wales coach. He was a very fast learner and assimilator of ideas. Four games in charge were enough to show Graham how his Super 10/12 philosophy needed to be tailored for a northern-hemisphere market. He found a front row comparable to the All Black version he'd had with the Auckland Blues and settled for a tight, simple game based on the power of Garin Jenkins, Peter Rogers and Dai Young or Ben Evans in the scrum and Scott Quinnell and Scott Gibbs on the advantage line, all backed by the managerial and kicking expertise of Neil Jenkins at number 10. Occasionally and gloriously, his vision of a wide, free-flowing game flowered – in two away games against France especially – but not too often. Wales's first-ever victory over the Springboks at the newly built Millennium Stadium probably epitomised Graham's Welsh Way better than anything else.

When Graham Henry applied to become All Blacks head coach in 2003, he exchanged emails with Nick asking how he should present himself at interview: 'Graham wanted to know his stats with Wales, but more importantly he wanted to get a sense of what he could bring to the table that would set him apart. I felt that his northern-hemisphere experience was a priceless asset. Graham's rival for the job, John Mitchell, hadn't appeared to make the most of his experience with England and went over completely to a Super 12-based style that looked good and could beat Australia by 50 points away from home but then lose to the same opponents in a crunch World Cup semi-final only a couple of months later. Eight All Black forwards couldn't budge six Englishmen one miserable inch on a wet night in Wellington earlier in the summer. So I said he could get the All Blacks playing closer to the tradition established by men such as Colin Meads, Ken Gray and Ian Kirkpatrick. "Exactly what I was thinking," he replied. And that's how it worked out. Carl Hayman was a fringe player under Mitchell, now he's the best tight-head in the world. Within two years, All Black packs had once more become an instrument of torture to opponents.'

Kevin Bowring was and is an advanced rugby thinker in the mould of Carwyn James. Just before finishing as coach of the national team in 1998, he produced a report on the elite game in Wales that was truly prophetic. In it he advocated, among other things, the formation of four regions in the tier below international rugby and the introduction of the Celtic League, the establishment of a distinctive playing style ('the Welsh Way'), centralised training for the national squad, and even the purchase of Iestyn Harris. But instead of being valued as a visionary asset, Kevin was frozen out. No role was found for him within the infrastructure of Welsh rugby. Eventually, he landed in England, joining the Rugby Football Union (RFU) in 2002 and becoming the Head of Elite Coach Development.

On 12 December 2007, Kevin received the Dyson Award, named after Geoffrey Dyson, a man who was renowned for his professional approach and who demanded the highest standards and utmost commitment at all times. Presenting the award, Rob Andrew said, 'Kevin thoroughly deserves the recognition and the award. The work and the coach development programme he has introduced at the RFU has benefited a huge number of club and national coaches. The programme helps the coaches' development and prepares them for the demands they face every day while on club and England duty. Kevin continues to be a major asset to the elite rugby department, and on behalf of the RFU I would like to congratulate him on his honour.'

Graham Henry returned to New Zealand with his work in Wales unfinished, and neither Allan Lewis nor Lynn Howells, his lieutenants, are now employed in Wales. Mike Ruddock and Clive Griffiths coach Worcester Warriors in the English Premiership. Kevin Bowring is the Head of Elite Coach Development in England. So, there's very little evidence of a desire within Welsh rugby to hang on to its winners, people who know how to create structures that will enable us to win and keep winning at international level.

Mike, Graham and Kevin were all very 'literate' in coaching terms and would readily absorb new influences into their coaching philosophies. Both Steve Hansen and Scott Johnson, on the other hand, were really quite conservative and struggled to move very far from their Super 12 backgrounds. Hansen in particular had no respect for rugby league and was stubbornly insistent that the Canterbury way was the right and only way to do things. In the week before the second Test on the tour to South Africa in 2002, he replaced Clive Griffiths – a significant 'leaguer' as both a player and a coach – and his defensive pattern with the model he'd used at Canterbury. We probably lost that game because of it, and the defence was seldom Test-match standard during his tenure. Canterbury thinking dominated the team patterns and selection. By early 2004, we ended up with lots of great ball handlers and athletes in the forwards but hardly anyone who could win the bloody ball in the first place.

Clive Griffiths always thought that Steve Hansen had the instincts of a successful chief executive rather than those of a head coach. He set out to change professional attitudes within the national squad, and he achieved that vital aim, but he always seemed far more comfortable in his larger role as David Moffett's cohort 'sorting out Welsh rugby', rather than attending to his immediate duty of winning Test matches. Poor selections continually hobbled the team, and, more often than not, our forwards struggled in the tight. The calamitous home defeat to France in 2004 – a game we should have won quite comfortably – defined the Hansen era as concretely, if not as memorably, as the glorious World Cup defeats to New Zealand and England the year before. A miserable return from the set-pieces – well under 50 per cent of our own ball from scrum and lineout – decided that game, and I think it will eventually decide Hansen's real stature as a coach of Wales when the dust has settled.

Scott Johnson formed close relationships with a core group of senior players, including Gareth 'Alfie' Thomas, Stephen Jones and Martyn Williams, and he could be a great motivator and innovative thinker. He played good cop to Hansen's bad cop very effectively, but I doubt he ever really wanted to be king. He always looked happier as kingmaker, or the eternal pretender-in-waiting who was really pulling all the strings behind the scenes. I suspect Scott Johnson loved nothing better than a bit of melodrama, but the continual swirl of emotional undercurrents and political machinations when he was around could be both exhausting and damaging. They had certainly exhausted Mike Ruddock's patience by February 2006. But that is the story of Welsh rugby over the last twelve years – a story of exhaustion and regeneration, culminating in the glorious renewal of 2008 and a second Grand Slam in the space of three years.

2

THE REDEEMER COMETH

'Mental toughness is essential to success.'

Vince Lombardi

'I am a winner. I just didn't win today.'

Greg Norman

'I just want you. I don't want your mate.' Those were the first meaningful words I heard come out of the mouth of Graham Henry. Graham was the first foreigner ever to be appointed coach of the Wales rugby team on a permanent basis. He had an ironclad five-year, £250,000-per-annum contract to prove it. He was going to get what he wanted, and on that fateful afternoon in my office at the University of Wales Institute, Cardiff (UWIC) at the end of August, it happened to be me.

The mate in question was Keith Lyons, with whom I'd been working as a notational analyst since 1994. The WRU were based at Cyncoed, on the UWIC campus in Cardiff. They were situated in a building called Queenswood, in a block of offices on the ground floor. Kevin

Bowring, the coach, and Terry Cobner, the director of rugby, had been based there since 1996. Keith Lyons and I were at the other end of the building from Kevin, which made for easy lines of communication.

I first met Keith as a student. Keith had been responsible for teaching the module on notational analysis at Cardiff Institute of Higher Education when I went back to college in September 1991 to start a degree in human movement studies. Two years later, the institute was given a contract to support the WRU with analysis services, mostly technical work plus an additional embryonic involvement with the national squad. Keith and Gareth Potter were driving the project. When I qualified in 1994, I joined the project, which was by then developing rapidly. At that stage, Keith was looking to relinquish most of his lecturing responsibilities in order to manage what was to become the Centre for Performance Analysis. His relationship with the union became even stronger when Alex Evans took over as coach in time for the 1995 World Cup – Keith had worked with Alex at Cardiff RFC and also knew Geoff Evans, the team manager, very well. So Keith went to South Africa, while Gareth Potter (who had done much of the initial groundwork) and I supported him from Cardiff.

There was a strong rapport between Kevin, Keith, Gareth, me and the other four researchers in the team. Kevin liked to wander down the hallway to our office, because it's fair to say that his relationship with Terry Cobner was a difficult one. Kevin recalls trying to develop a positive relationship with Cobner without achieving the ideal outcome: 'Because he was appointed after me, I was determined to give it my best shot. I certainly respected him for his playing achievements, but I definitely felt that things needed to be done differently to the way that Terry perhaps wanted.'

The WRU had set itself up for a fall by getting their appointments in the wrong order in 1996. First, they appointed a South African, Dave Clark, as the chief conditioner, then they made Kevin head coach and finally they installed 'Cobs' as the director of rugby. So, Cobner did not get the chance to select a coach with whom he knew he could work, and the two men were as alike as the proverbial chalk and cheese: Bowring a refined rugby visionary and an English-based London Welshman; Cobs a rough-edged, direct, earthbound man of Gwent.

The head of faculty at the Cardiff Institute, John Pugh – Vernon's brother – could see that Kevin was spending a lot of time at our end of the building and used to come up to me periodically and ask how their relationship was progressing. Although a native Welsh speaker from Ammanford, John always used to deliver the question in an impeccable Oxford English drawl, along the lines of 'Now tell me, Alun, how are they doing, old boy?' Unfortunately, the answer tended to be a bit more rugged and visceral.

By the end of Kevin's term in charge of the national squad, the relationship between the two men had deteriorated to the point that Cobner burst into a team meeting prior to the match against Canada on the summer tour of North America in 1997 and cut right across Kevin's pre-match team talk. As Kevin says, 'Our relationship did deteriorate, because we weren't getting the results we wanted and our methods were fundamentally different. We probably disagreed on how we should coach rather more than on what we should be coaching.'

Cobner had already sent a fax via team manager Trevor James complaining about Leigh Davies and the three Thomases, Alfie, Arwel and Nathan, who had all dyed their hair peroxide for the tour. Cobs told them in no uncertain terms to change it back again. Kevin remembers that 'we showed them a video clip where the referee had penalised them for offside when they clearly weren't. The players in question realised that the ref's attention had been drawn by the peroxide . . . They simply stood out like a sore thumb.' Terry had a very forceful personality. On at least one occasion, he had shouldered his way into Kevin's office to fiercely debate team selection. If he didn't rate someone, he would argue persistently enough for Kevin to change his pick.

So I think Kevin began to enjoy the walk across campus to our office at the main end of the building. We were something of a steam valve for him. He used to come up and chew the rugby fat with us, and he leaned on Keith for support with the issues that he was going through at the time. I think Cobs used to associate the analysis team with Kevin as well, because we had some typically forthright exchanges – as Pooler men – about the amount the union was paying for our services. It was £115,000 for the three years: Terry thought it was too much; I thought it was too little. We were at the cutting edge of analysis globally and needed to maintain our rate of development, but Cobs repeatedly questioned the value for money we offered.

The record 51–0 home defeat at the hands of France at the end of the 1998 Five Nations did for Kevin, and the suicidal summer expedition to South Africa that followed, under the temporary command of Dennis John, rang the bell for radical change. Deafeningly so. We were stuffed 96–13 by the Springboks at the end of the tour, and, as Colin Meads would have said, we were bloody lucky to get 13.

In retrospect, it's surprising how much of Kevin Bowring's vision has lived on. Kevin was the sixth most successful coach in Welsh history with a respectable 52 per cent winning ratio. Kevin's remarkably prophetic report on the way ahead for Welsh rugby was compiled after the disastrous defeat against the French. He began the report by pointing out the need to develop a distinctive Welsh style of play, based on keeping the ball alive, pace, continuity and tempo. At the end, he included 13 bullet points, outlining key requirements for a successful future:

- A clear commitment to KB as coach until after 1999 World Cup

- The appointment of a full-time assistant coach, regardless of cost [Kevin's assistants had always been part-time]

- Contract 25 players from clubs for the duration of 1999 Five Nations

- Contract core players up to 1999 RWC

- No promotion or relegation in season 1998–99

- Centrally supervised training from January 1999 until RWC

- Buy Iestyn Harris

- Financial consultant to negotiate remuneration package and contracts for players

- Individual/positional clinics on Wednesday a.m.

- A proactive, positive publicity strategy

- Create a more competitive club structure (Anglo-Welsh?)

- Create four regional teams to play in Europe

- Provide resource and finance to support the national team management requirements

Many of these points were addressed by the two Kiwi coaches who followed Kevin, Graham Henry and Steve Hansen, and a new chief executive in David Moffett. Graham Henry was brought in on a long-term deal, with a couple of full-time assistant coaches. From 2001 onwards, training was conducted from a central location at the Barn at the Vale of Glamorgan Hotel. Iestyn Harris was bought from rugby league in 2002. A more competitive club structure was introduced (the Welsh-Scottish, then the Celtic League) and the creation of four regional teams followed, again in 2002.

Both Mike Ruddock and I would experience at first hand the need for a financial consultant or some kind of independent arbitrator to negotiate contracts for members of the management group between 2004 and 2006, and the provision of resources for the analysis department was to be a bugbear throughout my time with the national squad. I always felt I had to fight for every penny I got.

The Welsh-born coaches from 1996 to 2008 never seemed to have the clout to get what they wanted, even when they had as crystalline a vision of the future as Kevin. It was always the New Zealand coaches who assimilated the need for those changes and pushed them through. They were the pragmatic ones who could force the WRU to act decisively. With a Kiwi in charge, the union acted; with a Welsh coach at the helm, they showed a lot more reticence, and the gap between promise and delivery yawned. We've lost intellectual property as a result: Kevin Bowring is now the RFU's Head of Elite Coach Development; in England, for goodness sake.

The WRU employed their own peculiar modus operandi in the search for a new coach, which has turned out to be a signature for them over the last ten years. While Terry Cobner was telling Mike Ruddock that he had the job in Wales, Vernon Pugh and Glanmor Griffiths were flying to the other side of the globe to hold secret meetings with then-Auckland Blues coach Graham Henry. And Vernon always got what he wanted at that time. As coach of a Welsh Universities side on a trip to Scotland, he once secured the five-star Balmoral Hotel for his charges.

Graham was parachuted in ahead of Mike in much the same way as Mike would 'gazump' Gareth Jenkins six years later, and Gareth would benefit from another late reversal to get the nod ahead of Phil Davies in 2006.

Having gotten to know Kevin quite well, I was saddened to see him go. At the end of his post-Five Nations report, he had submitted a list of options: 'Support me'; 'Sack me'; or 'We agree to part company'. The union chose door number three, and Kevin felt he had no alternative but to leave: 'I felt that I'd compromised enough and wasn't prepared to compromise my principles any more. The official decision was that we agreed to part company.'

So, it was difficult for me to make an immediate connection with Graham – I felt quite guarded and reticent at the beginning. When Trevor James came knocking on the door and said, 'Graham would like to speak to you,' I didn't want to know and avoided the meeting. It's fair to say that we didn't really get off on the right foot. The first time I met him, he came in to look around the offices, with Keith fussing around him endlessly like a mother hen. He was shown written reports on individual forwards in the Welsh squad, which I used to produce off the back of the statistical analysis. We also compiled videos of players' strengths and weaknesses, from which a selection of positive clips were set to each individual's favourite music track – research indicated that this provided a physiological stimulus. These tapes were lining the shelves when Graham arrived. It was obvious that he didn't like the overall feel of the place, because it so clearly had Kevin's stamp on it. I don't think it took him long to make up his mind that he was going to do most of his work from home, especially as he was staying in a small apartment not far from UWIC at the time.

But the main reason he came that day was to meet and suss out me and Keith. He left the talking to us and had his sour face on, which made me quite nervous at first. Nothing makes you more anxious than a face that doesn't reveal what the owner thinks about you, and Graham was a master at that. The visit didn't go well, and we heard soon afterwards that he was looking elsewhere. It was only when Trevor James happened to mention to Graham that I was a former Wales international and that Keith and I didn't necessarily come as a package that his ears pricked up and he returned for another look. He made a point of talking to me alone and outlined his main requirements. The key was the ability to quantify gain-line success. My answer must have satisfied him, because after a short pause he made that immortal offer: 'I just want you. I don't want your mate.' Suddenly, I was in business.

That one sentence summarised why Graham Henry was like a breath of fresh air wafting through the stuffy corridors of Welsh rugby, and why he had such a huge initial impact. Graham could be blunt to the point of being brutal, and he would always tell people what was on his mind, immediately and without reservation. It almost cost him friendships with the likes of Lynn Howells and Garin Jenkins, but you need that bluntness and simplicity in an environment where the habit of thinking one thing and saying another has become the norm. It's the dark side of the national-squad culture that flourishes whenever a coach has not got the strength (Gareth Jenkins) or organisational authority (Mike Ruddock) to control the environment. It was no accident when Gareth Jenkins was fired at the end of the 2007 World Cup that Roger Lewis and Dai Pickering went looking for a replacement in New Zealand. They specifically wanted a Kiwi coach who came with less political baggage and could cut through the crap and dominate his environment, and they got their man in Warren Gatland.

One of the immediate litmus tests is the ability of the new coach to create his own management team and get the right people in the right places, working as one unit without hidden agendas. Because he was expected to be the saviour of Welsh rugby, Graham had greater licence to get what he wanted than any coach up until Gatland took over in late 2007. Steve Hansen worked with at least three people he didn't really want. Mike Ruddock was saddled with Scott Johnson and never given the authority to create his own group from scratch. Gareth

Jenkins largely accepted the scaled-down backroom team he was given, with the exception of Nigel Davies.

Graham made most of his assessments during a two-day leadership course at Atlantic College on the Vale of Glamorgan coast. David Pickering, a businessman and another ex-international, was to become one of Graham's closest allies over the course of the next two years. During the dinner at the end of the course, Graham saw that South African-born Dave Clark didn't have the outlook or communication skills he was looking for in a conditioning coach. Dave wasn't a great communicator, and the work he did was power rather than aerobically based – neither sat well with Graham. He had a conversation with Pat Lam at Newcastle, and Lam mentioned a man at the opposite end of the scale from Clark, the ultimate 'empath' and feel-good communicator, and a rotund Geordie to boot: Steve Black. Graham drove up to Newcastle to meet 'Blackie', and the job was offered and taken on the same day. It turned out to be a key appointment.

There was never any sense during Graham's time in charge that the management group wouldn't present a united front publicly or that the public show didn't reflect the true feeling behind the scenes. At a meeting in a conference room in the basement of the Copthorne Hotel, Graham introduced the squad that had been selected for the game against South Africa in November. Every single one of us in the management group took turns to get up and explain what our role would be: Allan Lewis, a selector and the backs adviser; Lynn Howells, the forwards coach; Blackie, the motivator/conditioner; Mike Wadsworth, the team masseur; Mark Davies, the physio; and me, head of analysis. Trevor James, who'd been a mentor to Kevin Bowring and had extensive coaching experience of his own, fulfilled the role of team manager and administrator and provided some continuity with the past.

I remember the atmosphere so vividly. It was quite electric. There was total silence in the room when Graham began to speak. You could have heard a pin drop. It was partly due to his reputation but mostly to his style of delivery. Graham started by setting out his philosophy and what he expected from the players. He talked about South Africa not as an overpowering opponent, but as one we could handle – one we could surprise and beat. They would take us lightly, and we had a chance to catch them with their trousers down.

Graham wasn't passionate; he was measured and self-contained, and there was a feeling that if we could only apply what he said, it would inevitably bring positive results. His coolness and quiet self-confidence were infectious, and I could see from the players' faces that the infection was spreading throughout the room . . . Senior pros and dominant personalities within the group, such as the two Scotts, Quinnell and Gibbs, Rob Howley and Neil Jenkins, listened with rapt attention. Graham knew how to command an audience perfectly, and he was very well organised in his manner of expression. It was a defining moment. The other less well-known defining moment occurred when Allan Lewis got up to speak; he talked about being a passionate Welshman, willing and able to burn down an Englishman's holiday cottage for the cause. I noticed Blackie squirming a bit uncomfortably in the corner just before mentioning that he wouldn't be moving down from his home in the north-east any time soon.

The full force of that attentive silence followed us all the way to the Kensington Gardens Hotel on 14 November 1998, the day of the match against South Africa. Before giving his team talk, Graham walked quietly through an immaculate 'U' of 22 players to open a small window at the far end of the room. 'We can win this game,' he said. I'd bought a tape of rock anthems in Kensington High Street that morning which I intended to play on the coach – the boys liked to listen to music on the way to the ground, though at that stage it was all speakers and a few Walkmans in the pre-iPod era. I was arranging it all with Trevor James when the team emerged from the basement meeting room in the hotel. The atmosphere was just amazing; not a word was said from the moment the players stepped on to the bus to the time they disembarked. I looked at the tape in my hand – in that instant, it was surplus to requirements.

Graham was simply the best speaker I'd ever heard. He didn't waste words. He rarely lost his temper or his balance between motivation and the appeal to players' emotions and keeping them focused on the details of the task at hand. He had that knack of keeping them smart and hungry at the same time. The state of concentration Graham could elicit with his talks was worth the fourteen-point start on South Africa we got that day, and it was a conjuring feat he was to repeat throughout his first two seasons in charge.

As Allan Lewis put it, 'Graham was incredibly positive in his mindset. He didn't see the impossible, and he'd never let the players see that he thought there might be trouble ahead with our next opponents. That message would never be transmitted. And he had the rhetorical and motivational skills to build someone like Scott Quinnell up into a world-beater. I think that Blackie was a key component in Graham's success with Wales. Sometimes he'd spend the whole day with a player, just looking after him or taking him shopping, maybe offering him a shoulder to cry on . . . He'd reckon it was time well spent in order to get the player's head right.'

Blackie sat at the right hand of the redeemer. He was the single biggest factor in reinforcing self-belief within individual players, bolstering the positive atmosphere and getting the players to buy into Graham's vision of how Wales could play a game of international rugby. Blackie approached conditioning by looking at the whole person, not just the physiological aspects of his body. For him, conditioning was 80 per cent mind and 20 per cent body. Having explored North America from one coastline to the other, he always knew the latest conditioning theory inside out but didn't always trust conventional wisdom to give the best answer. He was always looking slightly beyond it to a more holistic solution, and Graham liked that unorthodox approach. He thought it would give him an edge.

I remember Blackie once asked Huw Wiltshire for some help, but when Huw turned up with his stopwatch, he just said, 'Huw, lad, you won't be needing that . . . Just look in their eyes, and when they're fucked, move 'em on . . .' At the end of a tough workout, Blackie would always finish with a 'feel-good sprint'. However tired you were, you had to do that last sprint at a pace and rhythm that 'felt good'. Absolutely magnificent. It was at the end of one such session during the 1999 World Cup preparation that Blackie, looking all the way down from the top of the pavilion at Christ's College, Brecon, at the players toiling below, spotted Allan Bateman. Spreading his arms wide, Blackie purred, 'Allan Bateman, ya've got an engine like a Roowells-Royce.'

In reality, there were two sides to Blackie's character. Garath Archer tells a story about how Blackie took a few of the Newcastle players to see his hero, Lou Ferrigno – the man who played the Incredible Hulk in the TV series – in gym action on a pre-season tour to North America. Blackie and the boys were watching Ferrigno work out on the Nautilus equipment, and Blackie asked one of Ferrigno's minders if they could meet the man in the flesh. After a brief consultation, he came back and said, 'No. Try again tomorrow.' So Blackie and the lads returned the next day to find Ferrigno knocking out two or three four-hundred-pound bench presses. He stopped and asked for a volunteer in the gallery to give it a go. Blackie's hand shot up in the air, and he promptly banged out ten reps of four hundred pounds without a second thought. Ferrigno was impressed and came over to shake Blackie's hand, but Blackie just gave him the bird. His parting shot: 'Sorry, mate, ya had ya chance yesterday.'

On the one hand, he was the most generous and kind-hearted soul you could ever meet; on the other, he had the edge of a street fighter in the late-night shadows – very aggressive, competitive and distinctly capable of sorting people out. It was no accident that when a liquor-soaked Gareth Thomas – the 'old' Alfie, dark and brooding and explosive – got in Graham's face after the 1999 French game in Paris and Graham started to react, it was Blackie who stepped in. No one messed with Blackie. If he was Graham's cheerleader-in-chief by day, he had no problem doubling as his minder by night.

Blackie really played the same role as Scott Johnson did five or six years later. He could talk to the players, and he was available for them 24 hours a day. We struggle with consistent discipline and mental toughness in Wales, and both Scott and Blackie had the ability to find the right words to get people back on track when they began to wander 'upstairs'. When he entered a room in the morning, he'd crack a joke or give a couple of the players a hug, and the atmosphere would be crackling in no time. Graham might have been the engine of the great revival in 1999, but Blackie was the essential oil that lubricated all the parts and enabled it to run smoothly.

Although Graham had been a back himself and tended to coach the backs, he always insisted on forward drills that were both live and opposed, fierce man-on-man contests in which people had to improvise solutions on the hoof. This was manna from heaven for an ex-Pontypool forward brought up in the Prosser school of ethics. He used to echo Pross so closely it was almost eerie. 'Train in an orderly fashion' was Pross's dictum. 'The way you train reflects the way you play' was Graham's. Blackie would quote the Olympian 400-metre hurdler Ed Moses: 'You develop concentration in training. You can't be lackadaisical in training and concentrate in a competition.' Then, off his own bat, he'd add, 'Practise your concentration, especially when we are together but also at other times in your lives. Make concentration a habit everywhere – the rewards will be enormous.' To me, this was the sound of that ominous silence that used to inhabit Pontypool changing-rooms before we ran out on to the pitch. Mental toughness. The discipline of running in your lunch breaks at work or after a hard shift at the pit. Thinking about your opposite number for the whole week before the game. Then Perk's wagging finger.

Mark Davies and I were lassoed in to help with the forward preparation for that first Springbok game. All I can remember is getting battered to the point of exhaustion and wondering what was that immense weight coming through the middle of the maul. It turned out to be a bloke – no, a monster – called Craig Quinnell, bringing his great mass and strength to bear. Time and time again, the exercise was repeated, until the lesson was tattooed on both bodies and minds, and could not be forgotten in the heat of battle.

Peter Wheeler, the old Leicester hooker, had brought the Pontypool thumbprint back to Welford Road with him at the end of the 1977 Lions tour to New Zealand. Pricey, Charlie Faulkner and the Duke were on that tour, and Terry Cobner ended up coaching the team after a disastrous opening Test, much as he'd done with Wales when John Dawes was off-colour. When Peter rose to a position of influence up at Leicester, he encouraged that edginess, the siege mentality in training: 'If you're not good enough in training, somebody better will take your position – no matter who you are.'

Mefin Davies will tell you that it's the same there now – Leicester are so old-fashioned in that respect they are like a throwback to those dark ages. Dark but good. Martin Johnson was the heartbeat of

England's World Cup-winning side in 2003, and he was born out of that culture, too.

Graham Price explains that 'Peter Wheeler was a member of the Lions team in New Zealand in 1977 when Cobner took over the pack leadership and, subsequently, control of the coaching of the Lions forwards. It was exactly the same coaching and philosophy as Pross at Pooler. We went on to beat the All Blacks up front. They told us it was the worst beating they'd ever had. They even used three-man scrums at one point.

'All the Home Nations teams benefited in some way from that tour during the next few years. Players such as Wheeler, [Fran] Cotton and [Bill] Beaumont took the methods back to their clubs and national teams. It was the same philosophy used on the 1980 tour to South Africa under Beaumont, and in the English Grand Slam team of the same year.'

At one point in the 1980s, Pontypool had three props in the national squad – Staff Jones, Pricey and, strongest of all, the Bear Mike Crowley – and another on the fringe in Paul Jenkins. The live scrum sessions were not for the faint-hearted, believe me. The first-team pack would scrummage 'downhill', and Pross would encourage the athletic forwards to climb into them all the way up and down the field. He was quite insistent about it. If things weren't fractious enough, he'd swap people around to get the edginess he wanted. He wouldn't stop scratching until he could see the inner steel – or lack thereof – in a player's eye.

Pross wanted to see a bit of 'nasty'. It was one of his ways of assessing a player's character. James Hook immediately noticed the same characteristic when Warren Gatland came down to help the Ospreys prepare for a crucial 2008 Heineken Cup match against Gloucester: 'He worked with the forwards and really got stuck in. There were a few scuffles among the boys, and he got them to show how much they wanted it.' This is a function of live forward drills, of the mano-a-mano contest that is still the essence of the game. It was refreshing to see it at a recent Worcester Warriors session in the lead-up to the European Challenge Cup final against Bath – a huge skirmish that reflected the competitive edge that had helped produce their upturn in results during the latter part of the 2008 season.

It is an area in which I believe another man of Gwent, Mike Ruddock, got it spot-on in 2005. We did live scrummaging and lineout defence drills, and absolutely nobody drove through us from the lineout that year. Ireland had scored two easy pushover tries in the 2004 Six Nations against Wales, but a year later they gave up on the tactic as early as the first quarter of the match. They never got a sniff. Under Steve Hansen and Gareth Jenkins, live and opposed forward drills were very much the exception and not the rule. Hansen in particular preferred scrummaging indoors on his customised machine, with the forwards wearing training shoes on a rubberised surface. His refusal to change in this respect meant that we were poor scrummagers from 2002 to 2004, at least until Mike Cron came on board for the 2003 World Cup and steadied the ship a little.

Of course it's not much good demanding total commitment to the cause from those around you if you're not willing to give it yourself, and Graham would usually be up at four or five in the morning poring over videotape or arranging the day ahead. An 18-hour day was de rigueur for him, and he didn't mind testing those around him to see if they could stay with the pace. Allan Lewis remembers idly wondering out loud how Graham went about the process of analysing games: '"You're always asking questions, mate," was the initial reply . . . Later, when I'd nearly forgotten about it all, he phoned me up at 6.30 one Sunday morning and said, "If you want to watch me, I'm starting in the next five minutes." Then he put the phone down. I tried to go back to bed but couldn't sleep, so I rang Graham again and said, "I'll be there in an hour." He would go over and over the same piece of action. His saturation level was so much higher than anyone else I knew. He'd go back and pick out different little details with each viewing.'

Allan goes on to recall another typical incident, which happened before the 1999 game to mark the opening of the new Millennium Stadium against an opponent we'd never beaten, South Africa: 'Graham was an organised workaholic who was always meticulous and never let the details look after themselves. Before the Springbok game, Braam van Straaten had come into the South Africa side as a late replacement. Graham had a tape of him and went to watch it on the evening before the game. He had a tiny combination TV–video recorder that he took with him everywhere, so he could continue to work while on the move. The bloody thing was always breaking down, and it chose this important moment to fold its arms and go on strike again.

'Graham sped back to his house in Marshfield to find another tape and some working machinery. The only problem was that by this time it was two or three in the morning, and he couldn't find his house key. He tried latches and searched for an open window to bundle his way in . . . Meanwhile, his wife Raewyn had been woken up by all the commotion and thought that an intruder was attempting to break into the house. Eventually, when Graham managed to gain access and review footage of van Straaten, the sun was coming up.

'I asked him why he'd bothered at such an ungodly hour, and he replied that he'd wanted to see if there was an adjustment we needed to make or anything else we could do to take advantage of the guy. As it happened, the additional legwork didn't pay any dividends on the day, but it did show Graham's remarkable desire to go the extra mile in preparation. He needed to win.'

Letting the little details look after themselves: it's a great phrase, and one that came back to haunt me so strongly during Gareth Jenkins' time in charge of Wales. The candle was being burned at both ends by some of the coaches then, too, but ironically on occasion more for social than for professional reasons. The little details were left very much to look after themselves for most of 2007. When I sat down in front of my TV to watch the Australia–Wales group game at the 2007 World Cup and saw that a callow young unknown, Berrick Barnes, had been brought in to replace the veteran Steve Larkham at fly-half, I asked myself whether Gareth and Nigel Davies would be making the same effort as Graham Henry had with van Straaten to find a little chink in his armour at the 11th hour. Within the first half-hour of the match, I had an answer. We attacked the Wallabies with the same plays that they had clearly expected us to run and didn't force Barnes to make a tackle once.

Graham was extremely good at highlighting those one or two key areas of an opponent's game that drove all the rest of it forward. He knew how to become specific, how to translate knowledge into training detail and how to work with an analyst to drip-feed the essential information to the players. The offensive moves from first phase would always be designed to break the type of defence the opponent employed, and Graham had brought with him from Auckland a huge, imposing playbook that his outside-half would be required to run. I think it included about 22 base moves from lineout and another 34 from scrums, all with subtle variations. He'd maybe pick out two or three that he thought would work for a particular game. New Zealand do it now, identifying a couple of moves, each with a sub-group of four or five subtle variations, that they think will break the defensive scheme, then they practise and refine them until they become second nature. It's why they tend to break teams from first phase more regularly than other sides in the world.

In the lineout, his 'Trifecta' formation – or 'Troifiktah' in Kiwi – had one outstanding lineout forward who would move fluidly up and down the line with the same two lifters. Graham had found his aerial athlete in the shape of Chris Wyatt, who up to that point had only ever been considered as a number 8 or blindside flanker. Just from seeing the trial matches, he felt that he could use Chris in much the same way as he had Charles Riechelmann with the Auckland Blues, a lock who could work around the field as a back-rower but had lineout athleticism to boot. Chris could go forward or back and manoeuvre in the air to beat opponents, or the hooker would hit him as he walked into the lineout with his lifters before it was formed or the opposition knew what was happening. The superb off-the-top ball he won provided the bullets for the backs to fire with Graham's vast array of set moves. It was key to our ability to lift the tempo of a game.

I guess every coach when he first steps up to international level tends to fall back on what has worked for him before in the lower grades. If he's lucky, his vision of the game at that level will translate successfully to the Test arena. By that measure, over the last ten years or so the Auckland Blues, Swansea and Waikato–Wasps models have largely worked. The Canterbury and Llanelli ones didn't. The common ground between the successful models is that they all had sound basics in the set-piece. Graham went out into Welsh rugby, and sometimes beyond it, to find people who were similar in terms of character and ability to those he'd left behind in New Zealand. For Sean Fitzpatrick read Garin Jenkins, for Royce Willis and Charles Riechelmann read Craig Quinnell and Chris Wyatt, for Grant Fox read Neil Jenkins.

Some of the pieces took time to come together. The scrum coughed and spluttered at first. Dai Young, our senior prop, was out injured for Graham's first six months in charge, and we endured a set-piece nightmare against our second opponents, Argentina, seven days after the South Africa game. They fielded a huge front three of Mauricio Reggiardo, Freddie Méndez and Omar Hasan. Due to their unique *bajada* scrummaging style, which funnelled power through the hooker rather than the props, they always picked a third prop in the middle of the front row, and they bulldozed us all around Stradey that Saturday evening.

As if that wasn't enough, Reggiardo turned out to be one of the smelliest and most aggravating men in world rugby. He always seemed to be involved in off-the-ball stuff or getting into people with a bit of niggle. And something in his diet gave him a most unpleasant aroma so that it quickly became a talking point among our players. Neil Jenkins got smother-tackled by Reggiardo and suffered right in front of the cameras. He was actually fanning himself and holding his nose on the ground. It was one humiliation heaped upon another, and an abiding image from that game for me. I didn't feel that particular account was squared until the second Test out in Argentina in the summer of 1999. Mauricio Reggiardo had had his way with Chris Anthony at Stradey, but there was a moment at the Estadio Ferrocarril Oeste when Peter Rogers beckoned Reggiardo into the next scrum with something approaching contempt. After the engagement, Reggiardo fairly galloped back over the touchline pursued by a snarling Rogers as the scrum crumbled to dust, and Argentinian hopes with it.

The big positive to come out of the Stradey game was the ability of Neil Jenkins to fill all of Graham's needs in the pivotal outside-half role. Despite being half-suffocated by Reggiardo and the power of the Argentine scrum, Jenks let all his skills breathe in the open spaces at Stradey. He was fundamental to Graham's plans and possessed a range of abilities that a lot of people in Wales never truly recognised, either then or now. 'Oi, Neil Jenkins, yew are ruining Welsh rugby, yew are,' as one wag up at Sardis Road once memorably put it.

Graham didn't agree. Neil could pass off his left hand superbly well, which increased our capacity to go both ways in attack – witness the 'miss two' pass against England at Wembley that allowed Shane Howarth to score in the corner after a dozen or so phases. He could remember all of Graham's moves and run them accurately, and the precision and timing of his passes helped us to score four tries from long-range backline plays, despite being obliterated in the forward battle by Argentina. He could also kick well out of hand, and, as everyone knows, he was a goalkicking artist. In fact, Jenks had all the basic skills you would have expected to find in a top All Black international. He was a Welsh version of Grant Fox. Before Graham arrived, he'd lost his place to Arwel Thomas, everyone's sentimental image of a Welsh outside-half, and even been shoehorned into full-back, a position he had occupied for the Lions Test team in South Africa in 1997. But Graham saw his talents and made him his first choice number 10 without any ifs or buts.

The games that stand out for me from the Graham Henry era would be the three against France – two victories in Paris in 1999 and 2001 and another in Cardiff in the warm-up to the 1999 World Cup – and the match versus South Africa to mark the opening of the new stadium. Those were the times at which the picture of 'the Welsh Way' Graham had in his mind came closest to being realised on the field.

Paris in the 1999 Five Nations was certainly a key moment. We were under the cosh, having lost to Scotland and Ireland in the first two games, and Graham had misread the emotional impact of the tournament. For the first game against Scotland, we'd stayed in the Balmoral, a fabulous hotel in the centre of Edinburgh overlooking the castle and Waverley train station. It's the ideal place to be for a Wales–Scotland encounter, and I remember sitting in the dining room, watching the ebb and flow of thousands in Welsh red, white and green rolling up and down Princes Street far below. I could see that Graham was staggered by the immensity of it all, this first taste of the Five Nations, and his eyes widened to the point of naivety. 'I couldn't believe everyone lived so close to each other,' he said. 'Where I live now, in Auckland, my nearest neighbour is over three miles away. I didn't realise the geography had such huge significance, that it could create such passion and intensity.'

It was the first time that he had encountered the 'binge culture' in Welsh rugby. His first reaction was to attempt to dilute it, if you'll pardon the joke. He had Trevor James wheel a fridge full of beer into the team room on Thursday evening. It was like pouring oil on a fire. The confusion etched on the players' faces was something to behold. They had no idea what to do or what behaviour was expected. The thinking in Graham's part of the world is that you can just relax over a couple of beers and then go to bed. He didn't understand that it's difficult for a lot of Welsh players to do that. The culture over the years has been that one beer tends to lead to six or seven others. It made the players nervous and uncertain, and that uncertainty was reflected in the performances against Scotland and Ireland in our first two matches.

He didn't know it at the time, but Graham had discovered the key to the Welsh psyche. We're emotional and tend to go to extremes quite easily, so if we drink, we have to go the whole hog. Alfie Thomas is a very good example of that kind of emotional excitability. In his book, he's honest enough to admit that at the time:

> I was probably not the easiest person in the world to coach. Put it this way, I wouldn't have wanted to coach me! I wasn't very stable at the time in terms of how a professional rugby player should act; in fact, in some respects I was as far from what a professional rugby player should be as I possibly could have been.

Although he saw Alfie as a talented individual, Graham Henry felt 'he couldn't be trusted in the really big games. But I think Steve Hansen was the making of him, and he owes a huge debt of gratitude to Steve for improving him so much in the second half of his career. When the Lions came over to New Zealand in 2005, Gareth was definitely the outstanding player on that tour, and he certainly got the Lions up for that second Test.' But even after the reformation by Steve Hansen and being made the Lions captain, it didn't stop Alfie Thomas participating in a huge binge in the small hours after the second Lions Test in 2005. There's another honest description of that evening in his book.

Warren Gatland learned from his time in Ireland that the Celtic temperament needs chilling rather than inflaming. There's never an absence of passion, eager to be conscripted. So I guess Gatland had a couple of games' head start on Graham. Instead of pandering to the players' emotions, Graham concentrated on keeping everyone cool and focused on the game plan for the French game. 'Use the top three inches' became his mantra.

We stayed at a quaint lakeside hotel in Enghien-les-Bains to the north of Paris, and I remember going out for an early morning run. It was a dull, overcast morning, and a soft drizzle began to coat my face as I began the 20-minute circuit around the lake. For me, it's always been about running. It brings me alive. Perhaps because I've spent so much of the last ten years indoors in front of TV monitors, I love the opportunity to get out in the fresh air, take in the outside world and clear all the junk out of my mind. Whether it's running up by the old railway track near my mum and dad's at Blaenavon, or completing those ferocious laps of Pontypool Park with Pross and Ivor Taylor waiting with their stopwatches and stern faces, it's always helped me cleanse an overheated mind. It's my way of keeping a cool head.

On the Lions tour of Australia in 2001, I used to go out with Andy Robinson three or four times a week. Scarcely had we arrived at one new venue before Andy pitched up and said, 'Run? Ten minutes?' Before we'd unpacked our gear or equipment. Before anything. We didn't care where we were going, running out on to the headland at Manly at the tip of Sydney Harbour, running through the undergrowth until we were completely lost. Until we almost ran straight over a cliff at the end of the harbour. We were like men possessed, Andy cutting the path ahead, no pause for reflection. When we finally made it back to the Manly Pacific Hotel for some breakfast, we met Dave Alred about to embark on his own morning run: 'What route did you take? Where did you go?' We gave him directions, telling him what a great run it was, hoping he'd find the same cliff edge as we had.

I ran around the lake in Enghien-les-Bains alone with my thoughts, soaked to the skin but feeling clarity return with each step. The cool, neutral climate gave no hint of the brilliant pyrotechnics to come later that afternoon at the all-new Stade de France. Just as I completed my circuit, I met Graham emerging from the hotel, also alone, head bowed. Impassive as a Buddha, he grunted minimally as we passed, then took himself away deliberately in the opposite direction. It was a weekend during which powerful but understated emotion was to prove more than enough.

We'd had a foretaste of the Stade on a visit the previous afternoon. It was magical – the plushness and size of the changing-rooms and the transparent roof latticing the spring sunshine on a perfect oblong of new turf sent me tumbling all the way back to my playing days. Suddenly, it was me running around like a sand-boy, fielding kicks and getting stuck into the training run like any other member of the squad. It was definitely a stadium built for a special occasion, and I knew we could all feel it.

Graham was back to his pre-South Africa prophetic best. On the Saturday morning at the team meeting, I can remember him having a special word with Neil Jenkins about the new cap playing at number 7 for France that day, Marc Raynaud: 'Jenks, he'll be flying early on . . . the show-and-go will be on – look for it.' Both Jenks and Rob Howley cut inside, taking advantage of Raynaud's eagerness to get up field quickly, and made telling breaks within the first 15 minutes.

Our all-new front row, featuring two massive one-hundred-and-twenty-kilogram-plus new caps at prop in ex-Transvaaler Peter Rogers and six-feet-four-inch Ben Evans at tight-head, as well as a scrummaging hooker in Garin Jenkins, did the business. They began to exorcise the ghost, if not the pungent memory, of Reggiardo. Even at the very first scrum, the combative French tight-head, Franck Tournaire, melted inwards and downwards under blowtorch pressure from Peter and Garin. We began to counter-attack from restarts deep inside our 22, going wide with miss passes and full-back Shane Howarth in the line, scoring tries or else tearing off huge chunks of yardage. Craig Quinnell finished off an 'end of the earth' score from one such restart at the end of the first half as our third try rode in swiftly on the back of the second, and belief flooded through the entire team. At last we had the clear-headedness to 'be bold' and execute Graham's high-speed, high-intensity game plan. What Graham Henry said would happen, began to happen. But I've no doubt that the brilliant sunshine of our rugby that Saturday afternoon began with the soft, indifferent rain of the morning – the neutral mental climate established by Graham Henry over the course of that long weekend in Enghien-les-Bains.

There were also some premonitions of the game at the same venue six years later, both good and bad. Like Graham, Mike Ruddock would exhort the Welsh players to be bold in their attitude to the key game in Paris, and our second-half explosion in that match mirrored the first half in 1999. Those two halves of rugby rivalled each other as pure examples of the Welsh Way in action. Coincidentally, in both games we were hanging on desperately at the end with some dogged defence and having problems getting the ball off the bloody field so that the ref could blow the final whistle. Dai Llewellyn, our reserve scrum-half in 1999, had asked me to come to his room on both Thursday and Friday afternoon to help him with some of the moves and calls. I went through them all patiently, and Dai got on late in the game. He duly forgot everything, had a dart up the middle (Dai was a typical Gwent scrum-half in the David Bishop mould) and almost got turned over with Jenks screaming in his ear to boot the ball straight off the field.

The one sour note afterwards was the sudden appearance of the dark side of Gareth Thomas on the bus home. Alfie was still smarting from his original omission from the match-day squad – eventually he joined the squad as a replacement – and he got in Graham's face with some provocative, confrontational chants. Graham didn't like it and reacted, and Blackie had to tap into his bouncer side and pull Alfie off him. The theme of Graham's build-up had been clear-headedness and now here was the opposite. I think it marked Alfie's card as far as Graham was concerned. He knew Gareth was a passionate man who sometimes wasn't in full control of his passion, and that pushed him to the fringe of Graham's thinking. Things would be both very different and very much the same in seven years' time when Gareth returned as captain of a successful Welsh side. However much of a senior pro he became, and however much responsibility he took on, Alfie never lost that volcanic, confrontational side of his nature. Alfie: the double-edged sword of Welsh rugby.

The French game also illustrated Graham's ability to think outside the box. He never ruled anything out, even the possibility of divine intervention. Allan Lewis saw that 'one of Graham's greatest strengths was that he looked at everything. He'd always be looking at the weather on match days. In 1999, just before we beat France, Graham, Blackie, Dai Pickering and Trevor had all visited the Sacré-Cœur basilica in Paris. Of course, we won the game, and Graham didn't exclude the possibility of even divine intervention, so that became a superstition with the management forever afterwards. They kept on going to church on the eve of internationals, until it got to the point that Trevor hired a helicopter to fly Graham down to St David's so that he could say a prayer before the Australia quarter-final game in 1999.'

Where Steve Hansen, Scott Johnson and Gareth Jenkins tended to be quite conservative about who they trusted as sources, Graham had a tremendous capacity to pull information from well off the beaten track. He was the first to use 'El Coreador', the ex-international referee Corris Thomas who wrote reports for the International Rugby Board (IRB) on the latest trends in the game. Corris based his work on statistics but had a great feel for those subtle shifts, and he could express himself energetically on paper. Sadly, his work was later to be thrown out as unusable by Steve Hansen, although I brought him in again in 2005 when Mike Ruddock took over. It was typical of the difference between the two men and their contrasting attitudes to Welsh rugby culture at the time.

In the summer of 2000, Graham also introduced me to Nick Bishop, who'd been corresponding with him for some time before he wrote a large report on the Wallabies for the 2001 Lions trip that was to form a significant plank in our preparation. I didn't know anything about Nick until Graham plonked this monster 70-pager in my lap with a glint in his eye. 'Although I'd always followed Wales closely, I don't normally send letters to coaches, but something within me felt strongly enough to start doing so in Graham's case,' Nick explains. 'He did have this atmosphere of "specialness" when he first appeared in the UK. He always seemed appreciative of the letters I sent, replying immediately, even when he didn't have much time or many words to spare. It got to the stage where I seemed to be reading his thoughts about selection and approach. "Your player comments are amazing! Are you sure you haven't got my home bugged?" he wrote in one reply.

'We arranged to meet one hot summer's morning in Bath at the end of July 2000. I think Graham had also gone up there to talk to Jon Callard over the "warehousing" of some of the Welsh players he had there at the time – Gareth Cooper, Gavin Thomas, Andy Williams and Andy Lloyd among them. A lot of them were simply regarded as squad players or were doing bench duty, and it wasn't doing their national careers any good at all.

'Graham was two hours late. We'd arranged to meet at the Recreation Ground without being any more specific than that, and I started alternating rather frantically between the ticket office, leisure centre and the far end of the ground. Eventually, at about one o'clock, Graham emerged up the steps of the leisure centre followed by a rather sheepish-looking Jon Callard.

'We began to walk around tourist-infested Bath in search of a lunch venue. Graham had a liking for all things Mediterranean and for Mediterranean food in particular, so we eventually landed at a Moroccan restaurant. After ordering something suitably exotic, Graham had another thought and said, "And I'll have some chips with that."

'I remember pointing out that he was almost certain to be appointed head coach of the Lions, as the majority of English players and backroom staff would probably knock Clive Woodward, Graham's only serious rival for the job, out of the equation. He grinned knowingly and thought about it, saying that he couldn't believe that the Lions would appoint a foreigner in the role.

'It must have been tongue-in-cheek, because Graham asked me to produce a report on the Australians later in the lunch. He wanted the full monty. Seventy pages and about eight videos later, the report was well received. It was typical of Graham's ability to think outside the box and trawl for information in remote places.

'Later, in the autumn of 2000, I visited Graham on a Heineken Cup weekend at his home in Marshfield, and we ran the rule over some likely Lions candidates who were playing in four games between Friday night and Sunday afternoon. On the Saturday morning, we went off to the local fitness centre to do a couple of hours of conditioning work. As we emerged from the session into the car park, a man rushed up to Graham with a great sense of purpose and pressed what looked like a supermarket bill into his hand. There was some writing on the reverse side. Graham chuckled: "He's always giving me these little mottos and quotes. Bit of a pest sometimes." Apparently, the guy had found a couple of good ones, and it had now become part of his job on Saturday mornings when Graham was at the club.'

I don't think Graham had trusted me to produce the motivational tapes for the players before the game in Paris, but I remember him sitting in on my presentation in the team room on the first floor of the hotel before the next game against Italy in Treviso. Immediately, I was very aware of his presence. The presentation included a sequence with Blackie storming on to the field to embrace the players at the end of the French game to the accompaniment of 'Hooked on a Feeling' by Blue Swede (later to be covered by the one-and-only David Hasselhoff), cross-fading to a shot of Blackie and Graham arm in arm with big, flushed, grinning faces, all framed by a nice fluffy heart. I began to feel inexplicably queasy.

Fortunately, the tape also contained a great deal of meat. The France game was the first time that the players had embraced Graham's philosophy unconditionally in the key areas: the powerful scrummaging and quick, mobile lineout delivery; the accurate skills under pressure; and the execution of set-moves, the bold and spectacular counters from deep using the whole width of the field. So, I felt I was entitled to get a little bit sentimental. The performance had released the kind of emotion you only get when you fully buy into something for the first time, without any reservations. It was a little like falling in love, and my suspicions were confirmed by a spontaneous, vigorous round of applause at the end of the presentation. I'd tuned in on the right wavelength, and, hell, I even cracked a smile out of Graham on a couple of occasions. I felt he'd bought into Alun Carter and felt confident enough to use me far more extensively as a resource, both personally and professionally. We beat Italy by over 60 points the next day and went on to surprise England a couple of weeks later to finish the championship on a real high.

Looking back on it now, I am amazed at just how fast my personal life was travelling from the time Graham took over in November 1998. Somehow, the speed and intensity in one area must have transferred to others as well. I married my girlfriend Catherine on 19 December

1998, six days before Christmas. We'd only been courting since June, and I'd moved down to Penarth from my apartment in Cardiff in no time at all. That was after 15 years in Pontypool. I had been playing rugby for UWIC but suffered a facial injury and nearly gave up just before we were due to get married. We'd decided on a winter wedding, and the ceremony was held at St Peter's Church on the outskirts of Penarth, which only had room for about 40 people. My best man was my cousin Ian – the best man among a host of best men there. We headed off to the Saint Germain district of Paris on our honeymoon immediately afterwards on the Eurostar, to ice the cake on what had been a whirlwind romance. We stayed at the Hôtel de L'Odéon near the Église Saint-Sulpice, in the café district of Paris close to the Jardin du Luxembourg. All these winter days were turning out crisp, clear and sunny. No room for second-guessing or hesitation.

Events followed with machine-gun speed. Less than six months later, on the Friday before the South Africa game to open the new Millennium Stadium, Trevor, Mark Davies and I had gone up to bid farewell to Dave Clark, the conditioning coach under Kevin Bowring. Late on in the evening, Trevor made a point of pulling me aside and having a private word. He asked me how I felt about going into business for myself. He was plainly unhappy that the college was using some of the money from its fat WRU contract to fund research into Welsh rugby and knew that Graham wanted individuals to split away and deal with the union on their own terms.

The idea of setting up my own business was mind-blowing. I was fairly settled as director of the department for performance analysis, in charge of ten staff members and administrating contracts with English and Welsh hockey and Welsh football plus a host of smaller contracts. I didn't sleep well on the Friday night and woke up with a hangover the next day – 26 June, a brilliantly sunny day with one end of the ground still lying open and the stadium only three-quarters finished . . . 27,000 people crammed into the available seating to watch the first-ever Welsh victory over South Africa, 29–19. I sat next to Graham, with Trevor on the other side. There was just us, no one else. After one more month of turmoil, I took the plunge and informed the college that they had lost the union contract – a substantial one at £115,000 per annum. I knew

I would only be receiving half of that sum and would be working like a dog, but the time had finally come to set out on my own.

That August was a stressful month. I more or less took the month off, with Graham's blessing, in order to get myself organised and was unable to play much of a part in the World Cup build-up as a result. The tapes on the opposition became the subject of a tug of war between the union and the college, and Trevor argued that they were the property of the WRU, as they'd been produced during the union contract. It was only a petty symptom of the real pain that my departure had caused. Keith Lyons hunted me down for some weeks over that, but I was too busy buying new office furniture, editing equipment and a computer, and trying to set it all up at home in Penarth. I'd already resigned from the college, and the WRU contract was theoretically up for tender, although I was obviously in pole position to get it. I vigorously threw myself into working long, long hours at home. I didn't always know when to stop in my eagerness to get the business off to a flying start.

Eight short months later, on 27 March 2000, our son Henry Lewis Carter was born, right at the end of the Six Nations. I'd finished all the work for the Ireland game in Dublin on 1 April and stayed behind for Henry's birth rather than travelling with the rest of the group. There is such a clear memory of seeing Henry for the first time: he was a Caesarean birth, and I remember this small bundle of living *me* being handed over, with one eye open and the other shut. Poor Catherine was stuck with the howling parcel of joy for two nights while I sloped off sheepishly to 'wet the baby's head'. Catherine was finally discharged on the Thursday, three days after Henry's birth. When she returned home, it was just perfect. I used to work in a little alcove in our first-floor flat. The apartment was Victorian with a beautifully high, whitewashed ceiling, and the trees outside used to speckle it with images, like a kind of cinema screen. Henry was asleep next to me in his Moses basket in the front window, four days old while I worked in my 'office'. For once, everything I needed in my life seemed within easy reach. All in the space of 16 months. Marriage, a new home, my own business and now a son.

There was the small matter of a World Cup neatly bisecting the start of the new business and Henry's birth. It was actually a blessed relief when it arrived, allowing me to focus on the task at hand and regain some stability. One significant oversight in our preparation turned out to be the failure to practise with the stadium's new sliding roof closed. We underestimated the effect this would have, even on seasoned veterans such as Garin Jenkins and Scott Gibbs. It was the only time I can recall Gibbsy close to tears as he walked out on to the field for the opening match of the 1999 World Cup against Argentina on 1 October – raw emotion replacing the habitual well-considered peer over those professorial spectacles of his. With the roof shut, it was as if a lid had very definitely been kept on all the swirling emotions beneath, and of course the level was continually being pumped up by the likes of Shirley Bassey in the pre-game entertainment. Control of our feelings and use of the 'top three inches' had been key to our success since the game in Paris, but the closed roof made it harder to hit that note again. It was a mistake on our part, and I felt it had a significant impact for the rest of the tournament. Predictably, the Argentinians made life awkward for us, and we only scraped past them 23–18 in a nail-biter that set the mood for some uneven performances in the qualifying stages.

We were up against Japan and won convincingly, but we were well down for Samoa and lost 31–38. Graham knew just how good the Samoans could be, and he painted a vivid picture of the likely reaction to their defeat by Argentina: they'd be in a tight huddle, praying and getting close, and they'd come out firing in much the same way as Graham himself responded to losses – with resilience, boldness and a show of inner steel. This was no coincidence, as Pat Lam, the Samoan captain and 'family leader', had been very close to Graham in his Auckland days and shared the same values. For that one time in ten, the performance indicators didn't reflect the result, and a dominant 70 per cent share of possession was overturned by four Samoan scores directly off our mistakes. That was the end of our 11-match unbeaten run.

It had been a very wet October in Wales. Graham was very, very edgy for the quarter-final game versus Australia. He knew how switched-on his adversary Rod Macqueen was from their shared Super 10/12 days as coaches of the Blues and Brumbies. And, of course, all Australian sporting teams are very smartly prepared. They look for any small edge they can get, and by whatever means possible. There was a guy called Huw 'Flash' Gordon up at UWIC who was best mates with the ex-Cardiff coach Alex Evans, and now Evans was the forwards coach with the Wallabies. Flash had done some coaching up at UWIC, and we'd become good friends over the course of time. For this week, however, Graham and Trevor were keen that all friendships should be put aside, and there was complete radio silence.

On the Wednesday, we trained at Sophia Gardens in Swansea, and Graham had decided to change the plan of attack for the game against the Wallabies. We would throw short to the front of the lineout instead of our usual routine – primarily targeting Chris Wyatt with the occasional back ball. From first phase, Graham wanted to hit around the tail of the short lineouts, where comparatively few Australian defenders would be stationed. But from the very beginning of the game, it was obvious that Australia had changed the defensive pattern that they'd used in all their other games and were ready for Graham's attacking plan. Graham was very dirty about it afterwards – to use an Antipodean expression – adamant that someone, probably Flash, must have observed that critical Wednesday session and spilled the beans. It wasn't the only time the Wallabies' talent for information-gathering was to prove a real factor in Graham's undoing. Eighteen months later, on the British Lions tour of Australia, there would be another heartbreaking defeat amid similar murky suggestions of Aussie spying missions, the truth of which Scott Johnson confirmed when he joined the Wales management group in early 2002.

There had been some signs of nervousness. Both our props, Peter Rogers and Dai Young, came up and asked me for some video footage of their opponents the day before the match, and Peter in particular was so self-confident that he would never do that under normal circumstances. That close to the game, most players don't have the time to absorb what they're seeing. They need to have been visualising their opponents and implementing counter-measures on the training field for most of the week. Then, when the game arrives, their responses are automatic, instinctive. But these requests came at the wrong time in the build-up. It was an anxiety call. As a result, a side as canny as the Wallabies was able to nullify our clear advantage in the scrums. They stood close and crowded the hit, or they stood up and tried to con the referee, Colin Hawke. They're the past masters at it and are still getting away with murder today – Michael Foley was their hooker then, and he's Australia's forwards' coach now, so he's probably germinal to their whole attitude to scrummaging. I think that was the start of Peter's decline.

The other key factor was the refereeing of two 'axe' moves Jenks called, in which there's a dummy switch and the ball is given to the blindside wing coming up the middle. Both calls sprang Dafydd James through a big hole in the Wallaby D, but instead of collecting seven points from each opportunity, we collected two penalties against for obstruction from Colin Hawke, who had a negative history with Graham from his New Zealand days. I couldn't bear to attend the after-game function, so went home after a few beers and worked on the analysis of the match. It was the best way I could think to drown out both my sorrows and my exhaustion.

Fast-forward to Paris in 2001. The last high watermark of the Henry era, Graham's last hurrah. We stayed in Chantilly, at a first-class hotel on the outskirts of the village with its own golf course. On the Thursday evening, we were led out into Paris in the care of Ian Borthwick, a New Zealand journo who knew Graham, and a legendary French liaison officer who I'd known from my days as a player in 1991. He offered me a job, playing for his rugby club in Paris and running a car park for him in my spare time. I graciously declined. We ended up at a fantastic restaurant in the Saint Germain district quite close to the hotel in which my wife Catherine and I had spent our honeymoon. Dai Picks, Trevor and Lynn were all there, and Graham introduced me to the pleasure of oysters for the first time. We ate good food and drank good wine over rugby talk well into the night.

In those days, we'd start early, at around 7.30 p.m., and be finished by 11 p.m. Although Graham only needed about six hours' sleep per night, he was always adamant that he'd get them, so he wasn't one for burning the candle at both ends. The emphasis within the management group was to enjoy our time together but not take things to excess, and Graham set a good example in this respect. We'd have a few drinks but were mindful of certain standards: 'Act sensibly and socially and look after your mates' as it said in our 'Standards of Performance' bible. It was all very different from the social culture within the group under Gareth Jenkins in 2006 to 2007, which wasn't nearly so sensible or restrained.

On the Saturday morning, I was woken by a loud grinding noise downstairs. It was about 6.30 a.m., and there was a constant rumble as I put on my training gear in preparation for my usual early morning run. I found myself getting drawn ever closer to the noise, as if hypnotically. Down the final flight of stairs, and there was 'heavy' Trevor James plodding – there could be no other word for it – on what appeared to be a nineteenth-century running machine. It looked like an instrument of torture, and it certainly sounded like one. Graham had been sucked towards the source of the melody, too, and appeared out of nowhere beside me. We chuckled as Trevor's Porthos-like figure threatened to wake the entire hotel.

A sense of humour and a real pleasure in each other's company was a big factor in our progress. You'd have Lynn Howells and Allan Lewis crooning Dean Martin songs at the front of the bus, while Blackie would impersonate Pavarotti singing 'Nessun Dorma' at the back. Then there'd be a response from the players, until the whole place was just alive with song. Graham would sit in his usual spot just behind the driver – emphatically not singing but with a huge grin on his face. Lynn Howells recalls, 'Before every international, Allan would be near the halfway line down on the touchline while I'd be up with Graham in the stand. We used to communicate through walkie-talkies. While the national anthems were going on, we'd be singing Nat King Cole songs to test the radios.'

Contrary to popular opinion, Graham also had a sense of humour, and he didn't mind being the butt of jokes himself. His speciality was to sneak up behind a player who might have been getting a little too comfortable or too big for his boots and say, 'What's the matter, clunk. Ya shit doesn't stink anymore?' I remember he did this to Chris Wyatt once, to startling effect. Chris almost jumped out of his skin.

Graham often used to stay with the BBC commentator Lynn Davies down at his home in Llanelli, and frequently he'd get up on a Saturday to go for an early morning run. Lynn's newsagent happened to notice this after Graham had run right by his shop a few times and planned an ambush one morning. As Graham jogged past, he jumped out with Lynn's paper and persuaded Graham to take it back with him. 'There's Graham Henry, my new paper boy,' the newsagent exclaimed delightedly as Graham beetled off into the distance.

Another hotel north of Paris, another wet morning, another run. As I circuited the golf course, I came across Mark 'Carcass' Davies, Peter Herbert and Allan Lewis playing an early morning round. We were all active, up and ready for the day ahead. As in 1999, the game and the occasion were both magnificent. After an unpromising start, we overturned a ten-point deficit, beginning with Rob Howley's sensational seventy-yard dart after Dai Young had nudged up on our tight-head at a scrum and S.Q. had exploited the open channel. Robin McBryde cemented his position in the Lions squad that day with a top-notch performance of close driving and accurate throwing to Martyn Williams at the tail of the lineout. Neil Jenkins was masterful at outside-half, dropping two late goals and scoring a last-minute try to secure the win. We were strong all the way down the spine of the team.

'The Welsh Way' under Graham Henry was pretty simple. For eight months in 1999, we dominated everyone in the scrums, even the South Africans and Argentinians. Cobus Visagie told us after the first game at the Millennium Stadium that the last 30 minutes of the first half against Peter Rogers and Garin Jenkins was the most searching scrummaging test of his career to that point. At that time, Peter and Garin took every tight-head they met apart, and it was Peter who resurrected the old 'walkaround' technique that Charlie Faulkner used at Pontypool, pulling the opposing tight-head away from his hooker and causing the scrum to slew and disintegrate. Not strictly legal, maybe, but with a hooker as strong as Garin it worked a treat. Then we'd launch Scott Quinnell over the advantage line with Howlers on his shoulder. Chris Wyatt gave us great off-the-top lineout ball from the Trifecta to launch set-moves from Graham's bible, resulting in tries against England,

South Africa and France between March and September 1999. The two Scotts and Mark Taylor kept us going forward through phase play, while Neil Jenkins navigated the ship and kicked nearly 90 per cent of his goals. Shane Howarth was secure and intelligent at 15. But it was really only in a couple of halves in Paris, in 1999 and 2001, that we ever opened up and had both the nerve and the puff to play Graham's all-court game consistently. We were great for a while, but Graham never thought of us as the finished article.

3

DECLINE AND FALL

'It's a certainty. We'll Beckham them.' Graham's nemesis during his time in Wales, both at home and on the 2001 Lions tour, turned out to be the England coach Clive Woodward. It all started one sunny day, on 11 April 1999, the final day of the Five Nations. In fact, it began in the week before the game, because we already knew that Woodward's England were confidently expecting a win to complete a Grand Slam of the other four countries. On the Friday evening, I'd been called into Dai Pickering's palatial suite at the Kensington Gardens Hotel. Trevor James was passing around a sheet of paper when I entered the room. A fax had been sent to Graham by a concerned Englishman earlier in the week: he'd been travelling by train and taken offence at some loud, unguarded comments made by five men who were clearly members of the English management group. I know that two of them were Clive Woodward and Phil Larder, the defence coach. Skulduggery was the main dish on their menu. There was talk of singling out Garin Jenkins and Craig Quinnell for 'the treatment' and getting one or both sent off – 'It's a certainty. We'll Beckham them.' All this mixed with a smattering of anti-Welsh jokes and the habitual English attitude of smug superiority.

The die had obviously been cast by this discussion, because we turned up at Wembley only to find the England team already ensconced in the home dressing-room, which we'd used for the games against Ireland and South Africa. We turned to the right through the big doors at the old ground, and there was a large red rose on the changing-room door. Woodward and company had gotten there first. There was a short confrontation, then Graham just said 'Fuck 'em', and we ended up using the away shed for the first and only time at Wembley. But these kind of shenanigans didn't hinder us before the game, or even with only ten minutes remaining when Woodward paraded in front of our replacements' bench loudly demanding English rosettes be displayed on the winner's trophy. They did, however, set the tone for Woodward's rivalry with Graham, which was to continue keenly through two Lions tours in 2001 and 2005.

The atmosphere at Wembley that day is something I shall never forget. It was a very bright afternoon, and the pitch was as flat and immaculate as the proverbial billiard table. The build-up featured the Stereophonics and Tom Jones singing 'Delilah' right in the middle of the English warm-up, but we hardly cared — any more than we cared about the fax or the changing-room fiasco. The feel-good factor was so strong that it swept everyone along in a carnival-type wave that reached its apex with Max Boyce's rendition of 'The Day We Beat the English'. The match itself was almost like an afterthought. The whole day was just like a celebration-in-waiting. I managed to get away for a few moments before the game started to give Catherine and my parents a call. Amazingly, Catherine was back in the Kensington Gardens Hotel watching the motor-racing grand prix, one of her great passions — she liked the McLaren 'Men in Black'. It was an accurate pointer to her opinion of rugby games, however historic.

I had a great view of the game right on the halfway line — with Terry Cobs on one side and Trevor James, Graham and Dai Picks on the other — notating the game by hand as usual. Having reviewed the match ad nauseam in lectures since that day, it's clear to me that Neil Jenkins' penalty in the 44th minute of the first half was key to the revival of our fortunes. It brought us back to within one score of England at 18–25, despite having a negative 3–0 try count against us. Graham always emphasised the importance of the ten-minute period after half-time in his team talks, and we duly came out and went through eight or nine phases before Jenks put Shane Howarth in at the right corner with that beautiful miss pass. That tied the score at 25 points apiece, and from then on it was nip and tuck all the way to the finish line.

Tim Rodber became our unwitting saviour with two bits of play: first, by giving us a lifeline deep in our own half by failing to wrap his arms in a big shot on Colin Charvis; and second, by missing Gibbsy as he went through midfield from the subsequent penalty lineout. I don't think Woodward ever forgave him for that – he certainly disappeared down the back-row rankings pretty quickly afterwards. The try was a classic, from the off-the-top win by Chris Wyatt walking into the lineout in Trifecta formation to Scott Quinnell's charge, semi-fumble and offload, and the other Scott's soft-shoe shuffle past four wrong-footed defenders on the way to a joyful Fijian dive in the late afternoon sunshine. Could Jenks convert to give us a one-point lead? Of course he could. Somehow it epitomised the euphoric spirit of the whole day.

I'll never forget the reception after the match, walking past the rows of shattered English players. They were completely shell-shocked. They didn't know where they were or what they were doing . . . Mike Catt sat there unmoving, just staring into space. Everything that happened before the game – and even ten minutes before the end, with Woodward's rosette demand – indicated that he had taken victory, the Grand Slam and the Five Nations Championship for granted, and psychologically it left Woodward and his team with no 'outs'. Just walking among them at the reception, it was obvious that the game had delivered a huge dent to their confidence, and Phil Larder confirmed later that they tore that match to pieces in their analysis more than any other during Woodward's tenure. Unfortunately, I couldn't enjoy the scene for too long before picking up Cath from the hotel and driving back down the M4. I had to catch a plane the next day, to take my place on a World XV tour to Argentina.

There were so many memorable events on that short tour: the stick Barrie-Jon Mather and Neil McCarthy (two English players who'd been part of the Wembley experience the previous day) received – not from the Welsh contingent, but three Scots in the shape of Craig Chalmers, Gordon Bulloch and Jamie Mayer – while we waited for our flight at

Schiphol Airport. Scotland had won the championship on the back of our victory over England . . . The first sight of 'the Claw' – Peter Clohessy – fag dripping from one side of his mouth, travel bag on his shoulder, zeroing in unswervingly on the drinks cabinet . . . The wonderful chats early in the morning with Bob Templeton and his old Prosser stories for company.

But the finest memory I have of the whole trip occurred at the end. The kick-off for the game between the World XV and Argentina was taken by none other than a greying Hugo Porta, but the occasion was really completed for me by the actions of Frenchman Laurent Cabannes in the changing-room afterwards. I remember Cabannes quietly getting dressed and leaving his rugby boots, shin pads and socks stacked neatly together on the bench before moving towards the door. Rod Snow piped up immediately: 'Hey, Laurent, you've left your boots, mate.'

Laurent turned around slowly and replied, 'No. They stay. This was my last game of rugby. I don't play again.' I didn't realise it at the time, but free spirits such as Cabannes were about to be left behind big time by developments in the modern game engineered chiefly (at least in the northern hemisphere) by Clive Woodward's England. Corinthian idealists probably didn't have a place in the brave new world delivered by England in the years 2000 to 2003. It was a wholly new statement of the meaning of professionalism.

Woodward certainly delivered his revenge in spades over the next two years. In 2000, with most of our World Cup side still intact, we were dealt with heavily by a score of 46–12 at Twickenham. In 2001, the scoreline at home was, relatively, even worse, 44–15. The Twickenham debacle was the first time I thought quite clearly that we were beginning to fall off the pace required for international rugby. England were developing their style rapidly then, using the whole width of the field to stretch us from one side to the other. They had any number of terrific ball players able to get the ball to the outside in the shape of Jonny Wilkinson, Mike Catt, Austin Healey (all with outside-half experience) and even the hooker Phil Greening, and I could see their players deliberately standing right out on the touchline in order to drag our defenders across and give them too much aerobic work to do. We struggled to do that work, especially in the final quarter of the match.

My impression that the adherence to professional standards in Wales was not as complete as it was in England was confirmed by another late-night binge in which the players ignored instructions to cut their evening short and rolled back in the wee hours of the morning. A couple of them even stayed on in London and continued the next day. This is the culture in Wales. I know because I participated in it myself as a player after a defeat by Scotland back in 1991. It was to reach another climax in the collective Passchendaele-like obliteration of the squad by alcohol after the defeat to Fiji in the 2007 World Cup.

Alan Phillips would try to excuse the relaxed culture during the Gareth Jenkins regime to me by saying that both Steve Hansen and Scott Johnson could drink equally heavily but still turn up and carry it off the next day. I couldn't agree. That was not part of my rugby background. Mike Ruddock says that as Welsh head coach he wouldn't even have a social pint on the Friday evening before a game because there was always a real danger of the conviviality escalating. You have to be individually accountable to yourself as a player, and the managers of the group have to set an ironclad example. There is no room for ambiguity.

When I was 19 years old, I went for a shandy the evening before one of my first appearances for Pontypool. The next Monday, Pross pulled me aside and said, 'Don't ever do that again if you want to play for Pontypool.' Proof (if proof were needed) that the Pooler web of pub spotters was working as well as ever. We often only had one training session per week because people were on shift work, but in that one session we would be beasted, doing fitness work that would hold its own and more in the professional era.

As Graham Price says, 'Ray Prosser worked us like dogs. There was no point turning up at training to get fit – you would die. I've seen grown men broken in half, left weeping, by our sessions. The onus was to be in fantastic physical shape before you ever went anywhere near the ground. That meant training on your own or with a small group, working hard running all summer, being honest with yourself. I lost count of the games we won by simply destroying the opposition in the final quarter. Pooler lost a big edge when other sides started matching us for fitness. For a while, we were miles ahead of our time.'

Mostyn Davies used to dread pre-season training. He would spend most of the day before a session on the toilet. When we arrived and started our warm-up laps, we knew we were in for a belter when Ivor Taylor disappeared up to the top of the Grotto in Pontypool Park. At a given command, everyone would sprint for the corner of the ground in a mad race, then move into single file for the ascent. Up the hill, along the side of the ski slope, then that killing final hundred yards or so where the slope is nearly vertical. A few words of encouragement from Ivor, then back down into the valley and up again to the top of a second peak with Pross waiting. By the time you got back to the pitch, you were half-dead. Then maybe exercises along the length of the pitch in team units. 'Oi, Madman,' Pross would say to Chris Huish. 'You follow Spring and Shaft . . . chasing them will straighten your eyes out for you.' Chris has a lazy eye. Finally, a game of 'Prosser touch'. That meant full contact with no kicking allowed. Huish had his revenge, bumping me back fully five yards as I went to tackle him. I looked up to see Pross bent double with laughter. 'Madman, you can't do that. He's only a youngster who doesn't know what he's got into. Penalty against you.'

I remember a local lad called Mike Whitson came up for one of our pre-season runs – a strapping lad from Cwmbran, about 18 or 19 stones. He hadn't done any summer work, and he started out on one of the Grotto runs. Well, Pross was ready to begin the pitch work when someone said, 'Wait a minute. There's someone still up there.' Whitson arrived about 20 minutes later, dazed and weaving, and promptly collapsed on the ground in front of us. After a cup of tea, he came back in time for the game of Prosser touch, and immediately set about using his size and strength, banging everyone around. At the end, Pross went up to him and said, 'Don't come back 'ere, butty, until you can do the full session.' Whitson never returned. He went down to Neath instead. As I say, there was never any room for ambiguity about standards with Ray Prosser.

The squad met the day after the England game at the Glamorgan Cricket Club for the debrief. We'd been sitting in one of the rooms of the pavilion, looking out over the ground, and I was packing away my equipment when I got involved in a discussion among the senior players who had remained in the room. Rob Howley, Neil Jenkins, Scott Quinnell and Dai Young were present. They were talking about some of the latest trends introduced to the England squad by Clive Woodward.

Apparently, the England players would be sent to Harley Street to have hair samples taken, from which the exact composition of their diet could be deduced. Our senior pros were talking in a state of wide-eyed awe at their detailed, scientific approach to nutrition compared to our own burger-and-booze ridden culture. Jenks happily admitted that he would be picking up a burger on his way back to Church Village, and I think it was the same for all the others, bar Rob Howley, who always looked after himself carefully. It was a pivotal moment because they were beginning to question our own methods and attitudes.

Rob Howley was always one you could rely on to take care of his body and mind. He was always very professional. He could do the work and do it on his own, unmonitored. He always took ownership and was fastidious about the specific details of his performance. One Christmas, he came into the office before we were leaving for the holiday break and asked me if I could prepare a tape of all his tries for Wales as a gift for his dad. I wasn't keen because it meant an intense day's work, but he surprised me again by producing a bundle of tapes, each wound on to the exact time of his scores. So, all I had to do was splice the footage together without the interminable research. That was Rob: very meticulous, an eye for detail, sharp as a pin.

The fact remained that we had finished poorly against England, and Blackie, as the conditioner, had been under a fair amount of pressure even before that. An article by ex-Wallaby coach Bob Dwyer had appeared in the press calling the Quinnell brothers overweight and fat, and the issue showed no signs of going away. In the run-up to our next game, versus Scotland on 18 March, Blackie turned up late to a training session with Rob Howley and Dai Young at the John Lloyd Centre. When he arrived, he just wanted to talk through the issues with them over a cup of tea, rather than do the meaningful fitness work that Rob in particular wanted. This proved to be the straw that broke the camel's back for the management, and they decided that Blackie had to go. Blackie, either nobly or foolishly, tried to convince me that it wasn't their doing during a private conversation at the health club, but I wasn't buying. My gut instinct told me that even in leaving, Blackie was attempting to do Graham a favour by falling on his own sword and shielding him from the growing pressure on his own job.

Blackie often suffered physical symptoms when the real pain was psychological in origin, and during that period he began to experience acute stomach problems and pass blood out through his groin. At Murrayfield, he walked out of the stadium in dire pain near the end of the match, and symbolically out of the Wales national squad for ever. I visited him in hospital at the Heath over the next couple of days. His wife Julie was there with him, and the atmosphere was sad and muted. I remembered the time when he'd sent Henry some little books of nursery rhymes when he was born, each with a little message inside the front cover. Blackie: the soul of consideration for others, and ultimately the victim of it. I gave him a hug. He resigned on the Monday afternoon.

Great coach that he was, Graham never hesitated to show a ruthless streak in any perceived it's-me-or-him situation. Lynn Howells would experience this scenario about 18 months later: 'I'd worked with Graham since the outset in 1998 as forwards coach, but nothing is clearer in my head than the way it all ended. Graham invited me over for dinner just before the start of the November 2001 campaign. At the end of the meal, he just said to me, "We've had a good time, Lynn, haven't we?" I replied, "Yes," wondering where this was all going. "Well, one of us has to go soon," he said, "and I'm not going anywhere." I just burst out laughing. If it hadn't been Graham – and I knew how insensitive he could be – I would have put one on him. I told him that before I got up to leave.'

When Garin Jenkins took control of the microphone on the team bus after an A team game in France, he was doing his best impersonation of Graham calling time on his international career: 'Hello, Garin, it's Graham. You're a stalwart – Wales's most-capped hooker. It's been an experience, hasn't it? You're in the As on Saturday.' I don't think Garin could believe how easily he'd been let go. He repeated it over and over again, as if trying to convince himself: 'You're in the As on Saturday.'

It was good that Graham Henry had the guts to tell players and coaches to their face when they were no longer wanted. But sometimes Graham could be a little too ruthless and too brazen about it. Allan Lewis felt that 'Graham had great rugby values, even if I felt sometimes that his values off the field weren't always as admirable. A lot of effort was made to attract overseas players such as Jason Jones-Hughes and Andy Marinos to come to Wales with the carrot of a place in the World Cup squad.

But if it became clear during management discussions that they might not make the grade, Graham could cut the ties very quickly: "Well, they knew the risks when they came over here. Stuff 'em.'"

The pressure on Graham to drop Blackie had built up from a completely unrelated issue: the so-called 'Grannygate' affair. Our 11-match unbeaten run included a couple of New Zealanders in the form of full-back Shane Howarth and openside flanker Brett Sinkinson. At the time, the rules regarding qualification were pretty lax, so players such as Stephen Bachop could go from playing for Samoa to the All Blacks and then back to Samoa again in the course of his career. There was a sense of interchangeability between the Pacific Islands and New Zealand, which resulted in the Bachop brothers, Graeme and Stephen, eventually even playing *against* each other on the international stage.

I think Graham brought this loose attitude with him to Wales. When push came to shove, neither Shane nor Brett could prove they had a shred of Welsh ancestry. Well, Shane *might* have had a shred, because he insisted that his maternal grandfather was Welsh, although documentation indicated otherwise. The truth was that Shane had a family secret he wanted to protect, though neither his tears nor his frustration could budge the Maori register's obstinate insistence on Hare Matenga Popata from Oturu as being his 'real' maternal grandfather.

Sinkinson's was a more clear-cut case. Byron Hayward, one of the players to lose out on caps directly because Shane Howarth was ahead of him, said that 'Brett had no idea he was Welsh until Graham phoned up and told him that he was.' He did have a paternal grandfather from Oldham in Lancashire, which as his agent said is 'not many miles from Wales', but then that same agent had already mistakenly attempted to qualify him for Ireland through the grandfather on his mother's side, and a substantial body of water separates Dublin from Lower Hutt, in the Wellington district of New Zealand. Trevor James knew that Graham was desperate to recruit anyone who could help Wales in a hurry. It was par for the course Down Under.

Graham wasn't happy unless he continually put himself under pressure. He liked to create an atmosphere of uncertainty among his staff in order to put pressure on them, too. He wanted to discover whether you had steel showing after you'd been scratched, but sometimes I felt he miscalculated and got it wrong. When he first gave me Nick's Wallaby report, he did so without a word, and I sat there in Graham's home reading this monster 70-pager, my head reeling, wondering what I should be thinking: what's going on here? Does Graham want someone else involved? Knowing Graham as I do now, I can see that it was a way of keeping me on my toes, but at the time it wasn't at all easy to handle.

When he first set about finding a replacement for Blackie, Graham interviewed two main contenders: Huw Wiltshire and Peter Herbert, the Llanelli fitness coach. I remember dropping a tape round to Graham's home in Marshfield one afternoon. When I entered the lounge area, he was talking to Huw, and I immediately made as if to go, but he said, 'No, mate, hang around. Take a seat.' After a couple of minutes, it dawned on me that I'd actually stumbled in on Huw's interview for the conditioning job. I knew Huw well and felt very awkward, and a short while later I found an excuse to leave quietly. But that was typical of Graham: he liked to play mind games with people and see how they reacted. Over that same summer, he designated two coaches for the development tour of North America – Geraint John and Leigh Jones – without saying who was to be in charge, just leaving it open. He was there as an observer, watching as Leigh automatically took control of situations, with Geraint just as automatically falling in behind. Peter Herbert eventually got the conditioning role ahead of Huw Wiltshire, as he seemed to favour the aerobic emphasis that Graham had inherited from his Auckland days with Jim Blair.

The WRU proved something of a mixed blessing for Graham Henry. Even though Graham had much more control over his destiny than any other Wales coach before or since and found a willing ally in Glanmor Griffiths, he still found himself in the middle of committee meetings far too often for comfort, always having to justify this or that expenditure. Often these meetings would end with an exasperated Graham simply saying, 'Look, you've employed me to improve the fortunes of your team playing the national sport. For goodness' sake, just let me get on and do it.'

Graham had to set a new professional standard in terms of the relationship between the national squad and the administrative apparatus as soon as he came to Wales. Before the 1999 friendly against Italy, I remember we stayed in a small industrial town called Mestre in the Gulf of Venice, landside of Venice proper but still within range of a barcarolle for an ambitious gondolier. This was the game in which the WRU committee men made their presence felt. The hotel in France for the previous match had been too small to include them, but they certainly made sure that the accommodation in Mestre was large enough and amenable enough to cater for their needs. This remnant of amateurism infuriated Graham, and accommodation was swiftly segregated thereafter so that players and committee members would only mix at receptions after games, and only occasionally at that.

Over the 12 years of my involvement, native Welsh coaches rarely experienced the same level of support as their New Zealand counterparts. Mike Ruddock and Kevin Bowring lacked the authority to effect the changes they really wanted. Both are now working in England. Mike suffered from a lack of support within his management group, and Kevin Bowring's visionary ideas from his 1998 report were taken on board and implemented by Kiwis, sometimes years later. Moreover, life has not been any easier for up-and-coming Welsh coaches, who have found it difficult to identify a pathway through the ranks to the top of the game in Wales.

Chris Davey was a hugely successful coach of the Wales Under-21 side, winning three Grand Slams and six titles in his nine years in charge. But Scott Johnson once told me that Chris was 'clogging up the system', and now he's back on the fringes as director of rugby at UWIC. When Leighton Morgan and Mostyn Richards told Chris that he was out of a job in 2005, it highlighted a problem in the relationship between the union and the regions. Chris needed a regional or national appointment in order to progress his career, but the national role was already filled, the A team had been disbanded the year before and the regions were outside the union's control. So, Chris Davey was left in professional no-man's-land.

Kevin Hopkins, another Level 4 coach (the highest level that can be achieved in Wales), lost his job in May 2008 at the Ospreys after Andrew Hore took over as Elite Performance Director. John Bevan, the British Lion and double union–league international, was a fully qualified coach who guided the Wales Under-19s to the World Cup final at Stradey

Park in 1999, but he'd resigned within two years of that success and now teaches at Monmouth School. Gareth Jenkins was peremptorily sacked after the World Cup in 2007 and hasn't worked as a coach again since, so that is another bank of knowledge that's been lost to the Welsh game, at least for the time being. You can't tell me that those men, and others such as Trevor James, don't have a great deal to offer the domestic game in Wales. Trevor has retired to his farm in West Wales and spends most of his time painting pictures. He's only a phone call away.

I don't feel that the perception of Graham Henry as the saviour of Welsh rugby helped him one little bit. It put too much pressure on him to succeed and too little on the infrastructure of Welsh rugby to evolve a winning formula underneath him. I remember a house-warming party for Graham and his wife Raewyn in the early days, which included many family members, friends and union representatives. The WRU chairman, Glanmor Griffiths, got up to make an impromptu welcome speech and heaped praise on Graham. Whilst it was understandable – ultimately Glanmor needed Graham Henry to be a success in order to justify the financial outlay of bringing him to Wales – Graham felt he hadn't done anything, and he was being built up too much, so, ultimately, it was embarrassing. Graham defused it all tactfully, but the balance between having a successful coach and a successful support structure beneath him clearly wasn't right. When Graham inevitably started to lose a few games, there was nothing and no one for him to fall back on.

After the magic spell of our eleven-match unbeaten run had been well and truly broken by the two heavy defeats to France and England at the beginning of the 2000 Six Nations, Graham tried to rebuild the team with a new generation of players. Shane Williams, Stephen Jones and Ian Gough all cut their international teeth under Graham, although at least two of them – Shane and Goughey – were to be largely ignored by Steve Hansen when Graham left. (It's great to see that Goughey in particular has finally fulfilled the potential that Graham always knew he had in the latter stages of his career under Warren Gatland.) The only unit of the team unchanged from the 1999 World Cup was the front row.

Graham's judgement deteriorated steadily as the pressure on him mounted. At the start of the year, for instance, he made crisp, clear and very effective substitutions. However, later that year he made one intervention in particular that perhaps cost us a victory. The away match against Ireland in the spring showed Graham at his best. Another new boy, Rhys Williams, had come in as a late replacement for the last match of the Six Nations against Ireland on April Fool's Day. Graham phoned him up, but at first Rhys didn't realise who it was. I think he was expecting a call from his dad, and Graham just let Rhys carry on talking until a suitable pause arose in the conversation. 'Graham Henry here. You're in the team on Saturday.' April Fool. There was a deathly silence while Rhys got himself together. With the cajoling and encouragement of new assistant Geraint John – who'd known him from Glantaf School – ringing in his ears, Rhys handled and counter-attacked quite faultlessly on a typically wet and windy Lansdowne Road afternoon. But as well as Rhys played, he wasn't the decisive factor.

Graham made two crucial substitutions in the last fifteen minutes to tip the balance our way, bringing on Robin McBryde and Neil Jenkins for Garin Jenkins and Stephen Jones. Robin put a neat kick through from a short-side attack that earned us a penalty, and Neil promptly converted it. That was the game won, although Alfie did have to make one last-ditch tackle on Anthony Foley deep in our right-hand corner to make certain of the victory. If you'd told me then, after watching Rhys Williams's dream debut at Lansdowne Road, that we would be shipping ninety points against Ireland over the course of our next two games, I would have laughed in your face, but that's exactly what happened.

Substitutions: they are a major part of the modern game. Gareth Potter and I had done a great deal of research on the impact of replacement players on the course of matches in preparation for the game against South Africa in November 2000. We found that their impact was wholly disproportionate to the amount of time that they spent on the field. All our calculations were time based, and we found that a replacement might have ten or fifteen significant actions during his twenty-minute cameo. The starter for the same position might only produce about 25 actions for the entire 80 minutes. So you could get 60 per cent of whole-game effectiveness from an individual in only one quarter of the match. The work rate was incredible.

Graham was well aware of this research, and I think he overreacted to it and made an error in judgement in the game against South Africa.

Jenks had made one kicking mistake around the hour mark, and Graham promptly pulled him off and replaced him with Arwel Thomas. Usually, Graham had a great feel for the game, and his substitutions were sharp and accurate, but on this occasion he got it all wrong. Arwel had a nightmare, and we ended up going backwards in the last 20 minutes of a game we had every right to win. It was a far cry from Dublin at the beginning of April, when Graham's timely substitutions had won us the match. I guess it was a sign of the times for Graham Henry.

As a squad, we were treading water in 2000–01 despite all the new faces. We were still capable of the odd startling success, such as the game against France in 2001, but we were losing heavily and regularly to England and couldn't reverse the process because our fundamentals, particularly in terms of whole-life fitness and financial resources, didn't match theirs. As soon as Graham made the decision after the 2000 Six Nations to accept the head coaching job with the British Lions in Australia the following summer, I believe he signed his own death warrant as Wales coach. The events of the Lions tour drained Graham completely and accelerated a process that was already well in motion.

For seven weeks, Graham had had to live with the huge advances England had made in their team development and with Clive Woodward's unsubtle animosity towards him. Donal Lenihan, the Lions team manager, had told Clive Woodward that he stood absolutely no chance of being appointed as Lions coach, and Woodward obviously resented the elevation of a Kiwi who'd coached Wales to two consecutive forty-point losses against his own England side.

Woodward almost seemed to make a point of associating with the Wallaby management as the tour started and as it progressed. He was picked up at Coffs Harbour Airport by Ewen MacKenzie and Scott Johnson, two of the Wallaby assistants, and seemed also to enjoy being seen in public with Rod Macqueen more than with Graham. In fact, he wasn't associated once with Graham in a media shot. Nick Bishop recalls strolling out of his Coffs Harbour hotel in the week before the first Test: 'I walked across the golf course to get my morning coffee and a paper and right into a Sky TV discussion. There were lights and cameras, and there were a group of the Sky regulars circled on the lawn, but the two principals were Rod Macqueen and Clive Woodward. My eyes almost popped out of my head. The timing and the obvious conviviality between the two men didn't seem at all accidental before such an important Test match.'

This very much tallied with my own experiences on the trip. Through no fault of their own, England were so far ahead of the Celts in so many aspects of their preparation that it created a split in the camp that could only be inflamed by Woodward's attitude. 'That wouldn't happen with England' became the mantra for the tour. You could hear it at every training session or meeting. On the analysis front, we had to use video for the player tapes, as this was the medium the Celtic players were used to at the time, but England, with their much greater resources, had already allocated each player his own laptop, with clips on DVD. There were grumblings among the England players when we had to use videotape.

Then Phil Larder demanded half of the coaching time to bring the Celts up to speed on his own advanced system of defence, which had a domino effect, with all the other coaches pushing for their own increased input and sessions. This boosted the players' workload dramatically. Even at our bonding week at Tylney Hall arranged by the Impact group, there were seven actual bonding sessions or activities and six training sessions, as opposed to eight and one in 1997. The balance between training and relaxation had been lost before we even reached Australia.

The other point of balance, between the Celts and the English, seemed to tilt progressively towards England as the trip wore on. When Graham tried to introduce player feedback into the analysis, which was something we did with the Welsh squad, Phil simply said, 'We don't do that with England. We just tell them what to do.' The next day, I woke up to find that the plan had been quietly shelved. Some of the English players ridiculed Blackie for his unorthodox training methods, comparing him unfavourably to the English conditioner Dave Reddin. Then there was the pod system, in which players operated in groups down their own channels of the field. It went on and on, until the grumblings inevitably exploded publicly through the press columns of Matt Dawson and Austin Healey.

I guess the 'English problem' reached a fitting climax at Sydney with the series tied up at one-all and everything to play for. Graham asked Andy Robinson to change the lineout calls, as the players suspected that they'd been rumbled by the Aussies. Scott Johnson confirmed that the code had indeed been broken when he joined Graham's coaching team the following season, because he'd been doing most of the rumbling – playing water boy at every lineout before the first Test while clandestinely noting the Lions' lineout calls. But Andy stubbornly refused to change the calls, and we lost seven lineout throws in the game, including a vital pinch by Justin Harrison at the end when we were looking to make a kill with our driving maul right on their line.

The Wallabies, meanwhile, shrewdly made the most of their opportunity to exploit the cracks appearing in a superior team on tour. They stole a march on us at the lineout with Scott Johnson's successful spying mission, they brought in an unkickable Summit ball that neutralised the goalkicking of Jonny Wilkinson – one of the Lions' greatest strengths – and knocked him back down to a miserable 52 per cent success rate, and they got away with a much higher percentage of collapsed scrums and mauls than was usual in Test rugby at the time. These were both strong points in the Lions' game.

That was enough to win them a memorable series 2–1. But as Graham pointed out to me afterwards, in some ways we'd done better than the 1997 Lions side in South Africa: 'We shared the try count with the Aussies seven apiece in 2001. In 1997, the Lions were outscored 9–2 on the try count over the three games, but they had Neil Jenkins kicking goals from everywhere to sustain them. They also benefited from South Africa having a novice coach who hadn't coached any high-level team at all at that point in his coaching career. The business of success and failure on both tours was a very fine line.'

Nick co-wrote Graham's account of the tour after it had finished, and he remembers a meeting in the final week before the third Test: 'I would meet Graham regularly throughout the trip for updates, and in the final week we found a small, quiet coffee shop in Manly, a suburb of Sydney. We sat down and waited for a couple of cappuccinos to arrive. This was an achievement in itself, because during the early part of the tour it had been almost impossible to find a private moment. In Brisbane, we'd gone out one night to find a café and ended up being pursued by a horde of well-meaning Lions supporters around the side streets for a good 20 minutes or so.

'I started asking Graham a few questions. He began to answer, but after a few token efforts a silence enveloped our table. Strangely, the silence wasn't uncomfortable; on the contrary, it felt very expressive. I could sense Graham's utter frustration at the way the tour had unfolded. It was quite unmistakeable. We sat there for about 20 minutes, saying nothing, watching the people going about their business in sunny Manly. When we walked back to his hotel, it felt like the fate of the third Test, and of the series as a whole, had somehow already been decided.'

It's never easy to tell an international with 40 or 50 caps that he isn't good enough at the best of times, and Welsh players whom Graham had built up as 'the best in the world' hadn't been first choices on that tour. Some, such as Mark Taylor, ended up hammering on his bedroom door in frustration, knowing that Graham was inside but unwilling to answer. So even Graham's positivity had a downside that he eventually had to answer for. He came back a broken man. Nick remembers calling him a couple of months later: 'I was shocked to hear a voice I didn't even recognise at the other end of the phone. I was used to Graham being quick-witted, dry, in control. What I heard that evening was a man who could hardly speak and didn't want to, who sounded lost. I spoke to him again a couple of weeks later. There was an unfamiliar ringtone, followed by the sound of peace and quiet in the background. "Hello, mate, how are you? What's going on over there? It's five in the morning here." I didn't mention that all hell was breaking loose in the media over here. He was holed up on his own, convalescing in a chalet on a picturesque lake somewhere outside Auckland. I didn't blame him one little bit after the experience he'd just been through.'

We all returned shattered after losing that series. I had my own health problems to worry about after returning from Australia. I'd been doing the analysis work down at Cardiff with Lynn Howells and Geraint John since November 2001, which meant that I'd been juggling three balls for more than a year – the work for Wales, Cardiff and the Lions, not to mention the pressures of bringing up a young family. It was all just too much, and I began suffering from long periods of exhaustion. I didn't know it at the time, but after going for tests I found that I had glandular fever. Something had to give with me, just as it did with Graham.

I managed to offload the Cardiff work on to one of my protégés,

Naomi Jones, who did a fine job of at first supporting, then bossing about the new coach Rudy Joubert. Naomi was a 'graduate' from the notational centre who had come all the way through the system from work-experience trainee to regional analyst. I took it easy throughout September. There was one match held over from the 2001 Six Nations in the spring due to the foot-and-mouth scare, and that was the game versus Ireland. Eventually, it was played on 13 October 2001, and we were heavily beaten at the Millennium Stadium, 36–6, with three Irish tries coming in the last ten minutes. There was a strong thread of anti-Graham Henry feeling coming out of the Irish camp after the match, with some of their players painting it as a kind of payback for what happened on the Lions tour – and, of course, Welsh players such as Mark Taylor, Colin Charvis and Darren Morris were disgruntled that Graham's 'best in the world' moniker wasn't enough to get them into the Lions Test team. So there was pressure from within and without, and Graham decided to take another two-week holiday before our next game against Argentina on 10 November.

Our conversations at the time tended to be negative in tone, and I think both of us were seeking a way out. Graham wasn't a quitter, but having been the 'Great Redeemer', he was now ironically looking for saviours himself: Iestyn Harris and Clive Griffiths from rugby league, Steve Hansen from New Zealand, Scott Johnson from Australia. In retrospect, Iestyn wasn't ready for the game against Argentina, even though at the time I'd agreed with Graham that he was. He'd had one outstanding individual display for Cardiff against Glasgow in the Heineken Cup and had a skill-set no other inside back in Wales could match, but Argentina had some wily old foxes – Les Cusworth on the coaching staff, Agustín Pichot and Felipe Contepomi in the team – who knew how to exploit his inexperience in rugby union. We lost 30–16.

The pivotal change was not Iestyn Harris but the appearance on the scene of Steve Hansen. I first met Steve back in May when Graham brought him to my flat to show him the analytical tools we had in place and the 'Focus' system we were using with the Lions. Everybody in New Zealand had been recommending him to Graham, and he duly joined up with us at the end of Canterbury's National Provincial Championship campaign in November. With Graham stuffed after the Lions tour, Steve

Hansen would change the whole dynamic of the coaching group and have an impact far beyond anything Graham could have envisaged or planned for at the time.

Graham had been looking to replicate the English management structure, with himself as a Woodward-like director of rugby and a tier of assistant coaches beneath him. By September, he'd already brought in Clive Griffiths as the attack coach, with Leigh Jones initially handling the defence (although Clive was to take over that area in due course). Lynn Howells was still managing the forwards, with Steve Hansen 'shadowing' him closely and uncomfortably. Trevor James had changed the training venue to Atlantic College to try and help find that spark – a new setting to go with the new personalities. My strongest memory of our time there was of Steve Hansen putting our new psychologist, Graham Jones, down in front of the players, arguing with him quite bullishly and, ultimately, belittling him. It was real. Graham Jones is a world-class sports psychologist who has coached top-class athletes, such as the swimmer Adrian Moorehouse and squash champion Lisa Opie, but by the end of the autumn campaign he, like Lynn Howells, was gone. Hansen then produced a dossier on what needed to change in Welsh rugby. It was pretty basic stuff and nothing we didn't already know after Kevin Bowring's report four years previously, but Graham Henry seemed to love it.

The introduction of Clive Griffiths into the Wales set-up was to prove highly significant, not just for the remainder of Graham Henry's time in charge, but for the next six years. Clive was an international rugby player in both codes, and he'd coached at the very highest level in both. He was nobody's fool. Maurice Lindsay, the ex-Wigan chairman and chief executive of rugby league, first encountered Clive as an arch-enemy playing for local rivals St Helens: 'Both as a player and a coach, Clive lived and breathed rugby. It's hard to overstate the passion of the man. At first, I formed a respect for him as a player during our derbies with St Helens – he was one of the great goalkickers in league at the time. Then I discovered a very intelligent coach after his playing career had finished. Clive was certainly good enough to coach at the very top level, and, in my position as chief exec of the rugby league, I invited him to coach the Great Britain side to tour New Zealand in 1996.

'Clive was well liked by all the players, and he was a team man through and through. I never heard anyone with a bad word to say about him up north. I had so much respect for him that when I tried to resuscitate the Orrell rugby union club in 2003 and we were struggling to find our feet under the Australian coach Ross Reynolds, the first man I thought of turning to for a little experienced help and a guiding hand was Clive. He'd just left London Welsh at the time, and he helped the club get its bearings again.

'He was very much part of a great tradition of Welsh players who'd left their homeland to settle in Lancashire and play league, the tradition which began with Billy Boston and continued latterly with Dai Bishop and Jonathan Davies. Lancashire and south Wales were very similar environments. The communities were based around the collieries, and there was a tough blue-collar mentality in the fabric of the rugby. Look at Denis Betts [with Gloucester RFC] and Shaun Edwards, two of my lads at Wigan. There's a great deal of common sense and a blunt, no-nonsense attitude with these players that can jump codes easily, and I'd put Clive in the same category.

'Clive's passion is so overwhelming that it simply has to be harnessed. I remember being on the Wigan team bus on the way to Wembley for the 2004 Challenge Cup final. We were coached by Mike Gregory, who'd been a mate of Clive's at Warrington, and he was already in the grip of the motor neurone disease that claimed his life three years later. He could hardly read or write even then, and Clive sent a text message to my phone wishing him luck. I passed the phone back down the bus towards Mike, but it got intercepted by one of our props on the way, and he replied telling Clive to get stuffed. I got a call from Clive immediately. "Who the hell do you think you are, then?" he said. We almost fell out over it until I realised what had happened. But that's Clive Griffiths. He wears his heart on his sleeve and rugby matters to him dearly. The people in rugby matter to him dearly, whether they are from Wales or the north of England.'

Clive himself had been enthused at the prospect of working with Graham: 'I'd been asked to coach the Great Britain rugby league team in the mid-'90s, and then Alex Murphy took me back to St Helens as a skills and fitness coach. We went all the way to Wembley for the

Challenge Cup final. I then coached at Warrington for eight years with Brian Johnson and returned to the Chalenge Cup final with 'The Wire' in 1990. I finally returned to the game as director of rugby at London Welsh, helping them towards a record-breaking promotion season in 1997–98. After achieving a Level 3 coaching certificate with John Plumtree at Coach Training HQ in Usk, "Plum" invited me down to coach both attack and defence at Swansea in the 2000–01 season, and I think we played an attractive brand of rugby on our way to winning the Welsh–Scottish League that year.

'That's when I first got to know Graham Henry. He was around Swansea a lot at the time, and he admired our style of play. By 2001, he'd invited me to help coach the Wales A side alongside Mike Ruddock – the start of a long and fruitful partnership between Mike and me. Our first game was against France A in Bergerac, and we narrowly lost, 22–21. It was Garin Jenkins's first game for the As after his demotion from the senior squad, and he kept us amused with his Graham Henry impersonation on the bus.

'Graham asked me to do some coaching with the senior squad in August and September 2001 before the Romania game. I knew I was being given the Henry litmus test, and he was constantly asking questions throughout the sessions: "Why are you doing this? Why are you doing that?" He wanted to know the rationale for everything. At the end of the second session, I couldn't resist it any longer and said, "Have I passed the test, then?" He just grinned at me with that twinkle in his eye, but not long afterwards he offered me the option of a three-year contract, with responsibility for the defence as my main area but a remit to coach across the board.'

There was, however, immediate friction between Clive Griffiths and Steve Hansen. As Clive recalls, 'My first meeting with Steve Hansen was in the build-up to the Argentina game. He was there as an observer and not yet contracted. It was a bit of a shock . . . I was in the middle of a Tuesday session with two defensive groups, alternating between the two. I was in the process of setting up the second group when I looked back to see Hansen getting involved with the first and actually changing the drill. "Look, mate, I was trying something different with 'em," was his reply when I went back over there and asked what he was

84   **SEEING RED**

doing. He didn't even have the professional courtesy to ask me first, and we coaches always like to have everything orchestrated in advance, knowing all the plans and the people involved for the session so that it runs crisply. Remember the saying, "You only have one chance to make a good first impression"? Well, no truer words were spoken.'

Somehow it felt like the changing of the guard had already happened, especially when Graham Henry disappeared for his son Andrew's birthday right in the middle of our team-building week before the beginning of the Six Nations. That had never happened before.

The week before the first match against Ireland was the first time I encountered the burly, long-haired, mercurial Aussie Scott Johnson. There was a lunch at the Glamorgan Cricket Club after a morning session, and Scott had arrived, larger than life. I recall trying to speak to him in the queue as we were waiting to be fed, but he just gave me a perfunctory acknowledgement and looked away. It was obvious he only had eyes for Graham.

Graham took his seat in the corner with Steve Hansen on one side and Scott Johnson on the other. A couple of files were lying open on the table: the Australian playbook from the Lions series in 2001 and the Brumbies playbook from the Super 12. Steve Hansen had recommended Scott to Graham as the 'best analyst in the world', and Graham had even suggested at one point that I might find room for him in my own budget. After sharing all the experiences I had with Graham since 1998 and going through the ferocious wind tunnel of the recent Lions tour together, it was sad to see him sitting isolated in the corner, with Steve Hansen pecking at him from one side and Scott Johnson chipping from the other. The dynamic in our relationship had changed as clearly for me as it had for Clive Griffiths. Rugby-wise, both of us were suddenly outsiders in our own country.

It was a windy Friday afternoon when the squad set off to Dublin for the first match of the 2002 Six Nations against Ireland, not suspecting that the real storm lay further ahead. We stayed at the Westbury Hotel, close to St Stephen's Green. Graham arranged to meet me for a quiet drink in the bar that evening. I felt he had something to tell me, but we never got the chance to talk. Even at dinner the following night, Steve Hansen and Scott Johnson were seated in between us: 'We should be doing this and that . . .' Graham would turn to me and say, 'We're already doing that, aren't we, Carts?'

It was obvious that Graham was finding it difficult to control the powerful new personalities just beneath him, and the dynamic within the group had changed completely. So, it was no surprise when there was a showdown of sorts soon afterwards between Graham and Steve in what both coaches thought was an empty team room. Graham felt that he was being undermined and said so, and he demanded Steve's support in no uncertain terms. They didn't know Iestyn Harris was there. Iestyn had found himself alone in the team room after dinner and slipped down on the sofa when Graham and Steve entered the room . . .

In the game itself, Chris Wyatt left the field after two minutes, and Jamie Robinson after seven, which left us with two front jumpers and two inside centres for the rest of the match. The selection was poor and muddled, and reflected Graham's state of mind at the time. We were stuffed 54–10, and Ireland scored seven tries. Perhaps the worst aspect of the whole experience was returning through the airport on Monday morning. Graham and I had drifted apart from the rest of the team, and we pushed our trolleys along in silence, with only the occasional look between us. The atmosphere was absolutely awful – I was aware of this constant background hiss, a strange compound of stony glances and half-whispered comments from the onlookers as we walked past.

I'd followed my usual routine to present the analysis and performance indicators for Graham later that day, but Hansen wanted something completely different. It hadn't been discussed beforehand, but Graham went along with it anyway. It was as if Graham had already accepted his fate and handed over the reins. On the evening of Tuesday, 6 February, I got the short, inevitable call: 'I'm finished. It's been great working with you, Alun. Are you going to be OK?' Ironic, that. If I'd had more energy, I would have asked him the same question. The following day, Graham told the players he was leaving. He had made the arrangements with Glanmor Griffiths for his succession, and Steve Hansen was going to take up his appointed role as head coach of the national team.

Clive for one didn't feel Graham had to finish so abruptly: 'I was bitterly disappointed to see Graham go in February. I don't think he needed to go. It was a freak result against Ireland. I felt he could've taken some time out, hung around and ridden out the storm. I knew I had a rapport with Graham that there'd never be with Steve Hansen. As soon as Graham went, Hansen cut down my responsibilities, restricting me to the defence, where Graham had wanted my input on both sides of the ball.

'"You're only the defence coach," was his stock answer to any input I might have. In 2003, he didn't take me on the summer tour to New Zealand and Australia for financial reasons, and during the World Cup he wouldn't let me do anything more than coach one-on-one tackling techniques. I "cheated" a bit and brought the players into some situational-defence drills! I felt that I could have contributed far more if I'd been given the chance, which only fuelled my frustration.

'I travelled back to Liverpool Airport separately after the Ireland weekend, but even there a Welsh wag spotted me and came across. "You're Clive Griffiths, aren't you? I didn't know you were coaching them to play fuckin' touch rugby now." OK, you got me, bud. I just had to take it and walk away.'

4

EXILED IN MY OWN COUNTRY

Broken down in the middle of an A road. That was my dominant impression after we first moved into the Barn in the Vale of Glamorgan. I arrived one morning, the day after dropping off my equipment, to find the doors locked by heavy-duty chains. I was left sitting on the steps outside in the cold December air, watching my breath freeze as soon as it left my nose and mouth, feeling colder and ever more uncertain inside.

Ever since the World Cup in 1999, Graham Henry had pursued the notion of a covered, indoor facility available 24/7 as a base for the national squad. We used to train at different venues, but none of them were permanent. One of Graham's favourites was the Equestrian Centre at Pencoed near Bridgend, an agricultural centre with a big barn. Always sniffing the possibility of rainfall with his New Zealand background, Graham never lost a chance to get to the barn and its luxurious combination of mud, dung and sawdust. Once upon a time, we were on the M4 heading westwards to St Helens, a field that always had good drainage due to the loose, sandy texture of the soil. It was a favourite of Trevor James, who'd coached down at Swansea. It was bucketing down, and halfway down the motorway Graham said, 'Right, let's go indoors.' The coach dutifully did a U-turn and arrived unannounced at the indoor facility at Pencoed – forwards at one end, backs at the other, agricultural smell: Graham was happy. The weather could no longer disturb his planning.

Graham and David Pickering had been having informal meetings with Gerald Leek, a Rhondda entrepreneur who was in the process of constructing the Vale of Glamorgan Hotel on a parcel of land formerly belonging to the Hensol Castle Estate. They persuaded him to put up a barn for the national squad as part of his plans for the property. Glanmor Griffiths was also involved to supply the necessary financial backing from the WRU.

Steve Hansen also preferred all members of the management group to work under one roof. I wasn't particularly keen, as I was quite happy working from home in my 'office', and I don't think Graham was too enamoured of the idea either, judging by his regular absences. But the die was cast, and in December 2001 I found myself moving all my equipment into a small office at the end of the Barn, directly opposite the head coach's room. The assistant coaches were located next door, and Hansen had the best room, with a view out on to the championship-standard golf course.

The changeover was not a smooth one. On three occasions between December 2001 and January 2002, I arrived in the morning only to find huge, thick chains around the front door, so that nobody could enter or leave. I don't know the background, but Gerald Leek obviously thought that the union had not been fulfilling its part of the bargain with him, whereby they would pay a certain amount towards the maintenance of the facility in exchange for promotional and marketing rights. Gerald was so furious that he'd marched up and locked the doors. It was quite farcical. One day, I'd dropped off all my equipment; the next, I couldn't get in . . . Standing there, I felt as awkward as a man whose car has just broken down in the middle of a busy A road. It turned out to be an uncomfortable portent of the Hansen years. Welshmen such as me, Peter Herbert, Trevor James and Clive Griffiths – who'd all been integral to Graham's planning – were to be left sitting high and dry. It was a lockout.

Graham's last act as Wales coach had been to ensure his successor. Having made such an exhaustive search throughout New Zealand to find the best right-hand man, it was understandable. He'd found the bloke he wanted to continue his work, and in talks with Glanmor the day or two before he resigned, he was at pains to get a guarantee that Steve Hansen would be appointed the next head coach of Wales. It was the only occasion I can recall a coach being able to act with such authority, and as it turned out it did not bode well for the fate of the remaining Welshmen in the management group.

Graham departed on Wednesday, 6 February, only ten days before our next Six Nations fixture against France at the Millennium Stadium, so we didn't have much time to think about the deeper implications. As far as I was concerned, it was still the same squad but with Steve Hansen navigating the ship instead of Graham. Anxious to make a big impression, Steve probably tried to do too much, too soon. One of the immediate changes was that backroom staff now had to get to the ground early to set up and test all the equipment. When I arrived for the France match, there was a radio expert already there, fiddling around with wiring in the box. It became apparent that he was enabling us to tap into the French radio feed, so that we would have a 'heads up' on the plans of the French coaches as the game progressed.

It takes time and a lot of trust between all members of the management group to get clear, concise messages on to the field 100 per cent of the time. It is an arduous business. Only recently I noticed that Irish coach Eddie O'Sullivan entrusted the water/message-bearing duties to his long-standing analyst, Mervyn Murphy. Yet here we were, trying to decode French intentions before we'd even streamlined our own lines of communication. It was bizarre, especially as they were French after all, and we didn't have a French speaker in the box. Yet exactly the same mistake was repeated during the Italy game.

We were held together by the emotion of Graham's farewell before losing an exciting match 33–37 against the French. There was a lot of residual feeling for Graham's departure among the senior pros such as Scott Quinnell and Rob Howley. They wanted to dedicate the game to him, and at the death S.Q. got within smelling distance of the try-line for what would have been a game-winning score.

We managed a decent home win over Italy in our next game, but the acid test, as always in that era, was going to Twickenham in late March to play an England side fast approaching its peak. There was a curious minor incident that weekend involving Trevor James. On the Thursday evening before the game, a group of us, including Trevor, Peter Herbert and me, had visited a pub across the road from the Kensington Gardens Hotel, and purely by chance we'd run into some of Steve Hansen's mates. Trevor lost his expensive, £150 fountain pen that evening, and although he scoured the bar and the nightclub below it the following day, it was nowhere to be found. Strangely, the pen had found its way into the possession of Steve Hansen and new team manager Alan Phillips, and they saw fit to wait until Saturday morning before returning it to Trevor. They portrayed it as a joke and were having their little game with him, all part and parcel of Hansen's cheeky humour. Both Alan and Steve shared a mischievous sense of humour, and I remember Hansen even winked at Clive Woodward as they passed each other on the way to their seats before the game – and no one did that to Clive.

But, rightly or wrongly, the incident certainly sent a definite message to Trevor. Trevor was a fine coach in his own right who'd guided Swansea and mentored Kevin Bowring to the point that he became national coach. He was an astute student of the game and had produced a dossier on elite rugby and the management of teenage rugby players through to the senior ranks that had astounded Vernon Pugh with its detail and scope when Trevor travelled down to his chambers in Cardiff in 1997 to show it to him. None other than Graham Henry had recognised him as one of his huge 'invisible assets'. He was much, much more than an administrator or 'Mr Fixit' – 'I'd rather be called Pinocchio than an administrator,' as Trevor used to say. But Steve felt an obvious need to step out of Graham's shadow and make his own mark, and he started by pushing Trevor out to the periphery of the national squad environment and sacking Peter Herbert, our conditioning coach.

Around November or December 2001, we'd also introduced a new analysis programme, which had replaced the Focus software developed by Scotsman Ian Donnelly. Unbeknownst to me, a Sportscode consultant called Jon Moore had met with Steve and Graham and convinced them to buy a single laptop using his software. I was not invited to that meeting. So we'd changed systems, offices and head coach in the space of about three months. It was quite an upheaval.

The change of system encouraged Steve Hansen to change my job description. Using the live feed through the laptop, I would code the game for Steve's use immediately afterwards, reinforcing stats where necessary with video clips – the single biggest advantage of Sportscode is that it's a visual tool. Before Sportscode, I'd take hand notation up in the stand, then pick up live stats from Gareth Potter and print them off immediately after the game. Graham would have both the stats and key-performance indicators 20 minutes later to take into the press conference with him. Although I was still receiving the live feed from Gareth, Steve made it clear that he neither trusted nor wanted Graham's performance indicators. 'Where's that coming from? Who's doing it?' he'd say. I felt that the interpretive factor was being taken out of my role. A big slice of my job satisfaction and much of my self-confidence went with it.

If we had any doubts about how things were going to be under Steve Hansen, the April to May period before the tour to South Africa in early June dispelled any illusions. All of us – Griff, Peter Herbert, Trevor and I – had verbal or written contracts taking us up to and in some cases beyond the 2003 World Cup, in line with Graham Henry's own contract. But we had no idea who or what Steve Hansen wanted, and Peter in particular became very nervous. As many times as Peter talked things through with Trevor and me and as many times as we offered comfort, nothing seemed to lift the dark cloud over any of our heads. With the glass panelling between offices, Peter's worried frown as he commuted to and from Hansen's room was painfully public, and always deeper when he left than when he went in. He was gone before the start of the South Africa tour, and Steve took over the conditioning role in the interim, before the arrival of Andrew Hore from New Zealand.

There was a depressing feeling in the air that being Welsh meant 'Not Good Enough' to Steve Hansen. The Andy Marinos story was another case in point. Both Steve and Jonno knew Andy from the Super 12 competition as a number 10 or 12 for the Stormers. As a footballer, he was limited and probably did not deserve his place in the Test side, but nonetheless he played in all the Six Nations matches in 2002. Andy's big plus was that he was a superb role model off the field. With his professional attitude to nutrition and fitness, Andy made sure he squeezed every last drop out of his talent, and he was certainly fortunate in the timing of his availability. So Steve and Jonno initially preferred his attitude and southern-hemisphere background to another of the assets Graham had striven so hard to acquire: Iestyn Harris. Even Andy would probably admit that he wasn't fit to lace Iestyn's boots purely as a rugby footballer.

As the southern-hemisphere influence expanded, so the Welsh influence contracted. A renowned scrum doctor from New Zealand, Mike Cron, appeared out of nowhere in May, staying for maybe one week in every three or four months. Dai Young had been coaching just down the road at Aberdare and Cardiff, was a British Lion and available 24/7, but Steve wanted Mike. It turned out that he was something of a father figure to Steve Hansen. They'd both been policemen in the Canterbury area, and it was easy to see the origin of Steve's approach to the scrum and most other things once Cronno arrived. Mike had been a Junior All Black tight-head but gave up the game at 27: 'Like an old horse, I broke down in the legs and couldn't play any longer . . .' He was an expert at biomechanics and had even been to Japan to study sumo wrestling. He used one-on-one technical clinics, emphasising the use of a 'mirror' or video footage in the manner of a ballet teacher. Balance and core strength in the stomach area were everything, as essential to a prop as they were to a dancer. Work Steve had already started, Mike continued with greater depth and refinement, as he spread the good word at Neath and among the Wales age-group sides.

Steve was really at his best in technical meetings with individuals. I know he helped Iestyn Harris a great deal, going through footage of Andrew Mehrtens with him to help speed up his transition from league to union. He'd stop the film when Mehrtens was about to make a tactical decision and ask Iestyn what he would do in that position. Iestyn would answer, and then Steve would spool the film on to see if he was right. There were one-on-one and three-on-three clinics with the front-rowers, concentrating on individual technique. Each practice would be filmed, and Steve would pick out items – body and foot positioning, arching of the back, hip height – and invite each prop to examine their own form in the footage being displayed on a big screen at the Barn. Every individual was constantly invited to look at themselves in the mirror with fresh, recently filmed evidence, and it was one of Steve's great strengths. He never let that evidence go cold. It was always the same day or next morning, an up-to-the-minute slice of self-reflection. Crisp and clear. Iestyn Thomas took a great deal from those sessions when he saw that he could shoot even big Ben Evans backwards simply by keeping good body mechanics and flexing his back at the right moment.

Steve also orchestrated a big week at Saundersfoot, on the Pembrokeshire coast, in preparation for the Barbarians fixture on 29 May. Saundersfoot has always been something of a safe haven in times of trouble for the national squad, even if we haven't always beaten a retreat for the right reasons. Sometimes we go there to gather our strength before putting in a mighty effort, as we did before Ireland in the 2003 Six Nations; at others, we simply go to hide from the pressure – Nigel Davies taking the wreckage of the post-World Cup squad down there before the one-off game against world champions South Africa in November 2007.

We stayed at St Bride's Hotel and Spa, and the outcome could hardly have been more positive in knitting together the youth and experience within Hansen's first proper selection. A number of young guns from Pontypridd's successful Parker Pen Shield team were included for the first time – Gethin Jenkins, Michael Owen, Rob Sidoli and Ceri Sweeney – and they added new energy and excitement. It felt like a definite departure from the Graham Henry era. Rupert Moon was heavily involved at the time, looking after the players' interests off the field, and he brought his own brand of 'leaping puppy' enthusiasm to the table.

We were split up into four different tribes: Shona, Xhosa and Zulu for the players, and Boers (appropriately) for the management. Apart from the usual spread of physical and team-building activities – clay-pigeon shooting, paintballing, a visit to Hetherington Park – there were also poetry-writing exercises. Curiously, many of the players used this opportunity to take aim at Alan Phillips, the team manager. The players made no bones about their preference for Trevor James over 'Thumper' via their poems – let's just leave it at that.

There was a spirit of playful irreverence that week that extended to the management's own fitness run right at the end, in steepling rain with the players all around baying at us. I still have some terrific film of Hansen lumbering down the sodden track with the players howling in the background. There was just the right balance between serious work (with Steve taking the fitness sessions himself) and jovial relaxation.

We flew out to South Africa only a couple of days after losing 40–25 to the Baa-Baas. The dramatic, or rather melodramatic, tone for the trip was set on the flight itself. The WRU committee man delegated to accompany us was Terry Vaux, my former solicitor and an ex-chairman of Pontypool. A good man. Like everyone else, Terry had a couple of glasses of wine on the plane and then fell asleep. A couple of days later, at a reception for the tour party in Cape Town, Terry slurred his speech responding to the welcome extended by the Western Province officials, and some of the players suspected that he was drunk. In fact, he had suffered a stroke. By the next morning, he was in hospital, and his wife had flown out to be at his bedside. Although we didn't know it at the time, the incident gave notice of a sequence of events on that tour that wouldn't have been out of place in a soap opera. The lid was going to be blown off some raw, larger-than-life emotions.

The Vineyard Hotel, a quaint colonial building near the Newlands rugby ground on the other side of Table Mountain from Cape Town proper, was to be our base leading up to the first Test against the Springboks. I wasn't able to enjoy the marvellous setting immediately due to a virulent stomach bug that confined me to quarters for the first three days. It didn't stop Steve and Clive requesting some clips from the Barbarians game, however, and I gritted my teeth and fought back against the bug.

During that first week, Jonno was almost Blackie-like in his ability to get inside the players' heads and supply positive emotional momentum. He was the king of fun. He conjured games of cricket out of nothing, just a tennis ball and bit of wood. We'd kept his four-group division from Saundersfoot – Shona, Xhosa, Zulu and Boers – and the players bought into the groups so deeply that they even used them as the basis for a fancy-dress party on the Wednesday evening. The two hookers, Rob McBryde and Mefin Davies, quickly caught on to the thread trailed by Jonno and kept us endlessly entertained on the bus journeys to and from training: Rob with his riveting reads from Jack Canfield's *Chicken Soup for the Soul* on the way out, and Mef with his terrible, interminable jokes on the way back. Sometimes they wound on for the entire journey, but I can say honestly that by the end we were all well and truly 'hooked'.

Steve and Rupert Moon also made sure that certain players were given the responsibility of educating the squad in the history and spirit of the places we visited. It might be Stellenbosch, the 'City of Oaks', with its incredible academic and wine-growing tradition and the true cradle of Springbok rugby – back in the early 1900s, Paul Roos was both the first captain of the Springboks and the sixth rector of the school – or Bloemfontein, the 'City of Roses', with its abundant gold and diamond mines and the historic Bethlehem–Bloemfontein railroad that still runs through the old prairie battlefields of the Boer War. The players were always encouraged to turn outwards towards the culture of the country they were in – it's a Welsh tendency to become rather introspective abroad – and empowered to take charge of small but significant situations during the tour. It was all very healthy.

It was impossible not to respond to the tremendous natural beauty of South Africa. Even our training venue at the Villagers School, with all the colonnaded buildings growing outwards from a central playing field, a brilliant green quadrilateral, was breathtaking in its elegance and symmetry. There was the vertical, swinging cable-car ride up Table Mountain and the nervous pictures at the top, and a visit to Stellenbosch and its winery still guarded by a bronze statue of Dr Danie Craven. He stood squarely outside with his dog Bliksem, surveying both the past and future of South African rugby, his left forefinger jabbing the way forward. There was a wonderful evening sponsored by the BBC at the Best of Two Worlds restaurant in the Constantia Uitsig wine estate – best meal I've ever had, sitting on a garden terrace looking out at the vineyards and Table Mountain. Away from the heavy talk on the coaches' top table, Mike Wadsworth and I just couldn't stop laughing all evening, probably at our own good fortune.

But if we were in any doubt that there were two worlds, and that they were indeed separate, it was resolved quite clinically by an incident at the Wednesday evening dinner. Clive Griffiths was one witness: 'Trevor James could be a little opinionated, and he and Hansen tended to rub each other up the wrong way. At one point in the evening, Trevor said, "Oh, it looks like you made a bit of a mistake there . . ." to Hansen, or words to that effect. He said it with a huge grin and in clear earshot of everyone, but it was still a shock when Hansen just cut loose and ripped into him with a stream of four-letter insults. Trevor just wobbled on his chair and took it all. We sat there dumbfounded. It went on for five minutes. I'd never heard anything like it before or since.'

It was the best of worlds; it was the worst of worlds. With all the emotional pluses delivered by Jonno and the players and the physical environment of South Africa, there was still a palpable split in the management group.

My own personal nemesis came in the milder form of a Llanelli analyst called Mark Davies. Mark had worked down at Stradey for Gareth Jenkins for a number of years, and Steve had approached me before we left Wales about using him on the Springbok tour. He bore an uncanny resemblance to Barry Evans out of *Eastenders* and worked full-time in the planning department of Carmarthen County Council. He used a little Zion hand-held computer to generate live feedback to the coach as the game progressed. I took a step backwards and filmed training sessions while Mark stepped forward to provide the live analysis that Steve wanted. Gareth Potter continued to supply me with stats from home, and over the course of time I found that Potts's conclusions seldom agreed with those of Mark Davies. To my mind, Gareth's analysis was exhaustive and accurate, as you'd expect from someone who had made it his life's work.

We'd moved up to Bloemfontein on the high veld a few days before the first Test, bumping along in an old Dakota with propellers. The atmosphere in the Free State was much harder and more unforgiving than it was down on the coast, just like the plane ride itself. We were entering the enemy's lair, the Afrikaner heartland. But we gave a good account of ourselves in that match, setting a solid platform with our work in the scrum and scoring early from a set-piece through Craig Morgan. Craig came from behind a left-side scrum, with Kevin Morgan and Rhys Williams standing out alone on the right and the remaining backs stacked in the narrow short-side corridor. Mogsy just ignored Rhys and Kevin, first dancing around Andre Snyman, who was probably their best defender, then cutting past Breyton Paulse at speed. Both looked like they were glued to the floor. We were 11–3 up after the first quarter and playing some great stuff but blew it by conceding two quick tries at the end of the half. That handed the initiative more or less permanently to the Boks. We eventually lost 34–19, although we were still showing signs of life at the end of the game, which was encouraging given the number of fourth-quarter collapses we experienced in the last 18 months of Graham's tenure.

Mogsy's try was Jonno's creation, the idea being to drag away most of the defence with the stack to the short-side and then release our fastest and most elusive runner from a hidden position tucked away behind the scrum. Then he'd be operating against a mismatched defender in space, a battle he should, and in the event did, win. Like the man himself, Jonno's offensive plays from first phase could be either brilliant or outrageous. Against England during the previous Six Nations, he'd concocted three special moves, but the backs only had the nerve to call one. From another attacking scrum on the left, the backs again loaded up in a ten-metre short-side, all except for Dafydd James, who split out wide to the right. The idea was to kick across to Dafydd in a one-on-one isolation play against their left wing, Ben Cohen. It was much more Super 12 than Six Nations, and it all went laughably, horribly wrong – as might have been anticipated against the switched-on England of that era. There were no more specials after that.

Scott was a hard man to pin down. He was a maverick spirit who appeared and disappeared genie-like, and at irregular intervals. He had no discernible contract with the union; instead, he had a handshake agreement. He was with the squad until the end of the Six Nations, then announced tearfully to the players that he had to return to Australia to sort out some family issues. Steve rubbed his lamp, and Scott was back for the start of the South Africa tour. He jetted off again after the Under-21 World Cup; he returned for the autumn internationals. There was always an air of melodrama surrounding him, a big emotional atmosphere that needed a big stage.

Like his innovative back plays, Scott's team talks could be highly inspirational, but on occasion he could just as easily misjudge the mood of a room. Before the 2005 game against Scotland, he narrated the story of the building of the Bell Rock lighthouse off the east coast of Scotland in the early nineteenth century and the pioneering spirit of the 60 workers who'd constructed foundations of solid Aberdeen granite that have stood firm for over 200 years. The players talked about it for days afterwards. They came back wide-eyed and on the crest of an emotional wave themselves, ready to stake their claim and lay hold of the Grand Slam the following week. On the other hand, his talk to the Under-21s just after the senior tour to South Africa in 2002 had contained some personal material that the players simply couldn't relate to and left them cold.

I remember doing a presentation to the squad before the Italy game in the 2004 Six Nations. There was a complicated lighting system in the room, and it was proving difficult to get the projector in focus with just the right amount of background light. Jonno came in late and started making his own adjustments. Eventually, I let out a curse in his direction, and after sitting through the player tape, Scott quickly left the room. Players came up to me afterwards and asked me to go and see him: 'Jonno's in his hotel room, and he's really upset.' I could hardly speak I was so surprised, but I went up to his room to apologise nonetheless. He stood in the doorway with his head down and wouldn't look at me. He just said, 'Don't ever do that to me again.' I felt that Scott liked the soap opera, the big feelings generated by his hellos, farewells, returns and confessions. He always had, and probably always will have, an air of the prodigal son about him.

The interval between the two Tests brought the clash of worlds to a head. In the latter half of that week, I was taken aback when Steve Hansen blustered into my hotel room and started tearing one of Corris Thomas's reports to shreds: 'I'm not happy with this, mate . . . What's this fuckin' bullshit? How does this help me?' He went through the entire report like that, finishing by screwing the whole thing up and slinging it across the room.

Now, Corris was highly rated by Graham and also, incidentally, by Jake White in his recent autobiography. Basically, Steve didn't like Corris's style of writing, and he didn't like anyone in his group interpreting the evidence or drawing independent conclusions for themselves. He used the referees department at the WRU after that, although none of the people there had Corris's depth of background or his research experience in the world of refereeing. Steve was the polar opposite to Graham, who placed a high value on people who could think outside the box. Another Welshman, just like me and Griff, had been reduced professionally to the bare essentials. Clive: 'just a defence coach'; me: 'just an analyst'; and now Corris: 'just a referee'.

On the other hand, Steve Hansen himself 'specialised', at one time or another, in coaching every area of the team. Graham had started him with the forwards, after Peter Herbert's departure he supervised the conditioning and at the 2003 World Cup he even took over the attack structure from Scott Johnson. Between the first and second Tests in South Africa, he took it upon himself to change the team's entire defensive pattern. Steve had done the same before the 2002 Six Nations game against Scotland, changing the lineout to the Canterbury scheme he knew best. But there had been no live lineout defence drills, and we'd conceded a couple of pushover tries to a Scottish pack of very modest pretensions, the first time we'd shown weakness against lineout drives since 1998.

So, on the Monday evening after the first Test, Steve got the entire squad and backroom staff together for a couple of hours pretty late on – it must've been about seven or eight o'clock. We'd already had a hard day's training, and the players' liveliness and attention span had long since dwindled. Steve got a couple of them up 'onstage' and asked them what they'd do as defenders in a two-on-one situation. When one of the 'actors' went as if to come in and make a tackle, Hansen said, 'Noooo . . . you've got to back off and buy time for the cover to get across.' Then he started going through the defensive system he'd used in the Super 12 with Canterbury.

I occasionally caught a glimpse of Clive out of the corner of my eye.

His arms were folded so tightly across his chest that I thought he might break in half. 'Mate, I know this system works. I've won two Super 12 titles with it at the Crusaders,' was Steve's justification to him later. But an entire change of philosophy and structure with a big Test match five days off? I felt it exposed Steve's lack of understanding of the difference between Test match and provincial rugby. It was certainly bad timing and probably an error in judgement. As it happened, we gave up a score and lost the game simply because a Welsh defender wasn't allowed to use his instincts and attack the ball carrier when he had the chance.

Clive Griffiths had a long and intense debate with Steve Hansen about the late change and the merits of the system: 'Our clash was firstly about the defensive play of the wingers. Steve did not want them coming in off their wing at all to smash man and ball. The other transported idea, to back this up, was counting from outside-in. This meant that the openside winger would nominate the last, widest, attacker and shout, "I've got one." Then the defender inside the winger – say, number 13 – would shout, "I've got two," and so on, with the rest of the players filling in from the inside.

'In the Test at Cape Town, South Africa scored just on half-time on our right. Rhys Williams stayed out as he'd been told, but both he and I knew that he would have taken man and ball in the wet, treacherous conditions. It was a crucial score and gave them a lead they never lost.

'We also argued about the stance of the defenders – Steve wanted the inside leg up before the drift began [it enables you to drift more effectively towards touch if you're pushing hard off your inside leg]. You have time for that at set-pieces, but not when you've just folded around the ruck after the previous tackle. You don't have time to do the quick step – just nominate and get off the line as quickly as possible. We were using a one-out drift at the time, and this exposed the front-rowers big time, as they were often left in a mismatch situation.

'I'd characterise it as a vigorous debate, but we always made sure we presented a united front to the players. After all, as the head coach, he rightly had the final say.

'My point is, OK, you must have structures, but there must be room for individual expression. Wingers should relish making the choice and coming off the wing to spot-tackle someone man and ball if there's a chance to kill the move. If Shane Williams painted by numbers in attack, he would be worthless. When an attacking play is called, do we stop him stepping or chipping over? So why stop defenders doing the same?'

I felt Steve Hansen's change of system in a match week betrayed his lack of experience as a head coach at the top level. The players always have a lot of information to digest in the build-up to an important match, and adding a complete change of philosophy to that overloaded both the players and our own time schedule. Whatever the merits of the defensive system, it was certainly poor timing for a change of such magnitude.

The other story to come out of our brave 19–8 defeat in that waterlogged Newlands Test was the performance of the referee, Tony Spreadbury. Spreaders really had an atrocious game in atrocious conditions, and Steve was like a dog with a bone about it afterwards. He would not let it go. We had a bit of history with Spreaders, dating back as far as a Wales–France game in 1996. It was refereed by a roly-poly Canadian called George Gadjovic, but poor old George was so overweight that he really struggled to keep up with the play. He was knackered by half-time. That was one of the first matches in which the ref wore a mic, and George forgot to switch his off during the break. With our live feed, we could hear George rasping for air and Spreaders squealing in that panicking way of his: 'You've got to watch those Welshies. They're creeping up offside . . . they're making you look a fool, George.'

The chief problem at Newlands had been the contact area. When we took the ball into contact, Tony penalised the tackled player for not releasing, but when Colin Charvis got his hands on their ball, he was pinged for holding on in the ruck. I identified seven clear-cut instances in the game when Spreaders hadn't been consistent in that area. So when we returned home, Steve called the director of the English referees' association and asked if he could go over a few points with Tony privately. I put together a package of 16 clips on the laptop, and Steve brought Tony into my office to conduct the investigation. Steve made sure he was sitting between Spreaders and the exit, and over the course of the next two hours he squeezed admissions of error out of Tony on about half of the clips. It was gruelling. I could almost hear Tony sweating. Every now and again, I'd look back over my shoulder at Spreaders, his eyebrows going up and down like they were on hydraulics – face flushed and appealing for help. Then the bell for round 14 would ring. 'Slugger Hansen' would start the pounding, and Tony would start squeaking. If it had been a real boxing contest, it would have been stopped to avoid unnecessary punishment.

It reminded me of Graham's reaction to fellow Kiwi Paul Honiss after our 2001 game with Italy. Paul was quite proud of his performance and had a bit of a peacock strut on. They met briefly in the doorway to the reception. 'How d'ya think I went? It was good, wasn't it?' he said to Graham. In fact, he'd been a bit of a disaster.

'You're a bigger prick than I thought you were,' Graham replied.

The end of the second Test triggered a huge shopping spree amongst some of the management, Trevor and Alan Phillips being the worst culprits. Cape Town Airport was sheer bedlam. I think Trevor knew that the writing was already on the wall for him and was determined to make the most of his last tour abroad with Wales. He went through customs with about three trolleys resplendent with spears, shields, leopard skins and assegais. True to form, Alan had snuck through early and had gone pretty much unnoticed, admitting nothing, but with a shedload of wine – a full skip weighing about 120 kilograms. He didn't even make time to thank our two liaison officers for the terrific work they'd done throughout the tour. When we unloaded our skips at Heathrow, one of them was literally bleeding Thumper's red wine all over the conveyor belt. But that was typical of the 2002 tour to South Africa – big splashes of colour but with more than a hint of spilled claret.

Probably the single most influential figure of the Hansen era was Andrew Hore, the ex-Canterbury conditioner. He arrived in Wales in late June and almost immediately announced himself with a stroke of sheer genius. He had plans for a new fitness regime and wanted to associate it with historic beasting places in Wales, such as Merthyr Mawr and the Grotto in Pontypool Park. I helped with the arrangements for the Pontypool visit and even took my son Henry along with me to watch the session. The squad changed in the Pooler changing-rooms, then made their way up through the Grotto and along the back of the mountain towards the Folly. The Folly Tower is a famous landmark on Blaenavon mountain overlooking the Usk Vale. It was demolished by the Ministry of Defence in 1940 in the mistaken belief that it would provide a sighting-point for Luftwaffe bombers targeting the ordnance factory at Glascoed – the same factory that would provide work for generations of Gwent rugby players to come. At one stage, whenever Junna Jones looked up when he was employed there, he'd see the current Dragons coaches Paul Turner and Leigh Jones working close by.

The Folly was rebuilt by locals and historically minded enthusiasts in the 1990s. On my runs up the mountain, I could see how thoroughly nature had healed the scars of industrial excess and war. The sheep would use the old derelict mineshafts and bomb craters as shelter in times of bad weather. Nothing went to waste. At the very top of the tower, the glorious view was restored, and I could look out across six counties, from Glamorgan in the west to Gloucestershire in the east.

I stood alongside Terry Cobner, with Henry in my arms, marvelling as a Kiwi fitness conditioner drove the boys between landmarks that had such an emotional charge for both of us. It was the first time a member of the Hansen clique had striven to build a bridge to the good Welsh earth on which they were standing. At one point, I tripped and fell, just catching Henry before he dropped to the ground. 'Typical Pooler forward,' said Cobs, grinning. 'Great hands.'

Horey gave me a point of reference in the Hansen years, and he was the main focal point of growth for the Welsh team over the following three seasons. He reminded me of Pross – always in players' faces, never afraid to confront or even humiliate them if they weren't producing the required effort. For both Horey and Pross, it was about honesty and sustaining the same standards in every corner of your life. Both seemed to have a sixth sense that detected any falling away from the levels they expected. At Pontypool, there'd be no talking when you performed exercises in pairs around the edge of the field. The main reason I played over sixty first-team games in my first three seasons while still a teenager was that I never missed a training session in all that time. I was there early, and I left late. Training at our own *blood-twmp* meant something to us.

On the domestic front, Catherine soon became pregnant with our second child, Isabelle. In fact, she was due on 21 November 2002, a couple of days before the climax of the autumn series of internationals versus New Zealand. We began to feel the walls of our cosy little apartment contracting, and we knew we'd have to move somewhere bigger. In order to sell the flat, we had to set up a management company with the other three freeholders in the building and establish responsibility for repairs and maintenance. Our neighbours were considerably older than we were – all in their 80s – so we arranged a meeting at 7.30 p.m. one Monday to sort out the details. In attendance were Bill, Joan Jones, and Leslie and Friedel. But 7.30 rapidly became 7.40, as Leslie had to go back and get Friedel's hearing aid. After a further 26 steps up and down, he had to repeat the journey to get his own asthma pump. Bill, meanwhile, was so dizzied by the ascent to our front door that he promptly fell into a nearby cardboard box after his grand entry.

Friedel refused our offer of sherry until everyone was in place – very Teutonic and businesslike. After a rough start, we began to explain the benefits of forming a management company in terms of increasing the block's saleability. But we hadn't reckoned on our neighbours' long-standing feuds. As Friedel was putting in her hearing aid with some difficulty, Joan shouted, 'Are you trying to find Radio Two? You won't get any reception up here.'

Friedel was not the best person to antagonise, as her first husband had been a National Socialist in Germany during the Second World War. 'You von't get me to zign anyzing . . .' When Catherine tried to help, she replied, 'Ah, I see you're ze kind of man who lets his wife do all ze vork.' Bill fell asleep in the corner once extricated from the cardboard box. It was hopeless. There was a complete meltdown as the meeting became a forum for airing age-old grievances. Catherine and I were in stitches about it afterwards.

Isabelle's birth was so different from Henry's. It was a little like the difference between your first and second cap. The first goes by in a blur and you don't feel you have the time to enjoy anything. The second time around, I wanted to drink it all in. It certainly helped that Isabelle was good as gold and the opposite of that screaming-machine Henry. For two days, it felt like nothing else mattered, not even the All Blacks.

Alan Phillips was appointed the first full-time professional manager of the Wales national squad on 7 August 2002, about six weeks after our return from South Africa. It's funny how some people seem to know what's going to happen well in advance of the event . . . My first meeting with Andrew Hore in June had not left a positive impression. I was leaving the Barn with Carcass when we bumped into Andrew coming the other way. 'I see the big man's gone, then,' he piped up. Mark and I looked at each other. 'The big man with the beard,' he said. Horey meant Trevor James, whose torture was actually going to continue for the rest of the summer before he was finally put out of his misery by WRU secretary Denis Gethin in September.

Thumper managed to get the manager's job without fulfilling all of the 'desirable' criteria advertised in the *Western Mail* on 12 July:

> The Welsh Rugby Union is seeking to appoint a full-time team manager for the Wales national squad. The successful applicant will be a proven manager with excellent man-management and interpersonal skills. He/she will be comfortable in dealing with the media and also have an understanding of the pressures that surround the Wales XV and its whole management team. A background in the game is desirable but not essential, as is a competency in IT skills.

At the time, competency in IT was certainly a glaring hole in the Phillips CV. Thumper has certainly improved over the years, with the help of such people as Caroline Morgan and Dan Kings, but at the time he didn't know a PC from a bar of soap. His only competition for the job was another man of Pontypool, John Perkins. I'd emailed Perk, suggesting he would be the ideal candidate for the role, although I think he'd already made up his mind to apply anyway. He was undertaking a masters degree in sports science and had asked me about the role of analysis. He had also managed the Wales Under-21 side the previous season, receiving a glowing tribute from none other than Stephen Jones: 'The best manager I've ever worked with.' I touted Perk to Steve Hansen as a hardened individual who would bring great values to the squad, but Alan had the inside track. He was nailed on to get the job.

Encouraged by their success with the African tribes, and with Caroline's ample assistance, Steve and Jonno came up with some new team divisions before the autumn series of matches. There were 'Coal miners' (tight forwards), 'Assassins' (loose forwards), 'Michelangelos' (halves and inside centres), 'Strike force' (outside backs) and the 'Brythonics' (management). Jonno was keen on having little booklets with plays that could be clipped into and out of the book game by game, and a statement of core values. You even had to sign a declaration at the end of the booklet swearing adherence to those values, just as you'd swear allegiance to the flag or to tell the truth in court. It was to be the players' bible. Jonno and Caroline worked long into the night to prepare the booklets in time for our week's preparation in Wrexham before the first game against Romania on 1 November.

We had a hard but productive week's training at the excellent facilities at the Shotton steel works near Wrexham. The week was so tough that we struggled to hit our straps against Romania, leading only 12–0 at the break, but we put together some good passages of play to finish with a handsome 40–3 winning margin. Tom Shanklin was outstanding that day, racking up over two hundred yards and five line breaks with the ball in hand. There was also a moment involving Rhys Williams that said a lot about Hansen's approach. Rhys took the ball into contact near touch and released the ball early in order to cover his head among the milling boots, and we lost control of the tackle situation. Steve showed this piece of footage repeatedly to the squad as an example of 'how not to do it'. He ridiculed Rhys for paying attention to his own welfare and not presenting the ball properly to secure possession. It was a gruelling, typically Kiwi public humiliation, but it also highlighted Hansen's attitude to the breakdown. Hansen used to teach armbars and head-locking techniques and even hair-pulling in order to win that all-important war in the contact area. No quarter ever asked for, or given.

We followed the Romania win with an impressive 58–14 trouncing of Fiji and a stodgy 32–21 plod against the Canadians. The Llanelli back-rower Dafydd Jones won his first cap against Fiji. I've always had time for Daf. I used to call him 'Cowboy' after the All Black flanker of the 1980s, Mark Shaw. He's like those hookers: Rob McBryde,

Mefin Davies and Garin Jenkins. They're effervescent and lively, real emotional sparkplugs who ignite the players around them. Daf was bouncing during the Fiji week, and he was lifting the whole squad. I actually told him he was in the team by mistake at dinner on the Tuesday evening, thinking that he knew already: 'It looks like you've got a start, Daf.'

'Yee-hah!' His eyes just lit up. I thought he was going to get up and dance on the table or fire off a couple of exultant shots from his six-shooter . . .

Dafydd did so well that he was included in the run-on side to play New Zealand in the key game of the autumn series. I felt we had a chance in that game because of the inexperience in their front five. They had new caps right across the front row in Tony Woodcock, Keven Mealamu and Carl Hayman, and a second row of Keith Robinson and Ali Williams had only four starts between them. That lot would look pretty formidable five years later, but at the time they were wet behind the ears in international terms.

While I was away at Llandough Hospital waiting for Isabelle's arrival, Steve Hansen was busy installing Gareth Potter and his camera in an apartment block under construction in Cathedral Road, overlooking the All Black training session at Sophia Gardens on the Friday morning. Steve paid particular attention to their lineout drills and decided to change our pattern of lineout defence for the game. He didn't bother to tell Griff but began showing the forwards the footage from Gareth's spying mission in a meeting room up at the Barn on Saturday. During the game, the players were too uncomfortable with the changes at such short notice to react correctly under pressure. Our lineout defence was non-existent. We either lifted the wrong man or reacted too late or didn't get anyone off the ground at all in our confusion. As a result, we didn't pressure their greenhorn locks and lost much of a set-piece advantage that ought to have been there for the taking. It was the same mistake Steve had made before the second Test in South Africa, changing the defence five days before kick-off.

The gluepot pitch at the Millennium Stadium did take the All Blacks' lethal backline out of the game and help keep the score within manageable proportions. Jamie Robinson scored an early breakaway try to give us a lead at the interval, and the scrum proved to be a very different story from our defensive lineout disaster. Iestyn Thomas and Ben Evans really dug into Woodcock and Hayman, and we were awarded a penalty try after the Blacks disintegrated at a pushover attempt in the 76th minute. That brought the score back to 17–22 with four minutes plus injury time remaining, but we conceded three quick-fire tries in that last nine minutes to give an unrepresentative 17–43 final scoreline. That probably would have been an accurate reflection of the gap between the sides on a picture-perfect day for rugby but didn't do justice to our efforts that murky afternoon. I was watching the match with Henry and was glad he'd fallen asleep by then – all the while Potts went on filming behind us.

That game against New Zealand was to represent the last significant success we had at any of the set-pieces up until the World Cup when Mike Cron took over the scrums full-time and fortified our driving play generally. Ironically, it was Cronno who reintroduced live scrummaging practice. As he said, 'To get reality, you have to get off the machine and scrum live, whether it be drills, one-on-one, three-on-three, four-on-four, or whatever.'

On the way back from the Wrexham training week, John Rowlands and Mike Wadsworth were towing the scrum-machine Steve had brought with him from New Zealand. We already had an elephant's graveyard of four scrum-machines at the Barn, ranging from Graham Henry's simple sled to the complex Rhino favoured by Kevin Bowring. They all just stood where they'd been abandoned, unwanted and unused. Steve's customised machine was like the Rhino, with hydraulic pads that could push back on either head and wheels underneath so it could be used indoors. We used to practise with the forwards in training shoes, scrummaging on a ridged, unforgiving rubberised surface laid over the Barn's artificial pitch. The forwards quickly found that their studs would pop through their boots on those ridges, so the whole exercise became unrealistic.

J.R. and Mike had gotten as far as Shrewsbury when they pulled up at a set of lights. Mike heard a 'graunching' noise to the rear, then watched impassively as one of the small wheels from the scrum-machine bounced happily past him in the overtaking lane. Hansen's pride and joy had to be abandoned until a lorry could be found to pick it up. It was a vision of Welsh tight-forward play in the year ahead: the wheels were about to come off with a vengeance and leave us high and dry, with the worst Six Nations result in our history.

Understandably, Steve Hansen had been keen to scale down the importance of the key figures from Graham's era. Neil Jenkins was literally hobbling along after the 2001 Lions tour, and although he clearly had something to offer both athletically and as a model professional, Rob Howley was marked *persona non grata*. Scott Quinnell served out his time under Hansen as a role-player on the bench, until he finally retired after the Canada match, to a standing ovation from the 31,000-strong crowd and with his three kids in his arms.

We'd been in camp for the autumn series at the Vale of Glamorgan Hotel. With his Super 12 background, where teams would go away from home as a group for three or four weeks at a time, there was a strong camp-and-curfew culture, and Steve made it quite clear that he preferred people to stay in rather than go out. But I don't think he understood the geography of the M4 corridor in south Wales, where everyone lives within an hour of any training base you care to nominate.

Scott Quinnell remembers the situation well: 'Steve Hansen had said to the players, "If you live within 20 minutes of the Vale of Glamorgan Hotel, you're allowed to go home overnight. More than 20, and you'll be too tired to drive." I lived about 45 minutes from the Vale, and the drive wasn't a problem for me. Hansen's rule seemed quite arbitrary. It didn't make any sense, and I felt quite restricted. But Hansen was looking for a commitment from all the players, and he wouldn't bend at all.

'Originally, I'd planned to leave before the start of the autumn games, but Hansen said to me, "Look, mate, I'll give you ten minutes at the end of the Canada game," which enabled me to say my goodbyes as I wanted to. Then Hansen approached me again on St David's Day at Rupert Moon's wedding. "When are you coming back, then?" he said. I was dumbfounded and asked him what he meant exactly. "We want you at the World Cup, mate." I replied, "Has the policy changed at all?"

"No." "Well, I'm not coming back, then." Hansen was never one to take kindly to "no" for an answer, and the atmosphere between us quickly became strained. Things got a bit ugly, to be honest.

'I didn't feel Hansen had any idea about balance in life. My family and home life have always provided a great balance to my life in rugby. They made me appreciate it more and added to the sense of privilege I felt at being able to pull on the Welsh jersey. Having the space to switch off kept me fresher.

'In Welsh rugby at the moment, and in cricket, there's hardly any sense of this balance. In cricket, people are identified at academy level when they're only young teenagers, and that's all they know. By the time they reach their 40s and retire, they've been on the road for ten or fifteen years, living in a bubble. They haven't acquired any of the skills necessary to deal with the real world, and cricket has the highest suicide rate of any sport. And that's the situation we're now in with professional rugby here in Wales.'

Another to go around the time of the Canada game was Dafydd James. Unlike Scott and Jenks, Daf was still in the prime of his career. Like Rob Howley, he was a model professional who took care of his body, and he was a top-class winger who'd proved he could handle life at the highest level in the Lions Test side in Australia in 2001. Clive Griffiths rated Daf as both a footballer and a pro: 'I think Jonno regarded Daf as a bit of a big-head and a loner, and too slow for an international winger. But he had great footwork and the ability to stand up in the tackle, and he was a very good chaser of high kicks and a solid, physical defender with an excellent work rate. If you've played in the same side as Jason Robinson, Brian O'Driscoll and Jonny Wilkinson and held your own, as Daf had, you must be a class act.

'Dafydd only got back in the squad for the 2005 autumn series when Mike was the head coach. He was outstanding and proved he still had it, and he probably won us the match against Australia with a try-saving tackle near the corner flag. But Jonno was just as vehement in his objections then, and it was only because Mike had the casting vote that Dafydd played at all.'

All hell broke loose on the Wednesday morning before the Canada game on 15 November. Steve called a meeting and began stripping the players off, asking how many had left the hotel overnight. About eight players of the thirty-strong group put their hands up. It turned out that Hansen had been on his way to the gym early on Wednesday morning and spotted Dafydd walking down from the hotel car park. 'Listen, mate, where have you been? What have you been doing?' Dafydd wouldn't admit to having gone home, so Steve – true to his police background – went to check the exhaust of his car. It was still warm. As Dafydd had been booked into the hotel, he kicked him out of the squad on the spot.

The analysis department underwent a huge technical expansion between the end of the autumn series and the beginning of the 2003 Six Nations. Up until December, we'd used a maximum of three laptops, with coding and visual data transferred from my 'master' laptop on to those used by the coaches. That all changed when massive ex-Bath and England back-rower John Hall shouldered his way through the Barn door before Christmas. John must have really struggled to find clothes to fit his enormous frame, because he always seemed to be ready to burst through the seams of his business suits at any moment. Allied to the intensity of his manner, it lent him a formidable presence. John was representing an Australian-based software company called Sportstech, which supplied sports software developed by a guy called Don Prior. Don was a top hockey umpire in the days I used to provide analysis for the Great Britain women's hockey team. He developed early versions of his software for the Aussie women's hockey squad, and then Sportstech bought him out with a view to adapting it for rugby use.

John Hall was the Sportstech agent in the UK, with assistance from Jon Moore. Jon was quite a familiar figure in Welsh rugby circles. He could be observed manfully towing his own scrum-machine behind him as he gave scrum clinics up and down the length of the M4 corridor. I experienced a couple of his sessions at first hand at UWIC and Newport when I was there as a player, and Jon was able to build his profile to the point that he was invited to take a scrum clinic with the national squad during Kevin Bowring's reign. Jon knew a lot about the technical side of the game but often struggled to impart that knowledge as clearly as either he or his charges might have wanted. There was always a certain stiffness in the atmosphere between us, probably because I hadn't been keen on handing him the consultancy role he so obviously coveted within the department when I took over.

The two Sportstech representatives planted a vision of future Internet solutions within the WRU psyche, which would mean that every player in the national squad would need their very own laptop. In the event, Jon Moore impressed Terry Cobner and Mostyn Richards sufficiently with his presentation for them to order 32 units in time for the beginning of the Six Nations. I wasn't included in the negotiations that took place between Messrs Hansen and Hall, but it was certainly a treat to watch these two bull-like men going at it over the bargaining table. Hall would make an offer, and Hansen would stop to think and then bluntly say, 'Go and sharpen yer pencil, mate' – Kiwi for 'Not good enough . . . make me a better offer.' John Hall would bulge and bristle until you could hear the seams in his suit stretch and groan.

In the event, the 32 laptops and a hulking server arrived only 12 days before the opening Six Nations match against Italy on 15 February 2003. It took me the better part of three whole days to get all the damn machines registered and set up properly. Then I had to create a record of all the players who'd received them and give tutorials on their use. Later on, there would be a major problem in repossessing laptops from players who'd been abruptly dropped from the squad. With what I thought was a certain degree of common sense, I suggested that we only take six machines for the coaches and team leaders for the opening game, as I'd already discovered that the rather feeble server could only support a maximum of eight units before it started to turn off-colour and slowed to a grinding halt. 'No, mate, we're taking the lot . . . including the server,' Steve replied. Stunned, I complained that that was unmanageable . . . 'Set it up immediately, mate.'

It was a nightmare to check all the players had their laptops to hand and then pack the huge server into a flightbox for the trip . . . When the players turned up for the flight in their glistening brand-new black leather jackets, with laptops in equally smart leather bags slung over their shoulders, they looked more like a brigade of yuppie businessmen on a freebie than a group of international rugby players on a mission. I perked up a bit when Alan Phillips had to shell out £600 on his

Catherine holds Isabelle whilst I hold 'Tess' and Gwyneth (mum), Brian (dad) and Henry stand on their own two feet. (Courtesy of Alun Carter)

A proud father surrounded by his children – Emma, Henry and Isabelle – 'fun and an inspiration to all who know them'. (Courtesy of Alun Carter)

Finally spending some quality time together as a family at Caerleon in 2007 – Henry, Isabelle and Catherine – I'm behind the lens! (Courtesy of Alun Carter)

The strain is beginning to show.
(© Huw Evans Picture Agency)

Having a laugh with Mike,
Argentina 2004.
(© Huw Evans Picture Agency)

Close to the end. Head
down walking off the field.
(© Huw Evans Picture Agency)

credit card for mice and mousepads for the entire squad. I do believe Thumper turned an Italian shade of azure blue during the purchase.

From every point of view, 15 February was a debacle. As usual, Barry Evans – aka Mark Davies – was sitting next to Hansen in the stand, while I filmed from behind the posts at the Wales end. This followed a tip from the French analyst working for Romania during the autumn, who suggested that players get a much better feel for what they see on film when the camera is located behind them. He was right.

After a buoyant start, our lineout lost its way. Communications between Mefin Davies, the thrower, and Robert Sidoli, the signal caller, broke down, and we lost five of our own throws. Midway through the second half, Colin Charvis, our captain, was substituted and caught grinning at the camera on the sideline as his team subsided to inglorious defeat on the field. At the final whistle, Italian celebrations were loud and prolonged, and it felt like they were singing inside our desolate, morgue-like changing-room. The chanting sheared through the paper-thin walls, and we couldn't get away from it. The atmosphere was awful.

I had been asked to merge Mark Davies's coding with my end-on footage and the TV film. When I tried, I found that there was more than two minutes' footage missing from his coding – it was simply incomplete. I was still working at 7 a.m. on the Sunday trying to resolve it all with our flight due to take off at 10 a.m. I had to make sure that the players still had their laptops with them, then Hansen and Jonno asked me to sit between them on the flight back and go through the analysis after my paltry two hours' sleep. When we got back to the Vale, there was an immediate 40-minute debrief. The lineout issue resurfaced, and Steve blamed Mefin for our problems in that area. With all and sundry too tired or too hung-over to think straight, Mefin finally bit back and was dropped from the squad for his trouble.

One of our main problems in the build-up to the Six Nations had been Steve Hansen's absence for nine days immediately before we went into camp before the Italy match. During those nine days, Steve was away in South Africa on a coaching self-development course. Ultimately, as a head coach of the national team he was being paid to win Test matches. Being absent for a significant segment of the preparation for the Six Nations could not possibly improve his chances of doing that. To me, it was the kind of expedition you only undertake in the off-season, when there's nothing more pressing at hand.

The Italy match had left us with a huge void at hooker. With Mefin Davies being unceremoniously dumped after the debrief, and Robin McBryde out with a toe problem, we were desperately short of number 2s. There was only Bridgend's untried Gareth Williams left. At this point, Hansen made an amazingly ambitious call. Jon Humphreys was asked to come down from Bath on the Monday and Tuesday before the next match against England. Humph had been plying his trade in the English Premiership for a couple of seasons and hadn't played international rugby for four years. At 33, he must have been contemplating a gentle downhill trot into retirement.

Partly because of his own absence before the Six Nations, Hansen knew little about Humph other than one live report from Jonno, which was negative in content. 'Too old and too slow,' it said. He hadn't evaluated him personally and wasn't familiar with his character or style of play. Compared to Graham Henry, Steve Hansen had a depth of knowledge about Welsh players that was at best sketchy. Graham used to maintain a depth chart on Welsh players that showed the top four players in every position, but Hansen had nothing like that and wasn't so sure of his ground if he had to go outside the squad. Moreover, Humph didn't know many of the players in the squad at the time, and they didn't know him. Nevertheless, within 48 hours of Jonathan Humphreys' appearance at training, he was installed not only as the starting hooker, but as the captain as well. A captain from nowhere.

I have nothing against Humph personally – quite the reverse. In my experience, he was a tough, high-quality forward and an outstanding leader of men. But I couldn't agree with the decision to bring in a new captain from outside the squad once the Six Nations had started and the group had gelled. It went against everything I'd learned throughout my Pontypool upbringing. I thought Mefin and Sid should have been given another chance to set the record straight in the lineout. They would've repaid the faith shown in them – just as they did in our 2005 Grand Slam campaign. After filming the Wednesday afternoon training session at the Millennium Stadium, I let my feelings be known to Steve. 'This is the guy I want to lead us into the next match,' he said, nodding in Humph's direction. 'I like his character.'

'But you haven't seen him play,' I replied.

He kept on gesturing to his belly: 'It's a gut check . . . It's in here.' For someone who as a rule insisted on thoroughness and precision in his coaching clinics, codes of behaviour and team structures, it was an astonishing exception. This certainly wasn't the same guy who'd barbecued Tony Spreadbury like a juicy swordfish steak for two hours six months earlier, pausing only to flip him over and make sure that he was done on both sides. I went back to the changing-rooms and sat by Iestyn Thomas. We looked at each other and thought the same thoughts. Neither of us could believe it.

Nonetheless, we turned in a creditable performance in the first half of a 26–9 home loss to England on the Saturday, although it owed more to the resilience Wales always show after a poor performance than to Humph's galvanising presence. Ironically, we lost the game because of the structural faults Griff had noticed in our defensive pattern. We couldn't get off the line quickly enough inside, and the requirement to number from the outside-in constantly left tight forwards exposed, defending large gaps to either side of them at second and third defender. Steve Williams and Gavin Thomas both missed tackles as England dutifully went through our weak midriff to score tries from Will Greenwood and Joe Worsley that put them over the hill and out of sight.

If it sounds like I was becoming quite manic, it's because I probably was. Professionally speaking, it was one of the most deeply unsatisfying periods of my life. I didn't feel as though I had a chance to get my foot in the door and prove what I could do, and the tension and frustrations of my relationship with Steve Hansen kept on boiling over in a stream of petty little incidents. I was in very much the same position as Clive Griffiths. We were both officially employed but underused, and there didn't seem to be any light at the end of the tunnel. In hindsight, it might have been better if both our situations had been resolved definitely one way or another, instead of this agonising professional limbo without any apparent end. It was probably harder for Clive to swallow than me. That he'd been a top-level coach in rugby league and an international player in two codes scarcely seemed to count in his favour. Ultimately, both of us needed the money we were being paid by the union to maintain our families, and both of us loved being involved with the national squad of our native land. That kept us both living in hope.

By the time of the Scotland game, I sought out John Rowlands, our baggage master, for a bit of solace, something I've not done before or since. I went into J.R.'s room on Thursday evening, and we ate chocolate, a lot of it, and played on his PlayStation. That was the night I started smoking again, even if it was just a one-night stand. When J.R. offered me a Hamlet cigar, I thought, 'Why the hell not?' Remember those Hamlet ads from the 1970s? That was me, sitting in the baggage master's hotel room on the Thursday evening before a Test that would decide whether we'd be a winning or losing team that season. Puffing away while the walls came crashing down all around me. With Barry Evans at Steve's side, I remained in the hotel on match day to do my work alone. We lost 33–20 and didn't get a sniff until the last ten minutes or so.

Before the fourth game of the Six Nations, against Ireland, we'd fallen back to Saundersfoot to lick our wounds. Once again, we enjoyed the unique hospitality offered by Andrew Evans and his crew, the best I've ever come across, as we trained at Tenby Rugby Club. For the first time in my experience of the Hansen era, we had live scrummaging practices. A young lad from Neath came down to make up the numbers in the front row and proceeded to cause all kinds of mayhem wherever we put him. We tried him at tight-head, and he made life uncomfortable for Iestyn Thomas. We moved him across to the other side, and after a couple of scrums Gethin Jenkins was shooting us dirty looks. He was a 22-stone man-monster, and hairy to boot. Hansen asked who he was. 'Adam Jones,' came the reply.

The live-scrum sessions paid immediate dividends against Ireland, and I can remember Andrew Hore running onto the field with an urgent message from Steve to remind Iestyn Thomas to get in under John Hayes's ribs and drive him inwards. Even this story had a twist in its tail, however. Horey misunderstood Steve Hansen's instruction, and instead of delivering the message to Iestyn Thomas, he gave it to Iestyn

Harris, our inside centre, instead. In the changing-room after the game, Iestyn H. said to Horey, 'What the fuck was all that about getting in under Hayes's ribs, Horey?' It was an echo of the confusion with the radio feeds against France and Italy when Hansen first took over. The truth was that Hansen only trusted fellow-Kiwi Hore to deliver the message onto the field, but Hore perhaps lacked the rugby knowledge to realise who it was intended for. The result was an avoidable breakdown in communications.

Fortunately, Iestyn T. didn't need any off-field assistance. We produced our best scrum of the tournament as Iestyn bulled Hayes across the tunnel near our own line. From starting somewhere near north-south, Hayes's axis turned all the way to south-south-west as he ended up greeting his own lock forwards behind him. It was our best scrummaging performance of the campaign and brought us to within a single point of victory. In the dying minutes, we were denied a deserved win when referee Steve Lander signalled for a penalty after a deliberate knock-on by the Ireland winger Justin Bishop as we were pressing for a score on the Ireland line, then forgot the advantage he was supposed to be playing when Stephen Jones missed the subsequent drop-goal. Even during the drop attempt, Malcolm O'Kelly was fully three metres offside and flagged by the touch judge, but Lander chose to ignore that as well. We lost 25–24.

One of the main themes of the Hansen era was that he always kept coaching and technical input in the hands of fellow Antipodeans. I remember Scott Johnson staying behind in Scotland after the game up there to spend time with Mick Byrne, a giant lefty Aussie Rules footballer who was then the kicking coach for the Scotland squad. Now he does the same job with Graham Henry's All Blacks. Scott had just been appointed kicking coach and obviously needed a crash course in the technical aspects of punting.

This incidentally cut across one of Clive Griffiths' few remaining coaching pleasures, which was to look after Iestyn Harris's technique as a punter and goalkicker. Fast-forwarding to the World Cup six months later, this would cause more unnecessary problems, both before and during the tournament.

As Clive recalls, 'I wasn't invited to the pre-World Cup camp in

Lanzarote or the summer tour to Australia. But Hansen promised me after a protracted discussion that I'd be in Australia for the World Cup itself, and, to be fair, he was as good as his word.

'I was still helping Iestyn Harris with his kicking at the time. I'd coached Iestyn since he was a 16 year old at Warrington, and from time to time he came to me for advice on his game generally, help with his kicking technique and for a bit of fatherly guidance. But in the first week at Manly, Iestyn was clearly uneasy . . . Turned out he was worried about his association with me jeopardising his place in the side. He'd been pressured into using Jonno as his kicking coach.

'It was a turning point in my relationship with Jonno. I'd kicked at international level in both codes and racked up the points in my rugby career, yet who was I to tell Iestyn how to kick?

'I was summoned to a meeting with Steve, Jonno and Thumper to discover what was up. Hansen explained that he wanted Scott to do all the kicking coaching, but I wasn't biting. I apologised for any misunderstanding and just replied, "OK, if that's what you want," and swallowed hard. There was nothing wrong with Iestyn's basic goalkicking technique, and he'd been very successful in league with it, but they wanted the change anyway. It certainly didn't help our cause when Iestyn missed a couple of crucial kicks against England in the quarter-final.'

Steve and Jonno both leaned heavily on information provided by the Aussie–Kiwi coaching network in Europe, which included Adrian Kennedy at Northampton and Ulster, Michael Foley at Bath, and Tim Lane and Steve Nance in Montferrand. Before the final game of the Six Nations, I'd downloaded previous French matches onto Scott's laptop to help him to prepare for a presentation that he was due to give on the Wednesday. On the Monday, I went into Jonno's office, which was next door to mine. I looked across at his laptop as I left his office and saw that the timing on the France–Ireland game that Scott had been analysing was 19 minutes. I pointedly asked Jonno if he needed any help, and he just said, 'No, mate. She'll be fine.' At the end of play on Tuesday evening, I popped into his office again, and he wasn't there. I looked and the timing on the game read exactly the same as before, with the presentation first thing on Wednesday morning. Subsequently,

I found out that he'd made a phone call to Tim Lane in Montferrand to get some background information on the French players. In the event, we lost heavily, 33–5, without firing a shot after the first quarter of an hour, and that was our first ever championship whitewash complete.

Steve was heavily involved in the restructuring of Welsh rugby on the strategic level, and one of the first cost-cutting exercises was to dismantle the A team. There was a furore about it at the time. Maybe it was necessary financially – I don't know. The WRU were in dire straits paying back the debt on the Millennium Stadium, but Mike Ruddock had been specifically wooed by the union to come and take charge of the As, and he gave up a perfectly good job with Leinster to do it. His results in 2002 were diametrically opposite to Hansen's, chalking up four wins (including England away) and only one loss, so the disappearance of the As certainly took the pressure off Steve and, incidentally, stopped the process of grooming a Welsh successor in its tracks.

Mike Ruddock remembers, 'It was back in 2000 that Terry Cobner approached me about working with Wales A while I was still coach of Leinster. That gave me the push I needed to come back to Wales and coach Ebbw Vale, but on the understanding that I'd get a crack at the As. Cobner indicated to me that it would put me in a much better position to have another tilt at the national coaching role when the job became available.

'But when Graham resigned early in 2002, the WRU appointed Steve Hansen without any apparent debate. Everything was signed, sealed and delivered very quickly. I was up at Wrexham preparing for a game against Scotland A in 2002 when I found out about Steve Hansen's appointment through Teletext. Then I heard the WRU were planning to scrap the As after the end of the Six Nations. Ikey Stephens, the manager, and I went to plead with Glanmor Griffiths to reconsider, but he said that there was no room in the budget to maintain the As.

'I don't think that fitness was as big an issue in Welsh rugby as the senior Wales camp made it out to be. Don't get me wrong, there was definitely scope for improvement. However, if fitness levels in Welsh rugby had been so totally off the pace, it would have been evident across all levels. When the senior team were being whitewashed in 2003, the

As won four out of five games that season, and Chris Davey won the championship with the Under-21s.'

Matters came to a head during the tournament debrief a few days after the France game. Remarkably, Hansen asked his New Zealand agent to lead this meeting, a Wales national squad meeting, so that we could all learn a thing or two from him. We didn't know him from Adam or what he was doing there. All the grievances during the season were dug up again. I remember Clive answering Steve's question about why he was getting such a negative response from the likes of Griff and me: 'If you talk to people like shit, you'll get shit back in return.' The Iestyn Harris kicking issue raised its head, and Steve talked about Clive 'cutting the umbilical cord' with Iestyn.

Hansen called me into his office for a private meeting shortly afterwards to discuss the issues raised. To my amazement, he ranted on about how Graham Henry had left the team in a parlous state, sent out the wrong messages to the players and paid them too much so that it wasn't a disciplined environment. Apparently, it was all Graham's fault now. He was at pains to convince me that his way was not only the right way, but the only way. This was part of a strange complexity in Hansen. However tough he appeared on the outside, there would always be these times when he craved your approval on quite a major scale. Shortly after the meeting, I had a chat with Gareth Potter and asked if he wanted to take my place at the World Cup. He agreed, and, surprisingly, so did Steve. After the 2001 experience on the Lions trip to Australia, I was in no hurry to return. At least I was grateful to Steve Hansen for that.

5

THE ROAD TO THE WORLD CUP AND A RETURN FROM THE WILDERNESS

Part of the World Cup preparation was a two-Test tour to the Antipodes over the summer, and both Clive and I were deemed surplus to requirements. They didn't have the money to take Clive, and I was replaced by Barry Evans, who managed to get enough time off from his job with Carmarthen Council to join up with the tour. Saundersfoot was once again used as a base for the pre-tour preparations, and the players were introduced to the new chief executive, Steve Lewis. What an introduction it was! Lewis gave a presentation in the lounge at the St Bride's Hotel, voicing many harsh truths in quite a confrontational manner. Martyn Williams was one witness who later wrote about the essence of the scene in his book. Steve Lewis made little attempt at diplomacy, telling the players bluntly that they were overpaid. 'That's all going to change,' he said. 'You probably won't have the brain to understand the new system . . . except maybe for you, Mark

Taylor.' I cringed as I imagined how someone like Colin Charvis would be taking it all. Charv is nobody's fool. Steve Lewis had thrown down the gauntlet, and without realising it helped to spark the players' strike a short time after.

The flight out to Australia was scheduled for Monday, 2 June 2003. The squad was supposed to leave the Vale at 11.30 a.m. to catch the afternoon flight from Heathrow. As usual, Mark Davies, Mike Wadsworth and I took care of the equipment, then went into the dining-room at the Vale for breakfast. No one was there. We looked at our watches –10.30 a.m. came and went, and we drank more coffee. The bus warmed up outside the hotel hopefully. Still no players in an empty dining-room. It turned out that J.R. knew that the players were holding a protest meeting about the tour wage scale up at the Cardiff West Service Station but had been sworn to secrecy. Eventually, Scott Quinnell appeared from the services for an interim negotiation with David Moffett while Hansen went apoplectic with rage. I think Scott thought he was getting the assurance he wanted from Moffett, but Moffett was a wily campaigner and simply wanted to get the players on the plane as fast as possible. An accident near Heathrow meant the squad missed their flight and had to stay an extra night at the Renaissance Hotel at their own expense. The next day, they couldn't all be accommodated on the same flight, so half flew westwards around the globe via the USA, while the other half flew eastwards via Malaysia to reach the same destination.

After a promising start against Australia, we managed only one try over the course of the two games against the Wallabies and the All Blacks. We were beaten up both physically and in a footballing sense by New Zealand, conceding 74 per cent possession and winning the ball only nine times in the first half. We made a massive 190 tackles in that game, with 36 misses, which was unfortunately typical of our inability to win and maintain possession at the time. The Test average was around 130 tackles per game, but we regularly used to have to put in 150 simply because we couldn't keep ball. We didn't tend to see much of it, and when we did we weren't trying to play with it in the right parts of the field.

We always struggled with possession-based sides such as England

and New Zealand, whose games usually featured a high level of ball-in-play time – around thirty-nine minutes, four or so more than Test teams on the next quality tier down. Our Llanelli halves, Stephen Jones and Dwayne Peel, would use a heavy positional kicking game under Gareth Jenkins down at the Scarlets, where Llanelli would aggressively contest defensive lineouts and get the ball back for them again. For Wales, they were also asked to do a lot of kicking, though nearly all of it defensively and from our own half. When Wales kicked the ball away, they weren't being aggressive, and they weren't trying to get it back – they were just trying to relieve the pressure.

Moreover, our lineout defence success – the ability to put a man up in the air to contest an opposition throw – was poor . . . well below 50 per cent, when the world-class lineouts of Australia and South Africa were achieving an 80 per cent success rate. Lineout leaders such as Gareth Llewellyn were very vocal on the training paddock but very quiet on match days, and players often suffered from both formation and information overload from Hansen.

The rigidity of the defensive pattern didn't allow us to attack the ball carrier and force mistakes when we had the chance, so we didn't turn over a lot of ball in contact. We were effectively playing rugby without the ball against any side who could field a big lineout or a big possession game – or both. Most teams tended to have one or the other. Some, such as England, were lucky enough to have both.

New Zealand beat us by a record scoreline of 55–3, and we lost by a margin of 85–13 over the two Tests. We conceded thirteen tries, and in one symbolic collision at Hamilton between the two rival back-row hard nuts Colin Charvis and Jerry Collins, we went down for the count. Literally, as captain Charv was knocked unconscious by the impact of Collins' hit. Barry Evans came back punch-drunk from Hansen's bawling-out sessions on tour and didn't look like he wanted to repeat the experience. I'd prepared some motivational tapes for the players and had them sent out by courier at a cost of almost £500 to the union. But when I asked Mark Jones how they'd gone down with the boys, he just said, 'What tapes?' with a bewildered look on his face. Once again, my contribution had proved to be a waste of money and effort.

At the time, it was quite easy for sides to suffocate us and make us play without the ball for long periods. Suffocation took on a whole new meaning when the boys returned from Oz to begin a three-month conditioning programme for the World Cup in autumn 2003. Thumper had made a deal and some oxyacetylene tanks appeared all around the Barn over the summer, with the laudable idea of creating an imitation Australian summer climate. I recall one of the workmen plodding up the stairs one day and asking what the tanks were for. When we explained, he looked concerned and said, 'If you try to do it with those tanks, you'll have no players left.' Apparently, the tanks were emitting carbon monoxide. The next day, I arrived for work as usual, and all the tanks had been abandoned outside the Barn alongside the unwanted scrum-machines.

Hansen had made a gutsy, or foolhardy, call that almost cost him his job during the World Cup preparation. The entire summer was to be dedicated to fitness and conditioning, with comparatively little emphasis on technical or game-planning elements, or on results. This approach to preparation in the few months before the 2003 World Cup strongly resembled that of Gareth Jenkins and the All Blacks management in the run-up to the same competition four years later. In all three cases, key players were withdrawn from major competitions – the Super 14 for the All Blacks – or from the warm-up games in the summer months. In my own view, this policy failed on all three occasions, without any shadow of doubt. None of those three sides entered the World Cup with any momentum, and none of them made it beyond the quarter-final stage of the competition. Only in one-and-a-half matches of all the games played by those three teams in the course of the 2003 and 2007 World Cups could either Wales or New Zealand be said to have played to their full potential (Wales v. New Zealand 2003, and the first half of Wales v. England the following week). The champions in both years, England and South Africa, threw themselves out on the road during the summer, playing their top players most of the time and ensuring that they were battle hardened and ready to think correctly under pressure when the real war began.

Ireland squashed us by 30 points at Lansdowne Road, but matters reached a head when what was clearly an England second XV came down and handed it to our first-choice side, 43–9, on the penultimate weekend in August. We didn't even score a try in front of our own people as all the old problems of winning and keeping ball returned. There is no question that Steve Hansen would have lost his job if we had lost the next warm-up game against the Scots. There was a huge amount of pressure on him.

Steve went up to Wrexham to keep Mike Ruddock company for the evening game against Romania on the Wednesday before the Scotland game. Gavin Henson and Shane Williams were in a side that won convincingly, 54–8, and Steve couldn't keep Shane out of his World Cup plans after an outstanding performance that included two tries. Although Mike was coach for the night, Hansen still couldn't resist trying to wrest back control mid-game when he disagreed with some of Mike's substitutions. We won 23–9 versus Scotland on the Saturday, and that was enough to save Hansen's job, and rightly so, for the World Cup.

They say it is always darkest just before the dawn, and, strangely enough, it was at this dark moment I got to see the finest side of Steve Hansen. The World Cup squad embarked on an intense five-day training stint to Lanzarote in mid-September. The first session was scheduled for 7 a.m. on Monday, and Ceri Sweeney appeared like some Aussie cricketer with his face covered in white sunblock. The only problem was that it was pitch black at that time in the morning. Occasionally, you'd see Ceri looming out of the murk like some ghostly, rugby-playing geisha . . . There were six sessions planned for the Monday alone – our first day there – and by Wednesday afternoon we'd racked up fifteen in total. This was the true World Cup squad: newly qualified Aussie lock Brent Cockbain got the nod ahead of Ian Gough, another Antipodean preference, and Shane Williams squeaked in on his form in the Romania game. There was no place for Gavin Henson, and the pendulum had swung back full circle to Captain Charvis (among three other co-captains) after the nadir of the Italy match.

It was one of the best weeks' training I'd seen. Steve armour-plated the defence in full-length body pads and instructed them to play hard-hitting, full-on D. Hansen himself took up a stance behind the attack and marshalled the positional play of the pods over multiple phases. It was all about getting the attack structures firmly planted in individual minds in the teeth of real defensive conditions. The running lines over five or six phases had to be right under live pressure. Angles of entry into the breakdown and realignments behind the ruck were taken apart and examined repeatedly. There was an emphasis on work rate and getting up quickly off the floor to add support, an advantage we'd noticed in Woodward's super-fit England. Support lines were not unopposed but filled with traffic, so that the pods would sometimes have to run backwards to go forwards again rather than simply taking the soft running line under no pressure at all.

I thought that it was a seminal moment in the team's development, and ironically it had come when Steve had decided to take over supervision of the attack structure from his blood-brother Scott Johnson. That week in Lanzarote set the platform for the outstanding ball retention and fluid phase play we showed against both England and New Zealand in the later stages of the World Cup, and gave confidence to the likes of Jonathan Thomas and Shane Williams to express their ability as attacking footballers.

After such an intense week, the boys needed some relief and descended on Puerto del Carmen for a drinking blow-out that was every bit as intense as the training. I don't think I've ever seen so much alcohol consumed so quickly as in the three hours we were there. On the bus back, the driver kept on having to tell the boys to sit down, as it was illegal to stand up on a coach in Lanzarote and he would cop the blame. At one stage, he even stopped the bus and refused to go any further. When we returned to the hotel, Club la Santa, some of the boys threw up in the lobby, and my abiding memory was of Steve Hansen, complete with mop and bucket, cleaning up the place in the early hours of the morning with everyone else safely in bed. Whatever else you could say about Steve, you couldn't argue that he didn't buy into the team ethic by concentrating on the small details, even if he was now clearing up a mess that was largely of his own making.

During the World Cup, Hansen relied on Barry Evans and Gareth Potter to do all the coding and analysis, and a young lady called Helen to do the filming, while I added a breakdown of the opposition and individual performance from 3 Ivy Street, Penarth. Mike Cron was accredited for the entire tournament to coach the scrum and, during the later stages of the tournament, the defence. Meanwhile, Clive was kept away from Iestyn Harris and confined to one-on-one tackling technique. Rather mischievously, Griff found some 'rogue' work to do anyway: 'A mate of mine, Terry Matterson, contacted me when we moved down to Canberra. Terry was with the Canberra Raiders and invited me along to the Grand Final, and I had a great time with him and the Raiders management. One of their star men was a back by the name of Clinton Schifcofske, and Terry asked me to take a couple of kicking sessions with him. Well, rugby league is big news in Australia – far bigger than union – and at the second of the sessions quite a few cameras were present.

'The next day, ol' Griff appeared in a banner headline on the sports pages: "Welsh Backs and Kicking Coach Takes a Look at Schifcofske". Steve was incensed, showing the photo to all the players on the bus, and Jonno's pride stopped him talking to me for at least the next couple of days. Scott and I were very good mates, and we used to get on famously, but from that point our friendship became strained. I tried to explain to him that none of it was planned, and it was not in anyway intended to upstage him, but he replied, "Mate, this is my country, my people. I want to know what's going on!" Originally, Steve had wanted me to introduce Mal Meninga – whom I'd known and played against in my league days – to the squad for a team talk, but the "kicking incident" robbed me of that chance.'

Once more, Jonno showed his aptitude for creating a stimulating environment for players on tour. He invited a succession of heroes from rugby league, cricket and Aussie Rules to address the squad, including Meninga, Andrew Johns and Matthew Hayden. He even organised a balloon trip over Canberra, which if you've ever been there you'll know is just about the best way to see the place. The players were well and truly won over by the coaching team during those six weeks, and I think Mike Cron's mature influence, as a kind of father figure to Steve Hansen, was a big factor.

After a slow start, we managed to gain revenge for our defeat against Italy in the Six Nations in the crunch game of the group stage. Then came New Zealand. Austin Thomas, the Buddha of rugby in north Wales, met Alan Phillips the day before the game in Sydney Harbour, right next to the famous opera house. Thumper had given the game up already; he didn't think they had a hope in hell against the All Blacks. Hansen's selection for the match was just a way of giving the second tier of players in the squad a game before the knockout stages. There was no grand plan and certainly no expectation of the explosive, try-scoring revival to come . . .

But the positive atmosphere engineered by Jonno and the attack structure put in place by Steve in Lanzarote now began to pay dividends. We kept the ball for long periods in the first half, maintaining possession through 12 phases before Alfie dropped the ball over the line in our first big attack in the eighth minute. This set the tone for our ball-in-hand aspirations throughout the match. For the first hour, Horey's conditioning programme ensured that we didn't wilt in a fast-paced game with a high level of ball-in-play time. Under Cronno's watchful eye, our scrum was even able to turn over the All Blacks at a crucial five-metre set-piece on our line in the 57th minute. Shane Williams and Jonathan Thomas poured all their frustration from being held back or overlooked by Hansen into that game. Both were outstanding. If it had appeared beforehand that they were being thrown to the lions, that night, as the game wore on, they became lions themselves, the hunters rather than the hunted.

The negatives only told in the final quarter of the game. We hadn't built up a winning mentality during the pre-World Cup warm-ups, and we'd lost games we should have won – against Italy and Ireland in the preceding Six Nations – because I thought Steve had taken refuge in his larger role as repairer of Welsh rugby, rather than concentrating on winning games as head coach. When you're tiring in that last 20 and you don't really expect to win and aren't used to winning matches, you start to remember all the stuffings you've had – you don't have that edge of mental toughness. Somehow you don't quite run or play as hard with the game in the balance. You lack conviction – a little voice nags away inside you: 'Uh-oh, it's going to happen again.' After the summer hammerings, there was only rust where there should have been hard, gleaming metal and competitiveness to the bitter end. From the 58th minute onwards, New Zealand took over, outscoring us 20–0 and three tries to nil. But to this day, I'm convinced that the All Blacks were there for the taking if we'd taken the trouble to build up a winning mentality over the summer and in the Six Nations.

It's interesting that Wales have been involved in the standout 'games of the tournament' of the last two World Cups. The match against New Zealand in 2003 and the one against Fiji in 2007 were high-scoring shootouts in which we scored nine tries of our own, while conceding twelve to the opposition. Both were prefaced by a sequence of summer warm-ups where the emphasis was placed squarely on conditioning, and we suffered two calamitous defeats to England – 43–9 in 2003 and 62–5 in 2007. In both tournaments, we had the opportunity to put teams away when we had a foot on their throats and didn't manage to do it.

The boys took a lot of confidence from the All Blacks game into the quarter-final against England. At half-time, with Wales leading 10–3, I thought we were going to win. We'd scored two great tries, one from a Shane Williams counter-attack and another from a drive off a lineout ball, and we'd created at least two other gilt-edged chances. But Woodward made a crucial change at the break, bringing on Mike Catt to add a kicker in midfield. Attention to detail is everything in winning Test matches, and we made a glaring error in our chase from kick-offs. We had Shane Williams chasing them, but he wasn't big enough to stop their chief returner, Lawrence Dallaglio, making about 15 metres on the runbacks and setting positions for Mike Catt to bang the ball another 50 metres downfield. On the summer tour, Mark Jones, who has more straight-line speed and physical presence than Shane, had performed the same role. Twice in the game against Australia, he'd thumped their big number 8, Toutai Kefu, deep within the Wallaby 22 after an outstanding chase, but we failed to use Mark at all against England. Then, at the beginning of the second half, Iestyn Harris stayed deep as an extra full-back after a deep clearance kick by Gareth Cooper, which allowed Jason Robinson a one-on-one with Gethin Jenkins, who was chasing him down. Robinson took him on the outside and set up England's only try of the game. These little things matter, and they gave England scoring chances and a territorial foothold in the game.

The feel-good factor was huge on the players' return from the

World Cup, and Rob McBryde told me that it had been one of the best experiences of his life. But I couldn't help thinking that with a better balance between conditioning and creating a winning mentality in the summer, and with a better selection policy and more attention to detail in the planning, we could have achieved even more.

The acid test of how far we had really come would be the 2004 Six Nations. First up were Scotland. Although the feel-good factor was enough to overcome a side tasting life under a new head coach, Matt Williams, the same niggles over selection and game management persisted. Adam Jones was taken off after half an hour just after scoring a try in the corner after a free-flowing move, and it was hard to understand. Adam was clearly pumped and could have easily lasted until the end of the half or the hour mark. But Steve was determined to pull him off after 30 minutes come what may.

Nonetheless, after beating Scotland, hopes were high of a first victory over Ireland in four years in the second match of the tournament. I remember we stayed on the north side of Dublin in a lovely setting right on the Portmarnock golf course. At the time, Ireland had an outstanding set of lineout forwards led by Paul O'Connell, supported by probably the best driving maul in the championship. I knew this was where the major challenge would come from and handed out one of Nick's reports to Rob Sidoli in the lobby of the hotel on the day before the game. We went through it in some detail: everything from O'Connell's facial contortions before he prepared to jump – he would really start hyperventilating when the ball was coming his way – and his tendency to repeat successful calls to himself. O'Connell was and is a dominator, someone who wants to pound you mentally and physically when he feels he has the upper hand. I thought Sid at least had to challenge him and show he wouldn't be stood over.

In the event, we played into a first-half gale, but the real gale was O'Connell. He won the first lineout of the game unchallenged, and Ireland got in behind him and effortlessly scored a pushover try from it, the first of two in the match. We didn't get off the ground to compete, even though O'Connell got into his groove and kept on calling the ball to be thrown to himself, six throws on the bounce. Sid looked thoroughly intimidated and beaten in his body language. We lost the first serious test of our World Cup resolve 36–15, and we were out of the game by half-time. Again, the absence of live intensity in the set-piece drills and a lack of emphasis on contesting first-phase possession within the Hansen culture cost us dear. Despite all the team bonding and attacking promise of the World Cup, we were still paper-thin where it mattered: in the trenches.

The defining game of the Steve Hansen era was the next match, against France on 7 March. Graham Henry had got in touch with me between the Ireland and France games, and we arranged to meet at Lynn Evans's house in Roath. Lynn is a sports psychologist and lecturer at UWIC and had co-coached the Welsh netball team with Graham's wife, Raewyn. Graham had just been appointed head coach of the All Blacks and was looking around for assistants. We had a long lunch, and he asked me about Hansen. I tried hard to be as objective and helpful as I could, noting that he was a good coach technically but a difficult personality to work with. I told Graham that he had made mistakes in selection and game management but that he could be a useful support coach. I believe Graham asked Trevor James the same questions but didn't get such flattering answers. When they met up, Trevor couldn't have known that he was face to face with Graham for probably the last time. To the best of my knowledge, they haven't spoken a word to each other since then.

The French game was really a damning indictment and showed more clearly than any other why Wales couldn't win important matches under Hansen's stewardship. We put the ball into twenty-seven set-pieces and won clean possession on only ten occasions. We won just half of our own lineouts (eight from sixteen) despite having four genuine targets in the team. It wasn't that we couldn't threaten the French when we got the ball – far from it. When we did win usable, off-the-top ball, we broke the gain line on three out of six attempts, a terrific success ratio. Our performance in lineout defence was just as poor. We put up a challenging pod only 37 per cent of the time, and half of those challenges were derailed by poor lifts – so, effectively, we were only contesting the French throw at one in five lineouts, despite the French jumpers using an obvious clap-hands signal for the hooker to throw the ball in.

The scrums were even worse. Due to Hansen's stubbornness in selecting Gethin Jenkins at tight-head and another non-specialist number 8 in Dafydd Jones at the base of the scrum, we only won clean ball at three of our eleven scrums. We were penalised four times, lost control of our channelling or made poor decisions at the base three times and were pushed off the ball completely on one occasion. We conceded one try directly from a retreating scrum when Jean-Baptiste Élissalde disrupted Daf at the base and then ran fifty metres off the loose ball to score, and another after a penalty from a scrum set up a lineout pushover from short range. The whole thing came to a miserable climax when Alfie moved to flanker for a patented Super 12 move in the second half, even though we were under such pressure that we'd be lucky to win the ball at all with one specialist forward absent. The fact that we lost by just seven points, 22–29, only fuelled my frustration with our shortcomings.

I remember Steve came into my office shortly after the game, and we began to talk. He rightly pointed out that we'd played a lot of top-tier nations during his time in charge and then asked me, 'Of all the games we lost, which could we have won?' Well, Steve, here's your answer: Scotland 2002 – inadequate live practice against lineout drives allowing a modest Scottish pack to push us over twice from close-range lineouts; South Africa second Test 2002 – changing the defensive policy five days before the game, which gifted the Boks their opening try; Italy 2003 – whipping Mefin off after fifty minutes and destroying our lineout confidence just when it needed support; and France 2004 – poor selection at tight-head and number 8 allowing France to score fifteen to eighteen points directly from our scrums. And there had been indoor scrummaging practice in trainers on a rubberised surface throughout. Even Steve's mentor, Mike Cron, probably the best scrum coach in the world right now, agrees that there is no substitute for live scrummaging practice. As Cronno says, live practice is when you get real about scrummaging.

We played our best game of the championship against England a couple of weeks later, only losing touch when Julian White came on as a replacement and began to bully our scrum around in the final quarter. We lost 31–21, but at least we hadn't beaten ourselves as we had done against France. With Steve Hansen's departure for New Zealand imminent after the final Six Nations fixture against Italy and Mike Ruddock already having been announced as the new head coach, I did my best to help foreshorten some of Jonno's emotional antics. He was in the process of milking the maximum amount of melodrama out of the should-I-stay-or-should-I-go scenario. Emotionally speaking, it was right up his alley, although I genuinely wanted him to stay in the picture. We badly needed some continuity, and there wasn't any shadow of doubt that Jonno had a positive effect on the boys.

Needless to say, I was glad to see the back of Steve Hansen, even if many of the players weren't. I don't think there's any question that he made a significant contribution to the Wales revival that led to the 2005 Grand Slam, but that contribution was much patchier than his apologists, such as Gareth Thomas and Martyn Williams, would have it appear. Having been involved in the world of analysis for about eighteen years now, I know that the statistics (treated with a certain amount of common sense) don't lie, and there were solid reasons why Steve Hansen's win-loss record as the head coach of Wales was so vastly inferior to the records posted by the two coaches who bookended his tenure: Graham Henry and Mike Ruddock. Whereas Steve Hansen achieved a 30 per cent win record, Graham and Mike were both above 60 per cent, and Mike had basically the same group of players available to him as Steve had.

The main problem was that Hansen lost the balance between creating performance improvement and creating a winning mentality among the players. Although Steve was an excellent technical coach and knew how to bring a group of players together, he didn't select well, and he changed systems too often and too suddenly. Under pressure from the media, he retreated towards the performance factor, to the point that it became an excuse for our inability to put people away when we had the chance to do just that.

Steve Hansen certainly didn't do Mike Ruddock any favours with his general distrust of Welsh rugby culture and many of the people who composed it. He introduced a professional consistency within the national squad that was probably long overdue – although there were still backslidings from time to time – but ultimately he threw too much of the Welsh baby out with the bathwater. Moreover, he would try to maintain a close interest in the fortunes of the Wales team, both personally and through the likes of Scott Johnson and Steve Lewis, well after his return to New Zealand in 2004. Just as surely as he put certain foundations in place between 2002 and 2004, so he guaranteed those foundations would find it hard to survive the stewardship of the next Welsh-born coach. It truly was a curate's egg, and the clergyman had left it with us and flown back to his homeland. The original cartoon that appeared in *Punch* on 9 November 1895 was entitled 'True Humility'. It pictured a timid-looking curate taking breakfast in his bishop's house. The legend under the cartoon read, 'Right Reverend Host: "I'm afraid you've got a bad egg, Mr Jones!" The Curate: "Oh no, my Lord, I assure you! Parts of it are excellent!"' Mike Ruddock was about to inherit a team bursting with excellent attributes, but within the shell of a thoroughly bad political situation.

6

TWENTY-SEVEN YEARS OF WAITING

'We need to talk about Jonno.' That could have been the byline for the process of selecting Steve Hansen's successor. Compared to Hansen's own blitzkrieg appointment, it was a drawn-out affair, like some kind of political Chinese water torture. We were still playing the final three games of the 2004 Six Nations while the duel between Gareth Jenkins, long-time coach of Llanelli, and dark horse Mark Evans, CEO at Harlequins, unfolded. The two Davids, Moffett and Pickering, were prominent in the assessment of those two front-runners. I think Mark Evans became a serious candidate mainly in response to Gareth's ever-increasing demands as they spun through the rounds of interviews. The more Gareth demanded, the more determined the union became that Mark should stay in the race.

I'd got to know Gareth Jenkins quite well on my regular journeys down to Stradey covering for Gareth Potter while he was away at the 2003 World Cup in Australia. I remember having a quiet word with Jenkins just before he went into one of those interviews, and he clearly felt that he had to work with people with whom he felt comfortable. This primarily meant his assistant Nigel Davies, which in turn placed Scott Johnson in a difficult position, as Nigel fulfilled much the same role down at Llanelli as Jonno did for Wales. Both the union and the players were still very much in love with Jonno, so it probably spooked the WRU when Gareth set down his marker with Nigel Davies.

The tide began to turn against Gareth, and negative reports about how he had interviewed mysteriously leaked out, apparently from high places, to the media. They made him look like something of a country bumpkin. With the added turboboost of these regular updates, the whole process became painfully public, at least for Gareth Jenkins.

It quickly became obvious that a major criterion of the process was the need to accommodate Scott Johnson and keep him happy, and Gareth was repeatedly told that a job was his but only if he could work alongside Jonno. Quite late on in the process, on 11 March, Gareth came up to the Vale to see if he could sort out the issues face to face with Jonno. Gareth wanted Nigel to work underneath Scott and learn from him, which would effectively make Scott his mentor. I was working next door when the conversation took place, and it was certainly loud and explosive. In fact, I didn't need to be next door to hear it. I could've been at the far end of the corridor and still made out the intent on both sides quite clearly. While Gareth's approach sounded humble and conciliatory, Scott's emotional pitch was at the top end of the scale. Every few minutes, Jonno would explode, and Gareth would try to calm him down again. 'Why should I want to work anything out? What have I got to gain from all of this?' ranted Jonno in the next room.

Back in January, Mike Ruddock had picked up his phone and been surprised to hear the voice of Mark Davies, the Wales physio, at the other end. Carcass, it turned out, was testing the water on behalf of his good mate Jonno: 'How would you feel about coaching the Welsh forwards with Jonno as the head coach?'

Mike wasn't enthralled by the prospect: 'I'd been through a tough season with the Dragons. There'd been a lot of political in-fighting, and Marcus Russell had had a difficult job maintaining the balance between Newport and the rest of Gwent. The WRU sent Steve Lewis to sit in on the Dragons board, and I found myself being drawn into the politics. In the circumstances, it was difficult for me to just concentrate on coaching. On the playing front, everybody thought of us as a bunch of rejects, despite the fact that we'd been successful and were still in contention for the league title on the last weekend of the season.

'When the national coaching role became available, I didn't feel comfortable with the prospect of working within an existing regime, so I didn't apply. I had unfinished business with the Dragons. Clive and I had done a lot of the hard graft with the boys there, and I wanted to continue developing them.

'Then I got a call out of the blue from Mark Davies, the Wales physio. He told me he was canvassing support for Scott Johnson, who was considering applying for the head coaching job. Mark asked me if I'd consider being an assistant coach in Jonno's set-up. My initial reaction was that if I wanted to be involved at all, it would have to be as head coach, so I declined the offer – but I was still curious to hear what Scott had to say, so I went along to the Vale to meet him as Mark suggested. Scott was clearly a passionate man, but I wasn't at all sure I wanted to give up being a head coach at the Dragons in order to go and work for someone else, especially someone I hardly knew.

'Then everything turned on its head. I was taking a training run at Cwmbran Stadium when I received a phone call from Steve Lewis. He said, "Can you meet me within the hour?" Whatever the matter was, I naturally assumed it was Dragons business. But when Steve turned up at the stadium 45 minutes later, he was accompanied by Terry Cobner. We went to the Parkway Hotel in Cwmbran, and they told me that the early rounds of interviews with Gareth Jenkins and Mark Evans hadn't gone well, so would I reconsider applying for the job. "We believe you're the man for the role," they said.

'They guaranteed secrecy if I agreed to interview, and I liked the forthright manner in which they were talking. A memory popped into my head: I recalled watching Wales getting slaughtered at Lansdowne Road in the Six Nations by a team including several of the Irish players I'd coached at Leinster. Ireland had scored two driving lineout tries in the first half, and they'd looked far better drilled technically than Wales at forward. I remember thinking, "I'm sure I could add definite value to this side as a forwards coach." I was of a mind that I could help with the set-pieces immediately.

'Although I only had a couple of days to prepare for the interview, I had a clear idea in my mind of the statement I wanted to make. I relied heavily on a video CV that Gareth Potter had previously put together for me – only two or three minutes long but including career highlights such as Swansea winning the cup and league and beating Australia, and other feel-good clips from my time with Leinster, Ebbw Vale and Wales A – and made sure this video was played at the beginning of the interview in order to give the panel a visual idea of the rugby background I grew out of. It was an exact, pocket-sized picture of how the basic traits of teams I coached would remedy the weaknesses of the current Wales side. The main thrust of my PowerPoint delivery was that while Wales needed to carry on playing with width and tempo, the scrummaging, general set-piece accuracy and all aspects of defence could be improved. I made it clear at the interview that I could only accept the position if I was able to appoint a defence coach to work alongside me. The interview must have gone well, as the next day Steve Lewis rang to offer me the job.'

By 12 March 2004, emotions were running high before the announcement of the new head coach. It was probably the best-kept secret in WRU history. The team manager, Alan Phillips, received the key phone call early on Thursday morning, and although he told Steve Hansen, between them they managed to keep it quiet until Mike was ushered into a small room in the Millennium Stadium ten minutes before the press conference was due to start. Andrew Hore, Alan Phillips and Scott Johnson were in attendance as Steve Lewis presented Mike: 'Gentlemen, I would like to present the new national coach.' Then he just left the room and shut the door. It was an odd, embarrassing moment for Mike. Then, a few moments later, Lewis came back in, grabbed hold of him and performed the same little ritual with the committee, a few doors down in the 'Wrex' room.

That wasn't the end of it. When Steve Lewis announced the new coaching group to the players up at the Barn later that day, Horey came thundering out of the room with steam jetting out of his ears. It's fair to say that he was less than enamoured of Clive Griffiths'

reappointment as defence coach. His attitude was 'Over my dead body
. . . No way is that going to happen.' I pointed out to him that he was
in fact the conditioner rather than the CEO, so it wasn't his decision
to make, but he wasn't to be deterred. I think that both he and Steve
felt they had a short cut to the seat of power as long as David Moffett
was the chief executive. We continued our vigorous debate by phone
later on, while Horey was in his car, and I reminded him that we'd
paid the price for the absence of a specialist defence coach at the
World Cup and couldn't contemplate another season without one.
The banter was only interrupted by a familiar voice: 'Aw . . . I think
that's enough guys.' It was Steve Hansen in the unaccustomed role
of jovial peacemaker, and I'd been on speakerphone throughout the
conversation. That caught me unprepared: 'Oh . . . hullo, Steve . . .
how are you?' I muttered.

Mike himself was soon drawn into the debate: 'I still had to see out
the season with the Dragons and was regularly travelling up and down
the M4 between Newport and my home in Swansea, so it gave me a
natural opportunity to stop off at the Vale to hammer out the details of
the new set-up with Alan Phillips and Scott Johnson. They were both
negative towards Clive's reappointment. However, Alan did say that as
I'd compromised by taking on board existing staff, he would encourage
those same coaches to compromise in order to create a positive working
environment.

'As soon as they realised that Steve Lewis had given me unrestricted
approval to hire a new defence coach and that that coach would be
Clive, they sought assurances that Scott would be recognised as my
number two. I had no problem with that, but I was worried that they
were losing touch with the bigger picture, in which we all had to work
together to the same end as a team of coaches. Instead, they seemed to
be obsessed with the pecking order.'

Personally, I felt a lot of sympathy for Gareth Jenkins, as I believed
he'd conducted himself in exemplary fashion during the interview
process, but at the time I didn't fully understand his relationship with
Nigel Davies. Nigel is very much Gareth's ideas man, and they are an
inseparable team, so if Gareth took the job, Nigel really had to come
with him. Mine wasn't the only sympathy call. Clive Woodward – who

already had his eye on Gareth as a support coach on the 2005 Lions trip to New Zealand – also phoned to commiserate. By the end of the cycle, I felt emotionally exhausted and in very much the same psychological position as when Kevin Bowring had resigned in 1998. For the time being, I was frozen in a 'grieving' phase for Gareth, just as I had been for Kevin.

It quickly became obvious that the triumvirate of Steve Lewis, Alan Phillips and Scott Johnson wanted to keep the Hansen philosophy alive and kicking, even if the man himself was now coaching on the other side of the globe in New Zealand. I felt that Steve Lewis in particular wanted to carry the Hansen torch onwards and therefore tended to view himself more as a director of rugby than an administrative executive. The wish to preserve many of the positive results from the past regime – especially the higher standards of professional behaviour both on and off the field, upon which Steve Hansen had always insisted – was laudable and natural, and it needed a nucleus of people in positions of power, such as Steve, Alan and Scott, to achieve that continuity. However, every new head coach has to begin with a clean slate and have the authority to create the environment they want, and it was clear right from the start that Mike Ruddock wasn't completely free to do that. In certain important respects, his hands were tied.

Quite naturally, Mike was of a mind that all coaches should report to the head coach in the new management group: 'However, I was aware that Scott Johnson had no job description as such, other than his skills coach title, and had no apparent contract of employment with the union.'

It wasn't until I attended a meeting between Gareth Jenkins and the new group chief executive, Roger Lewis, on 6 October 2006 that I discovered for myself that Steve Lewis (not the head coach) was the line manager for both Alan Phillips and Mark Davies, and Gareth categorically stated that he was unwilling to work within that structure. This structure had been in place throughout Mike's time in charge, so there were elements of the group that were outside the head coach's control right from the start.

Mike didn't feel able to sign the contract he was offered: 'Because of the swiftness of my appointment, there was no contract available for me to look at at the time of interview. Steve Lewis brought it to me just before we were due to fly to Argentina. I had a quick look through the 50-pager and made some notes at the end, thinking for the most part that it was unsignable. Then I handed it on to my solicitor, Tim Jones, to examine while I was away in South America. On my return, Tim Jones confirmed my suspicions that it needed a number of clauses removed or altered before he could advise me to sign it.

'There was no sense of urgency from the union for me to sign, and no one asked me at any time during my term as national coach to present the signed copy. The contract was for two years, it was for significantly less money than my predecessors had been paid and it was non-negotiable. But that part didn't matter to me, as it was never about the money anyway.'

For me, the arrival of Mike Ruddock and the resurrection of Clive Griffiths represented an exciting opportunity to re-establish my credentials after the Hansen years in the professional wilderness. Mike's first task was to select a squad to tour Argentina and South Africa in June, and many of the top players had been written 'sick notes' by Hansen and Hore after their efforts during a long World Cup season. There was a week's training beginning on 17 May, and we'd mustered a squad somewhere in between first-XV and A-team strength. Twelve or thirteen of the front-rankers were absent, including Stephen Jones, Gareth Cooper, Martyn Williams and Rob Sidoli, for the warm-up game against the Barbarians. The pleasing aspect of that game was that we 'nilled' a talented Baa-Baas line-up 42–0, which showed that the defence now had the opportunity to develop into an attacking weapon under Griff's stewardship. We ran a blitz scheme in that match, and Clive was keen to explore the potential of an aggressive D that forced turnovers for our corps of splendid counter-attackers – led by Shane Williams – to run back at the opposition.

Mike Wadsworth and I flew out ahead of the squad on 2 June. There were tearful goodbyes to Catherine, Isabelle and Henry, as this would be the first time I'd been away from my young family on tour since South Africa in 2002. I remember Henry slapping me on the head in front of his mates before announcing triumphantly, 'Look, my dad's got no hair.' Twelve hours to São Paulo, then another two down to

Buenos Aires. Interestingly, our liaison officer at Buenos Aires airport turned out to be a familiar face: Manuel, who'd met me off the plane on the World XV tour back in 1998. On the drive from the airport, the landscape was composed of eight-lane highways, gleaming skyscrapers and unfinished blocks of flats. There was a temporary reunion with the family at the hotel, by conference call on the PC. Isabelle couldn't work out what was going on and kept on reaching behind the monitor screen to check if her dad was really lurking behind it.

I don't think it's possible to overestimate the importance of backroom staff such as Mike Wadsworth in creating the right atmosphere within a squad of players at the elite level. Will Greenwood recently wrote an article praising the efforts of Phil Pask, Richard Wegrzyk and Tony Biscombe with the England team of Woodward's era. They are essential bits of connective tissue, giving advice to the players on everything from their opponents' strengths and weaknesses to diet and the correct maintenance of joints and muscles. It is they who reinforce the coaches' messages during the (often prolonged) periods of time they spend with the players.

When Graham Henry invited Mike Wads to join his team in 1998 as chief masseur, Mike already had a rich pedigree: he'd been in charge of a key department at Whitchurch Secondary School in Cardiff, and he was a top-level ski instructor who could coach soccer and rugby teams to a very competent standard. In 2003, Steve Hansen asked him to provide a massage service for the regions, extending his remit from the international level down to the regional tier underneath. I'd always hit it off with Mike, and we arranged to meet for dinner on the evening of our arrival in Buenos Aires. We only just made it to the waterfront restaurant after a close shave on the eight-lane highway. We sauntered across the first couple of lanes but then noticed a large lorry in the outside lane already beginning to rev up as the lights changed. I sensed it was going to be a close-run thing, and by the end we were sprinting flat out as the lights turned green and the lorry shaved Wads's backside as he flew past. The lorry driver didn't even make a token effort to slow down.

I immediately felt more energised than I had at any time under Steve Hansen, experiencing a professional 'second wind'. With Rhodri

Bown doing the individual player analyses back at the Barn and Gareth Potter taking care of the team stats, I was able to throw myself into a PowerPoint presentation of Argentina. Mike supported me fully – 'You know all the stuff, don't you?' – so I gave a 45-minute talk in the large team room at the hotel on the Saturday evening. The feedback was very positive, and I felt that once again I was moving forward.

As in South Africa in 2002, we really began to respond to a country where sport is a high priority. On the bus rides to and from training, we would pass a seemingly endless stream of soccer pitches, cycle tracks and tennis courts. A group of the boys went to watch the *superclasico* local derby between Boca Juniors and River Plate on the Thursday evening, and they came back trembling with excitement, saying how they could feel La Bombonera, the home of Boca, begin to move and sway as the fans jumped up and down in rhythm. Researchers have discovered that the stadium – especially at the end occupied by the stand with four tiers stacked one atop the other – actually begins to move a few inches in the air when the chanting and stamping begin: *'La Bombonera no tiembla. Late'* ('The Bombonera doesn't tremble. It beats'). As in 2002, Mefin Davies sparked a lot of positive energy and good humour with his jokes and tall tales on the coach journeys, and there was also much good-natured banter between the coaches: both Mike and Scott are musically oriented, and they'd take turns to guess the next track on the radio or tape from the first couple of bars: 'I'll name that tune in . . .' In our spare time we were well looked after by Manuel's colleague, 'Billy Patagonia', who had some Welsh ancestors in that region of the country.

On Friday, we flew up to Tucumán for the first Test. Tucumán is about as far removed from Buenos Aires as you could imagine. From a diet of top-class sport, steak houses and the urban high style of Argentine tangos spontaneously igniting in the streets, we suddenly found ourselves in a rural backwater. When we arrived at the ground for training, a workman was precariously balanced on the roof of the stand, making repairs with no safety net to catch him if he happened to fall off. That was par for the course in Tucumán. The universal form of transportation in the town seemed to be horse and cart, and we knew that one of the newsmen covering the tour had found himself in questionable accommodation, to say the least. Upon discovering a large mysterious blanket hanging next to the wall in his hotel bedroom, he went to pull it back and found nothing more than a ragged hole. It looked like a small bomb had gone off. There was no glass and no window frame, just fresh air and the sounds of the street beneath. When we turned up for training at the stadium, we found the carcass of a large dog on the terraces. It had just been left there to fester, surrounded by a cloud of black flies. Argentina like to use outlying areas such as Tucumán to soften up touring teams, which is probably the reason why the All Blacks tend to play only one Test, in Buenos Aires, when they go there. We were drawn into playing the first Test in Patagonia in 2006 because of the Welsh population and background in that area, but like Tucumán it was a defeat waiting to happen.

Mike Ruddock began live scrummaging sessions in the week before the first Test against the Pumas. At first, it was forced upon him, as the scrum-machine at the training ground was little more than a heavy steel skeleton with no pads to push against. The same thing had happened to Graham Henry when his squad arrived in 1999. Curious, that, in the land of the fabled scrummagers. It was an important moment, because Mike wanted to establish a culture of intense, physical, live contact sessions as part of Test-match preparation, and some of the players weren't too keen on the prospect. Mike addressed the moans from Charv and Gareth Llewellyn forthrightly and immediately. To the best of my knowledge, he was in full view of all the players at a meeting when he did so, not in his van reading periodicals. (In the fallout after he lost his job as national coach in 2006, Mike was accused of reading a paper in the WRU van at a Wales conditioning session. In fact, he had been reviewing footage of the opposition on his laptop.) It was certainly not Mike's coaching style to avoid confronting problems as and when they arose, but even before the end of the Argentinian leg of the tour, he was to discover that there was opposition to some of his methods that was well beyond his control.

Although Mike didn't want to change too many things straight off the bat, he did feel that there were three areas in which we could make almost immediate improvement. At the scrum, in defence, and in what he called 'momentum' situations. Apart from the insistence on live contact and scrum drills, Mike was very conscious of building attacking momentum through offloads in or before contact, spinning away in the tackle or even rolling on the ground to get those vital few extra feet after the collision. These were all ways of building the tempo of our attacking play without having to dominate the collisions straightforwardly, which Mike knew we would find difficult.

Predictably, the 'Tucumán Effect' was overpowering in the first Test. The Irish referee Donal Courtney was a very nervous type. Twenty thousand people were packed into the small ground by kick-off, and when they began baying for Welsh blood you could almost see him shrink to half of his normal size. He looked intimidated by the primal atmosphere. Although we'd talked to Courtney about the scrum and our intention to use a blitz defence before the game, Duncan Jones was penalised four times at scrum time, and Shane Williams was pinged for offside after jarring the ball loose in a perfectly judged man-and-ball tackle that resulted in a try at the other end of the field. The Argentines also ran two excellent scoring moves that found out our blitz from first phase and gave the senior players all the ammunition they needed to force Griff to dump it in favour of something a little more conservative. Meanwhile, I found my pocket being picked by a small lad while filming from the terraces at one end of the stadium as we lost a weird eleven-try game 50–44. Tucumán, Tucumán.

On a rare Thursday off, I went with Horey and Professor John Williams to watch the return game between River Plate and La Boca. We arrived three hours before kick-off to find sixty or seventy thousand River Plate supporters already crammed into the stadium. I could feel the constant drumming and chanting vibrate through my entire body during the game, as if I'd become some kind of sporting tuning fork. A father behind us kept on holding his son at full stretch above his head as if he'd won a trophy as the firecrackers exploded . . . Then a pure dead silence as Boca scored the winning goal at a ground from which their supporters had been excluded because of crowd trouble in the first game. I could clearly hear the whoops of celebration by the Boca players on the field as the crowd became a coliseum of statues.

As Donal Courtney was due to take charge of the second Test back in BA as well, we thought it well worth the effort to put together a package of clips that we felt showed how much his judgements had been tilted towards the Pumas by the Tucumán effect. Mike and Griff went to Courtney's hotel to meet with him, and the clip package proved to be one of the most influential reels we ever produced. I believe Courtney even received a caution from the IRB referees' panel as a result of it. It must have done the trick, because we were awarded the first five penalties of the game at the Estadio Ferrocarril Oeste. That helped give us a platform to overwhelm the Pumas with our high-tempo attacks and build a 25–0 lead by half-time. Shane Williams scored a spectacular hat-trick, and Nicky Robinson made a superb debut at outside-half. I can still picture the Argentine full-back's embarrassment as Shane put a double step on him for his second try. Poor Hernán Senillosa just fell over backwards and didn't even look like getting in a position to make a tackle. Although Argentina came back at us in the second half, we held on comfortably to win 35–20.

There was some tension in the camp as we headed off for our third summer Test in South Africa. Griff had noticed that although his relationship with Jonno seemed to be OK, Andrew Hore kept his distance. Alan Phillips, Scott Johnson, Horey and Mark Davies tended to behave as a unit in social situations, which often left Mike and Clive in limbo. Even at team meetings, you would always see those four sitting together as a group. When we arrived at our Johannesburg hotel at about six o'clock on the evening before the Test match, Mark Davies mentioned to me that there was a dinner planned for later. I relayed this information to Mike and Clive, who were quite surprised as they knew nothing about it. In fact, they hadn't been invited to join the fab four, so I ended up having a sandwich with them in the hotel bar instead. Somehow, it didn't quite gel with Hansen's departing declaration: 'You're all in it together.'

As in 2002, we stayed at the Vineyard Hotel in Cape Town for the first three days before moving north. We trained at the Diocesan College, otherwise known as Bishops, in the shadow of Devil's Peak. Len Kaplan, the long-time head of sports there, told me that they'd produced over sixty rugby internationals and at one stage had a team that included players who would go on to represent five different countries. He clearly lamented the loss of the likes of Matt Stevens and Stuart Abbott to England, Dan Vickerman to Australia and our very own Hal Luscombe, training there in front of us as we spoke. They were all people he'd coached, and although he was pleased that his charges had achieved success at the top level, he still regretted the drain of both their talent and sinewy character to other nations. I felt an immediate sympathy with him.

On Thursday, I had one of the best days off on tour I'd experienced, in the company of Jonno and the Prof. We drove up to the Platteklip Gorge and started out on the steep ascent to the upper cable station on Table Mountain. This is where I got my revenge on the Aussie longhair for his conclusive victory in our bike race in Lanzarote back in 2003. The large thick steps were ideal for a man of my proportions, while Scott was soon blowing on the zigzagging climb, hampered by his own relatively stubby pair of legs. I'd left him far behind by the time I teetered along a narrow, nerve-racking path just below the cable station, with a sheer drop of about 300 feet on one side. Reaching the top, which was guarded by two enormous boulders – as Peter Munday said all the way back in 1634, 'wondrous steep, the rocks on each side like massive walls' – I experienced the same thrill I used to get running up to the Folly in Pontypool. I looked out and the whole world seemed to be below me. Whenever I feel right, whenever I feel that I'm a real part of things, I take pictures, and on that Thursday I took plenty.

The South African leg of the tour did, however, represent a poor piece of planning. We'd flown out from Buenos Aires on Sunday night after the second Test to cross both water and time zones to Cape Town. After an uncomfortable eight-hour flight, we landed on Monday afternoon, with the Test match only five days away on Saturday. Because of the short turnaround, I'd sought help from Mervyn Murphy, the analyst for the Ireland team that had just lost its own two-Test series against the Springboks in controversial circumstances. Mervyn kindly left me two outstanding Sportscode files on the South Africans to make life easier for my Tuesday-morning presentation. On top of the time-zone change, however, we were training at sea level in Cape Town and only moved up to Johannesburg at altitude the day before the game. We seemed to be permanently trying to catch up with ourselves from the moment we arrived in the Republic.

The day of the game was, predictably, a tough day at the office. I was shepherded into the coaches' box to do my filming by none other than Kobus Wiese, the retired Springbok lock and captain. Kobus was dauntingly large but extremely patient and considerate as I struggled with my equipment. Nicky Robinson pulled his hamstring during the warm-up and had to leave the field after only 15 minutes or so, to be swiftly followed to the changing-room by Deiniol Jones with a leg injury. When Alix Popham tried to put in his second big hit of the game, he was knocked cold in a collision with Schalk Burger. Mark Davies spotted his distress immediately and ran on to the field as play continued, and both the paramedic and touch judge watched it all coolly from the sideline. Fifty minutes into the game, we'd lost three starters and had substitute hooker Huw Bennett playing as a flanker.

Gavin Henson disappeared as a tackler at full-back, and when Darren Morris came on as a replacement prop in the second period he took such a hiding from 'Ox' du Randt that Mike promptly had to 'give him the crook' after only ten minutes on the field. Mike sent on a warning with Carcass after five minutes, and when nothing happened, Darren was off after ten. It was carnage, and we ended up on the wrong end of a 50-pointer. When I returned to the hotel early to get a head start on the analysis, my chauffeur was a massive Afrikaner policeman who narrated with some relish the story of how he would feed his two pet pythons live rabbits for dinner . . . Quite delightful, and very much in the spirit of the day's events.

Scott had gathered together some clips from the game footage and asked me if I'd give his presentation the next morning, as he was taking a flight back to Australia that same evening. It had been OK'd by Mike, and I was glad to oblige, but I did feel that Clive Griffiths – with his experience as a backs coach – would have been a more natural choice. It was a niggling reminder that the management group was not completely unified, which was confirmed by a full-blooded argument between Clive and Gareth Llewellyn in the debrief about the merits of the blitz defence. Llew had been caught out on the short-side in the lead-up to one of the Springbok tries, staying out and 'numbering' in good Hansen style rather than stepping in to sack the ball carrier. Gareth went on arguing the toss with Clive for some time, and it was hard not to feel a basic negative attitude towards Griff in the shadowy background throughout.

For both Mike and Clive Griffiths, the whole debate about the style of defence quickly became the focus for a power struggle within the camp. Clive Griffiths recalls: 'Mike and I got the call from Wales on the back of our results with the Dragons. We'd finished third in the Celtic League that year [2004] and beaten just about everyone at Rodney Parade. Much of our success was due to the blitz defence, which we operated very effectively. South Africa had won the Tri Nations and Wasps had won the Heineken Cup using different variations of blitz, and I was keen to plant my own version in the national team during the 2004–05 season. I'd also used it to great effect in rugby league, so what was the problem? It worked! The Dragons boys were fully behind it. In fact, we employed blitz principles in one form or another all the way up to autumn 2005, until the groundswell of player protest among the non-Dragons became too strong and too hard to ignore.

'I felt like I was a car salesman. I was having to push this brand of defence to the players so hard. I knew we could be successful with it, but some of the players dug their heels in, and we eventually had to go with the flow . . . It worked brilliantly against the Baa-Baas, but we struggled to run it in Tucumán, and the Pumas got around us on a couple of occasions. Then it worked a treat in the first half at Buenos Aires, and we had that game in the bag by half-time.

'Even when we moved over to drift, I kept some of the blitz elements in . . . We told Tom Shanklin to defend on Brian O'Driscoll's outside shoulder all game in the Grand Slam finale, and he took to it like a duck to water. Prior to the 2005 Six Nations, I showed the players some clips of a recent Liverpool–Chelsea soccer match in which the Reds systematically cut down Chelsea's space and simply refused to let them play, and that became the theme for our defence. A couple of the boys were Liverpool fans like me, so they liked that. "Look," I said. "No space, no time."

'Another wrinkle I tried to carry over from rugby league was the split-centre defence, where the wing and centre on either side would operate as a pair on the edge – say 12 and 11, and 13 and 14 – while everyone else filled in on the inside. That worked well on the summer tour to the USA and Canada in 2005.

'There were just too many dissenting voices within the management group, constantly chipping away at the players with little negative comments about the blitz. A strong mass of opinion was built up over a period of time which made it impossible for me to continue with the blitz by the autumn of 2005 . . . I began to call it the dritz instead, a strange hybrid version of blitz and drift.'

Scott Johnson didn't rate the blitz, right from the start. It was a hot topic of discussion on the Argentina tour, and Scott said, 'I don't think this is going to work at international level. Sides will break it down too easy.' Interestingly, Stephen Jones then used almost exactly the same words as Jonno to criticise it later that year in November: 'I don't think blitz is going to work at international level. It can get broken down too easily.' It rang a bell in my head, and I picked up on the similarity of the language right away.

Meanwhile, Sonny Parker had smashed his hand into a mirror in a non rugby-related incident and was injured for the first couple of months of the season. To cap it all, the flight captain's voice came over the intercom with 400 people already on board the plane back to the UK: 'Will passenger Rowlands please identify himself?' No one stood up. J.R. had slipped off the plane for a contemplative cigar on the airstrip just before take-off, so we missed our time slot and had to wait a further 45 minutes before we could leave South Africa. We were indeed still playing catch-up from the Hansen years.

Mike flew out to Australia with his family later that summer and stayed in a beach-house belonging to a mate of Jonno's for two or three weeks. It was an important meeting of minds, although the trip did end on a significantly bizarre note, according to Mike: 'I was really knackered after the Argentina tour . . . I'd put a helluva lot of work into the Dragons, then there was the unexpected invitation into the race for the Wales coaching job and all the fallout from that, then the tour to Argentina and South Africa. It was a wild ride, but by July–August I was ready for a well-deserved holiday with the family. They flew out to join me after the first week.

'Scott had generously invited me out to stay with him in his home town just outside Gosford in New South Wales, and we had a good time. He took the trouble to show me around a number of the rugby league clubs in the area and take a look at their set-ups, and at the time I thought it helped to develop our relationship. There was a good balance between working with Scott, including taking a couple of sessions with his local team, Penrith, and spending time with the family.

'Everything was going smoothly until the end of the trip when I mentioned to Scott that we should meet up with a fellow Welshman who was staying nearby, Frank Burrows. Frank had a lot of ideas about coaching philosophy and had written some interesting articles. I thought it might be useful for us to meet with him.'

Frank Burrows had gone to Liverpool John Moores University and specialised in football coaching and philosophy. He published two pieces in the *Football Association Coaching Journal* as part of his degree. When Mike came over to Australia, he taught physical education, and his uncle had just interviewed Mike for a Welsh rugby magazine. The meeting between Mike, Scott and Frank occurred in a seminar facility between St George and the Rocks in Sydney, and Frank began by outlining his view of the fundamentals of coaching philosophy. Mike was encouraging, but Scott said nothing until after he'd finished.

The meeting left quite a bruise on Frank Burrows: 'My first thought was, "Hey, these two seem to have a 'good cop, bad cop' approach." When I stopped talking, Scott burst into life. He said he didn't give a flying fuck about any of the issues I'd raised. When we tried to discuss the importance of leadership, Scott said, "I just want to challenge you every step of the way." He didn't agree with the idea of fundamental principles, with everybody taking responsibility and having a say in their own role and behaving according to an agreed code of conduct: "If Shaquille O'Neal [an American basketball star] stayed out on the tiles every night, you wouldn't fuckin' drop him, would you? Fuck the other players. You'd still pick him."

'Mike remained very quiet and patient throughout all of this, until he'd finally heard enough: "Right, it's my turn to speak now, Scott." I formed the impression that there was deep contradiction in Scott. He had this hippie image and liked to appear a blue-collar man, a man of the people, but in reality he was quite conservative and reactionary.

He just went straight into this negative emotional red zone and never backed out of it. He kept on referring to the Wales team as "*my* team" and "*my* boys". He didn't want to discuss the possibilities. For several hours afterwards, I felt utterly exhausted by the experience.'

Back at home, Alan Phillips caught me by surprise again by suggesting, quite out of the blue, that I needed a new contract – I'd been working for the best part of a couple of years without one. Thumper hustled me over 'blindfolded' to Golate House in Cardiff, where Steve Lewis was ready for me to put pen to paper there and then. No time to think it over – just sign on the dotted line.

Contract negotiations with the WRU always put me on edge. In sport generally, I feel you have got to help people get the deal that's right for them if you really want them – it has to be a win-win situation. With Steve Lewis, I thought that he was making my life awkward with the manner and timing of his approach. I'm sure he was just doing his job and doing it well, getting the best deal on behalf of his employer, but, of course, it didn't look that way from where I was standing. Negotiations were never plain sailing but frequently long, drawn-out and highly stressful affairs. I suppose it depends which side of the fence you're standing on, as an employee or an employer.

One immediate improvement this time round, however, was the full-time acquisition of Rhodri Bown as a support analyst. I'd placed Rhodri with the now-defunct Celtic Warriors while organising the analysis staff for the new regional structure in 2003, and, of course, Rhodri had lost his job when the Warriors went under. I'd used him on a casual basis, but now I could afford to take him on as a full-time employee of Alun Carter Rugby Analysis. Rhodri was to prove a fine asset for the WRU, and it was a pleasure for me to watch him develop. Room in my budget also appeared to recruit Corris Thomas and Nick Bishop on an ad hoc basis to provide a view of the opposition and trends in the modern game, and I started feeding through Nick's big reports on the opposition to Scott and Clive. I felt that getting Nick on board in particular was a big plus. There's a lot of 'unknown' research and planning that goes on in the background, which the public never get to hear about, and has a critical bearing on the outcome of big sporting contests. Nick was an important part of that planning. A rugby match is like an iceberg: 80

per cent of what contributes to the result is underwater, invisible. Like Graham Henry, Mike was very aware of the value of information from outside the box, and I felt we were assembling a powerful group of rugby intellects. I had more practical help now than ever before.

There was a return to the organised approach that characterised Graham Henry's methods, providing clips of the opposition on disc for the players to assess and comment upon – a test of rugby intellect, and part of Mike's plan to empower the playing squad. This was very important, because we discovered that the game had undergone a significant shift in emphasis during the summer Tri Nations tournament. South Africa won that competition under their new coach, Jake White, by implementing an aggressive new 'umbrella' defence, not dissimilar to Clive's, that created turnovers by forced fumble or interception. Twelve of their sixteen tries derived from defensive pressure, rather than creative play with ball in hand, and they'd produced an outstanding defensive performance in trouncing New Zealand 40–26. This was a reversal of the statistical outlook up until then.

Our first autumn opponents were Jake White's new South Africa, and we were in a similar situation to 1998 when Graham took over the reins, having slumped to a heavy defeat on tour and urgently needing to redeem ourselves at home in our very next competitive game against the same opponents. Mike immediately put a solid foundation stone in place by showing the key individuals who had been rested during the summer – including Gareth Thomas and Martyn Williams – a thirty-slide presentation on his picture of how Wales would play the game in 2004–05: solid scrummaging with specialists in all three front-row positions, upping lineout stability on our ball and contesting the opposition throw; high-tempo attacks, moving the ball wide from scrum through quickly channelled possession, a departure from Hansen's policy of looking to hit up close or in midfield; setting targets in midfield with off-the-top ball from quickly formed lineouts, and then using the offloading game up front behind them; and quick tapped penalties and exploiting momentum with bursts of inter-passing close in. It was a very complete picture, presented with total clarity, and we'd had nothing like it in the Hansen era. Mike gave a captaincy role to several of the senior players to monitor and provide feedback on their local areas of the game. It was a rock-solid structure, and there was no room for ambiguity. Everyone knew their roles and what was expected of them before those key autumn matches.

After a poor start, we mounted a strong second-half comeback to come within a couple of points of victory in a 74-point thriller against South Africa. We scored three tries against the strong Bok defence and showed signs of buying into Mike's vision. There were quick tap penalties and even a pushover try when the South African replacement front row were destroyed by Adam Jones – happily running a full course – in the 83rd minute of the match. But the glimpses were too fitful and inconsistent to deserve the win, in all honesty.

New Zealand was probably the single biggest game of the autumn series. There was the big fear factor of playing the most dangerous attacking side on our schedule and not wanting to be humiliated in front of our home crowd, and the heady emotional charge of Graham Henry and Steve Hansen's first return to Welsh shores in new colours. The boys applied themselves diligently in training and in presentations on the local areas of the match that they were expected to manage. Our game planning was strong, and the players' intellects were engaged early in the process. We made adjustments in our style of play to counter the All Blacks. We were determined not to let them dominate the gain line or the heads at scrum time in order to get position to move the ball wide quickly, and we set out to control the edges of the ruck and go forward onto the ball in defence. All this was in place by Monday, and Clive Woodward, who was on a fact-finding mission for the Lions for the entire week, was amazed that the game-planning foundation was set so quickly.

Quite by chance, I also came across a historian in Corris Thomas's office up at UWIC, Gwyn Prescott, who pointed out to me that on New Zealand's 1905 tour of Britain, the Welsh national anthem had been sung as a response to the haka. I mentioned this in one of the autumn planning meetings, and Andrew Hore immediately jumped on the possibility of gaining a psychological advantage before the game had even started. After the All Blacks had finished their haka, a single Welsh opera singer strode on to the field carrying a Welsh flag and singing 'Bread of Heaven'. With every pace he took, more and more of the crowd gathered behind him until the entire stadium was a towering wave of sound threatening to engulf those black shirts. We rode that wave all the way to a handy 11–3 lead after the first half-hour and lost by just a single point, 25–26, while finishing the game stronger than the Blacks. Tom Shanklin and Mefin Davies scored tries in each half, and Gavin Henson hit an upright with a shot at goal that would probably have been enough to win us the game very late on in the second half. But it was our domination of territory and possession that gave us the game-winning opportunities, and the confidence that came from outplaying the Blacks for much of the match gave us a tremendous base to work from for the 2005 Six Nations. I recall Alfie saying that he didn't want Japan next up; he wanted New Zealand again. He knew we could take them.

Two elements of our play that had immediately changed under Mike's leadership were the efficiency of our scrummaging and cleaning-out in contact. We had a very accurate and detailed method of measuring our effectiveness in contact, and Gethin Jenkins really stood out in this area. He hit an extraordinary number of rucks for a prop and always had a positive impact when he got there, being not only very physical but also a good decision-maker. Colin Charvis and Dafydd Jones were also highly impressive for much the same reasons, and Richie McCaw told us afterwards that he couldn't remember a game in which he'd been targeted so accurately by the opposition flankers: 'I didn't get near the ball all day with those two jokers around.'

Much of our increased effectiveness was due to correct selection by Mike. Gethin had been returned to his natural role at loose-head and freed from the anxiety of scrummaging in an unfamiliar position. Mike also dumped Hansen's long-running experiment of playing three number 7s in the back row and picked a specialist number 8 in Michael Owen, who was quickly to become one of the stars of the show. This in turn freed up Daf and Charv to do their stuff at 6 and 7 without having to worry about how to control the ball at the base of the scrum and give our 9 the space and time he needed. There was a good balance of characteristics in the middle row, with Gareth Llewellyn and Brent Cockbain. It all made much more sense than what had gone before.

The game also proved the reliability of Mike's selection of captain. He'd initiated an exhaustive interview process in which people had to present themselves for the job and speak effectively to an audience: 'I didn't feel the need to change the captain before we went to Argentina, and the captain on tour had been Colin Charvis. I wanted to see how things panned out before I made any long-term decisions about the captaincy, and, anyway, I had a lot of time for Colin Charvis after working with him at Swansea. In fact, I'd first brought Charv down to Swansea from London Welsh back in 1995, so I knew him well. But we ran into some problems, because after I'd offered and he'd accepted the role, Colin felt the time was right to negotiate some extra financial reward for being captain. Whilst he might have had a point, as the position of captain does carry extra responsibilities, this wasn't well received, especially during a Test match week. That gave me a reason to consider a change.

'I decided to conduct a series of interviews and open the captaincy up for competition. Colin was invited to throw his hat into the ring along with other candidates, and I felt at the end of the process that Gareth Thomas came out a clear winner. I'd just finished reading Clive Woodward's book in which he talked about "sappers" and "energisers", and Gareth came across as being an outstanding energiser. This fitted the general plan to create a positive environment in which both staff and players were encouraged to take responsibility for their actions.'

Steve Hansen stayed on in the UK for a couple of weeks after the All Blacks tour had finished. Mike met with him briefly and showed him a players' handbook that he had formulated, which included codes of conduct, team moves and a history of Wales. There was a diary for players to plan and manage their own time. Mike's PA, Caroline Morgan, who had also cooperated with Hansen and Scott Johnson on their player bibles, reckoned it was the best of its kind.

I made Steve a conciliatory cup of tea in the Barn, and after the history of some of our previous disagreements had been given a brisk, humorous airing, Steve was actually very helpful in demonstrating some of the latest analytical developments in New Zealand. He showed me and Rhodri the system developed by the Verusco company in Palmerston North that was currently used by the All Blacks. They had thirty people trained to code matches, and the All Blacks would employ eight analysts each working on a separate ten-minute segment of the game. It took each analyst about eight hours to work through his segment, frame by frame and action by action. Every action was graded on a zero-to-ten scale of effectiveness – so a tackle could be a complete miss (0) or an offensive hit producing a turnover (10), or somewhere in between. Both the opposition and the Blacks would be coded in this way.

The Verusco system was incredibly exhaustive and even allowed the All Black coaches to access a database including all the provincial players in New Zealand rugby. If the coaches wanted to rate all the hookers for instance, they could simply press a button and access average ratings for all the number 2s playing rugby at provincial level or above, for every action from tackling to lineout throwing to scrummaging. It was well ahead of its time, and indicative of the financial resources the New Zealand Rugby Football Union plough into their technical support services.

Although I was very grateful to Steve for the technical heads-up, there was a negative side to his visit and his general wish to stay close to the Wales environment. In his recent autobiography, Jake White detailed the difficulties that he and Hugh Reece-Edwards experienced after taking over at Natal from a strong personality in Ian MacIntosh. Senior players were still in close touch with their former coach, which made it very hard for the new coaches to stamp their own authority on the team. When a coach leaves, I think it's essential that he distances himself from the players he has worked with. Friendships can be maintained, but there is a boundary that you cannot cross. I think Graham always maintained this distance after leaving Wales, but I am not so sure that Steve Hansen followed suit. The new coaches struggled terminally at Natal because they could not get past senior player power and an influential former coach lending them a sympathetic ear in the background. Steve Hansen's visits and on-going conversation with a group of senior players in the Wales set-up created the same kind of problem for Mike.

Many of the difficulties orbited around Clive Griffiths, who'd been excluded by Steve and whom Scott seemed to view as a rival. Mike had made a conscious effort during the autumn to bring the management group together with the odd relaxing drink after a hard day. On one such occasion, he found himself walking back to his hotel room with Scott Johnson: 'As we walked back to our rooms, Scott said very seriously, "There's something I've got to say to you, Mike . . . The boys don't think Clive Griffiths is a good man. He wants your job. They're starting to have doubts about you, too, Mike, because you align yourself with him."

'I was nonplussed and expressed my disappointment immediately: "Scott, thanks for the feedback, but you can tell the boys that they don't pick the coaching team, I do."'

At the time, however, incidents like this were kept firmly in the background by the positive momentum we'd built over the autumn period, spilling over into the New Year and the challenge of the 2005 Six Nations. There was a very pleasing sense of complementary roles being established when the coaches delivered their message to the players. Mike brought a clarity of purpose, and was capable of making tough decisions and getting the call right. Scott Johnson knew the players very closely and had developed a tight understanding, especially with the senior players in the group, such as Alfie, Stephen Jones and Martyn Williams. Clive Griffiths and Andrew Hore were experienced coaches who knew their own areas, defence and conditioning, inside out.

Energy levels were high. Rhodri and I threw ourselves into the preparation for England, and I made sure we left no stone unturned. We got hold of end-on footage from England's autumn games, and film with natural sound only – no commentary and little crowd noise. From one, we picked out a clear trigger. When England were preparing to drive and box-kick from lineout, they'd stand the chasing wing directly behind the lineout; if he stood behind 10, they'd be moving the ball outside. From the other, you could hear lineout and scrum calls with some clarity, and we tried to decode their intentions. It all helped build the players' confidence in the completeness of our preparation.

We started a countdown to the game in the office, and little notes appeared on the walls, picking out the strengths and weaknesses of the England players and team patterns on the back of Nick's reports. England were everywhere you looked in the weeks leading up to 5 February 2005. Mike knew how important it was to beat the old enemy, not just because they were England, but because we'd lost two very tight games against South Africa and New Zealand, and we needed that elusive win to put us over the top and confirm the progress we believed we were making: 'There was no doubt in my mind. Looking at our schedule, we only had two home games and three visits to places we'd found it hard to win at in the recent past – Rome, Murrayfield and Paris. Then there was Ireland with their "golden generation" of players waiting for us in Cardiff at the end of the tournament. I felt if we didn't beat England, we could have been looking at a wooden spoon. It was that finely balanced.'

We'd identified tight-head Julian White as critical to the success England had had in their autumn games against South Africa and Australia. White had dominated the redoubtable Ox du Randt in a 32–16 victory; as well as pressuring the Springbok scrummage, he'd given a platform for Martin Corry to roll into midfield from the set-pieces, and England gained most of their attacking momentum from that. Mike brought in Stuart Evans, the ex-Neath and Swansea tight-head to help with our scrum, and he noticed immediately that White and the English hooker Steve Thompson were binding up first before scrums. This was the opposite of normal practice in which the hooker and loose-head would bind first. It showed where the arrowhead of their pressure would come, as the tight bind enabled White to spear in on the opposition hooker. Mike and Stuart oversaw some terrific live, fractious scrum sessions in which the B pack imitated this bind, and Mike made it clear to Gethin Jenkins and John Yapp (who would be White's opponents) what was expected of them in no uncertain terms. England had only run away from us the previous year when White had come on in the last quarter and given Duncan Jones a real working-over in the scrum.

Mike had a great sense of the value of information, and our preparation was given a further boost by his invitation to regional coaches to give talks on our opponents before each Six Nations game. It was a political masterstroke in firming up the relationship between the national set-up and the newly formed regions, and it provided a new voice to concentrate the players' minds on the challenge ahead just prior to the matches. Gareth Jenkins presented on England for 20 minutes, and the players came out of his talk feeling alive and passionate about the game. Martyn Williams said to me, 'I feel I'm ready to go out and play against

England right now.' I used the opportunity to get more concrete detail into them while they were still 'hot'.

The final cherry on the cake preparation-wise was Mike's talk with the referee Steve Walsh on the eve of the match. Mike had changed his style of approaching referees before the game, trying to keep the mood relaxed and friendly rather than going hard at them. Knowing that Walsh was very much a feel-good ref attuned to the southern-hemisphere style, and that no ref likes to be told how to do his job, Mike concentrated on the positives rather than focusing on English transgressions: how we wanted to keep the ball alive and quicken the tempo and pass the ball. Fitness, agility, skill, tempo. We only mentioned English barging at the lineout right at the end, supported by an instant PowerPoint image, and Steve Walsh threw his arms up in the air and shook his head. I've no doubt he left that meeting convinced that Wales wanted to play the kind of game he wanted to referee.

Selection-wise, there was a question mark about the back row that had played so well against the All Blacks. Colin Charvis would definitely have started against England on the openside flank but had picked up an injury, and Mike did a thoroughly professional job of examining the form of three possible replacements – Martyn Williams, Robin Sowden-Taylor and Ritchie Pugh were all in the frame – before adding Martyn to the starting mix: 'I'd made up my mind to base the pack on the Pontypridd unit that had displayed a lot of guts and cohesion around that time under the tutelage of Lynn Howells. Six of the forwards came from Sardis Road, if you include Martyn Williams, who is really a Pontypridd boy anyway. I tried to get a seventh, Duncan Bell, but unfortunately found he'd already been "warehoused" by England after a lot of political jockeying with the IRB. So the only gaps we needed to fill were at tight-head prop and number 6. I wanted the club combinations to give us confidence in what we were doing.

'I also felt it was important to grow Rob Sidoli's self-belief. Rob is a confidence player, and he was our lineout captain, an area in which we needed to go well against England. I selected Mefin Davies as our hooker, and we held an extra lineout defence session on the Thursday. Rob told me that he really felt confident after that because we'd gone into their lineout plays in tremendous detail.

'Another key was the selection of Michael Owen. A lot of people had argued that Michael was best used as a lock, but I saw him as a number 8 in the high-tempo style I wanted to play. He wasn't a power player or dynamic off the base of the scrum like Ryan Jones, but he had great hands and incredible passing ability. He could help us get the ball outside the 13 channel quickly from scrums – which was one of our aims against England – and throw these superb 15- or 20-metre passes to change the focus of attack in phase play in an instant. I didn't want a number 8 who would always be picking up at the base of the scrum, because I wanted to use the backs from first-phase scrums and then utilise Michael's talents in midfield when the ball came back from that initial wide ruck.'

Michael Owen was to make two try-scoring passes in the opening games, against England and Italy, and formed an almost psychic understanding with Dwayne Peel at the hub of the team. They proved to be the heartbeat of the 2005 side.

The game went pretty much according to plan. We negated Julian White at the scrum, and he was replaced; we won clean ball from a well-policed lineout. We got under Charlie Hodgson's skin and were as physical as we'd been against the All Blacks in contact. But the most pleasing aspect of the match was the way in which we dominated the last 15 minutes, the period in which we'd lost the game in 2004. Our play off the bench was really powerful, thanks to John Yapp, Ryan Jones and Gareth Cooper, and we finished by almost scoring a try that would have created a margin of victory that truly reflected the balance of territory and possession. As it was, Gavin Henson kicked a wonderful winning goal from a position similar to the one he'd missed against New Zealand, having steadfastly ignored the numerous and ever more urgent requests that Mike sent on to the field for him to take over the kicking duties from Stephen Jones.

Even then, Clive Griffiths recalls that the reaction from one member of the coaching staff was slightly off-key: 'All the coaches were elated down in the dressing-room after beating the old enemy – the win was a real breakthrough. Then Scott got up and insisted on a moment's quiet from the squad and mentioned Steve Hansen. He asked the players to remember Steve's standards during their celebrations, as he felt we could play a lot better. I was gobsmacked, with Rudds sitting there looking on . . . I couldn't stand it and got up and went into the toilets until he had finished his speech. Maybe I should have swallowed hard again, and, of course, it meant that Jonno and I didn't speak to each other for another month or so. We only started talking again after a very blunt man-to-man meeting before the Scotland trip, and we ended up shaking hands.'

Mike Ruddock was elated by a great start to the Six Nations: 'Later that evening, just before the reception, Clive and I were enjoying a pint together – rather smugly, I might add – when Phil Larder, the England defence coach, walked in. The England coaches of that era were always good value and would always come over and have a bit of a chat after the game, win or lose. Phil Larder and Andy Robinson were both very good like that. They always made the effort and mixed well. Anyway, Phil came over and congratulated us on the win, but with all the emotion, he caught me off guard. I didn't recognise him and blurted out, in true Trigger style, "All right, Dave," thinking that he was Dave Alred. I panicked, and Clive almost blew the top clean off his Guinness. Phil maintained his composure and just said, "Oh, it's Phil, actually," but whenever we talk about Phil now, we always refer to him as "Dai Larder".'

The second game away to Italy gave us a chance to exact revenge for the events in Rome in 2003. I made a big point of this in my presentation, reminding the players of that empty feeling in the pits of their stomachs as Italian whooping penetrated the changing-room wall. I don't think revenge was uppermost in Gavin Henson's mind, however. He hadn't played in 2003 and had recently struck up something of a romance by text with Charlotte Church. I even remember a large group of players surrounding Gav *in the process* of texting Charlotte at our Roman hotel. It was, in fact, a unilateral text and represented the input of about seven or eight different members of the Wales squad. Gavin had made the mistake of asking, 'What shall I say to her?' and invited a whole raft of dubious advice.

After leading by 19–8 at the half, we ran away from the one-paced Italians, scoring a further 19 unanswered points to log a convincing 38–8 win. Most of the tries came out of counter-attack situations, and

Jonno would go through the clips afterwards picking out moments in the game that fitted his view of the team's identity. 'That's us . . . That's who we are!' he'd exclaim excitedly. But the outstanding aspect of our first two games was Clive Griffiths' dritz defence. We knew we could attack, but until 2005 we didn't know we could also defend. We hadn't conceded a try to England and only given up one to a blocked-down kick against Italy, and that against the run of play. Nick's reports on the opposition were proving their worth in our preparations. They demonstrated a fine intuition of how and where our opponents intended to attack us, and Clive used them as a base on which to build and adapt a very resilient defence week by week.

Despite the longer two-week break between the Italy and France games, there were more obstacles in the preparation. I was becoming edgy as the players were becoming too lax and not viewing footage of France with the same enthusiasm as they'd shown for England and Italy. I rattled a few cages, and Gavin Henson even came into the office and apologised for not having spent enough time in front of his laptop, which I think is typical Gav. Once he knows he's really an integral part of the team, he works very hard at his preparation, and his comments about the opposition players were always among the most perceptive.

Although Leigh Jones of the Dragons gave a presentation on the French forwards, following on the heels of Andy Moore and Alun Donovan's for the Italy game, our preparation had been patchier and a couple of notches below the smooth build-ups to England and Italy in quality. The rustiness showed during a first half in which we couldn't get our game on track, and France scored two tries to lead 15–6 at the half. In truth, it could have been a lot more had it not been for a string of saving tackles by Gareth Thomas at full-back.

Mike knew that he had to do something quickly during the interval: 'Just before we got back to the changing-rooms, the first thing I remember was Griff throwing down his clipboard and saying, "That's it . . . I resign." He was only half-joking, as we both really felt that the bubble was in danger of bursting. I made three clear points, the three Ts: turnovers – we were either knocking on or turning ball over in the contact area, and that had to stop; tackles – we were falling off first-up tackles; touch – we were missing kicks to touch, allowing waves of

French attackers to come back at us. I felt if we could correct these areas and get the first score after the break, we'd be back in business.'

Two tries early on in the second period saved our bacon. First, Martyn Williams scored from a counter-attack virtually from the restart, then he got a second from a quick tapped penalty close to the French line after a Michael Owen-inspired momentum assault close to the ruck had broken the French defence. Suddenly, we were leading 18–15, and some of the preparation began to kick in. We'd struggled in the scrummage with the starters on the pitch, with Adam Jones receiving his first official international 'lesson' from Sylvain Marconnet, but with a rush of replacements from both teams and Marconnet switching sides in the scrum, we went on the offensive.

Referee Paul Honiss had for the first hour been as helpful as his Kiwi colleague Steve Walsh with an 8–2 penalty count in our favour. Like all Antipodean refs, he really favoured the side that was trying to keep the tempo high and the ball in hand. During one of our second-half inter-passing breakouts from deep, you could hear him (with the benefit of the referee's mic) breathe out heavily as he struggled to keep pace with play – an 'aw' of disappointment – when Rob Sidoli knocked on with no defenders left in front of him.

Then there was a lineout around the hour mark that changed everything, and the game entered its critical phase. Mefin Davies and Rob Sidoli were conferring at some length before a lineout throw, and Honiss told them to hurry it up. When he didn't get the immediate response he wanted, Honiss started screaming at them to get the ball in. Where previously he'd been applauding our constructive play, now he was bawling at our lineout captain and hooker, and using some pretty agricultural language to boot. We lost the next four lineout throws and conceded the next five penalties.

But unlike Steve Hansen against Italy in 2003, Mike didn't pull the thrower off immediately, instead giving Mefin and Rob the chance to right the ship. To their eternal credit, they stabilised the lineout, and we began to see some ball again: 'I'd been under pressure from various people in the management group to start Robin McBryde at hooker. But I resisted the pressure, because Rob had just come back from injury and Mefin had been playing very well. The other point is that I knew I had to move Melon [Gethin Jenkins] across to the other side of the scrum when Adam Jones started to tire after the first hour. Being a novice tight-head, he could only really manage the transition if a big, strong scrummaging hooker such as Rob came on around the same time to help look after him. And Rob had a huge impact with his physical presence when he came on for the last ten minutes against France. In fact, I remember us even pushing them backwards during the closing stages.'

Another piece of preparation slotted thankfully into place as we battled for our lives in the last five minutes when France seemed to be permanently camped on our line. We'd made a big point to the players about the ability of the French ball carriers, especially their hooker William Servat, to make 'yards after contact', or YAC. YAC has been an important measurable for American football running backs for many years – the great Chicago Bears running back Walter Payton was especially good at it – and we'd recently introduced it as a statistical category. It measures the number of yards a runner picked up after the first contact with a defender, and players such as Servat and Yannick Jauzion had outstanding figures in this area. When Martyn Williams came off the field exhausted, he came up to me and said, 'All I could think of in those last five minutes was, "Hang on to him," as I felt Servat's legs pumping and his big second effort coming on. "Don't let the bastard slip out."' It was a great moment for us as analysts to see the wit and courage of the players translating the information they'd been given off the field into a 'winning action' on it.

The boys were on a real high after seeing off France 24–18. They were fast approaching their championship best, and there was a game of 'conditioned touch' early in the week before the Scotland match that was a wonderful showcase for the footballing talents of everyone in the squad, even the tight forwards. The team talk before that game, when he told the story of Bell or Inchcape Rock, a sunken reef off the Firth of Forth estuary that wrecked around six ships every year and had in 1804 sent even the mighty HMS *York* to the bottom of the sea with the loss of all hands, was probably Scott's very best during his time with Wales. By 1807, a young engineer by the name of Robert

Stevenson had been engaged to build a lighthouse on a reef that only peeped above the waterline for four hours per day. The work was not finished for four more years, and workers were crippled by accidents or even killed during its construction. It became acknowledged in due course as one of the seven wonders of the industrial world:

> 'Canst hear,' said one, 'the breakers roar?
> For methinks we should be near the shore.'
> 'Now, where we are I cannot tell,
> But I wish we could hear the Inchcape Bell.'
>
> They hear no sound, the swell is strong,
> Though the wind hath fallen they drift along;
> Till the vessel strikes with a shivering shock,
> 'Oh, Christ! It is the Inchcape Rock!'

'Inchcape Rock', Robert Southey

Scott used the story as a parable of the team's own development. A granite foundation course had been laid during 2002 to 2004 that couldn't be disturbed by tide or stormy weather, and now, in 2005, the lighthouse was sending out a signal to all comers about how Wales wanted to play the game of rugby football. He gave all the squad members little Bell Rock key rings to help maintain that understanding, and they returned from Scotland clutching them as if their lives depended on it. It was wonderfully stirring stuff at that time, though it would all sound pretty ironic less than one year later. As Southey's poem ends:

> One dreadful sound could the Rover hear;
> A sound as if with the Inchcape Bell,
> The Devil below was ringing his knell.

The first half against Scotland was our peak performance of 2005. We were 'in the zone', and the game broke all kinds of statistical records. Our forwards made more passes in that first half alone than their Irish counterparts made in the entire Six Nations. There was the highest ball-in-play time for any game of international rugby up to that point and most passes made successfully in a match. It was the game in which Ryan Jones, one of Mike's original selections, came into his own as an international forward. He was on the end of an inter-passing movement after only four minutes, having burst between the two Scottish locks to make the initial line break in midfield. Rhys Williams scored a second a few minutes later, when he backed his instincts as Griff demanded and went fully 80 metres for an interception score. That was a 14-point turnaround. Thereafter, the floodgates opened, and after 50 minutes we were up by a remarkable margin, 43–3. Although the Scots came back into it in the second half, scoring three tries of their own, we still emerged with an astonishing away victory, 46–22.

Cardiff, 19 March 2005. It's one o'clock. I'm standing in the middle of a brilliantly green Millennium Stadium pitch, taking photographs. The stands are already beginning to fill up with a mixture of red and green shirts. I go back inside and watch the boys shaking hands as they prepare in the changing-room. There are easy, balanced smiles, and an inner belief that this is our day shines through. Even Rhys Williams, who has been named in the starting XV but will mysteriously pull a hamstring in the warm-up, is comfortable with his role. His replacement, Mark Taylor, knows that he will be starting on the right wing, but Ireland will not know until the game kicks off. There is the same strength of purpose that I see in Warren Gatland's Wales before the Grand Slam decider against France three years later.

Fast forward, four hours later, same changing-room. I'm grinning from ear to ear at Rob Sidoli, knowing that this time round he's fronted up to Paul O'Connell and made up for the failure of the year before in Dublin. Rob and Brent Cockbain, or 'Cobers', clattered into Ireland at the first lineout, and that set the tone. They couldn't set up any of their imposing driving mauls, and with only ten minutes of the game gone, the Irish forwards gave up on the tactic. Pure Mike Ruddock.

Ireland turned to their backs. They came at us with an inside ball to expose Shanks's wide positioning in midfield. Suddenly, Denis Hickie was running free in open space. Still, we somehow scrambled back, defending it right on our own line and turning over the ensuing scrum. Pure Griff, pure Mike. Then, in the middle of the second half, they launched the attack from lineout we'd been waiting for. Rather than chasing Brian O'Driscoll out towards touch, Tom Shanklin came up and planted his feet for the hit as Ireland's captain began to curve outside him. 'Bod' was smashed in the tackle. It was the blitz that 'couldn't work at international level', and it just levelled Ireland's attacking talisman and gave the team a huge lift. Pure Clive Griffiths.

We'd broken the early deadlock, Gethin Jenkins pouring through on to Ronan O'Gara as he hurriedly cleared the ball towards touch. It was something Mike had been hammering home all week: 'Do whatever you have to to get to Ronan O'Gara. Get in his face. Rattle him.' Gethin blocked down the kick and followed up to score. By the middle of the second half, we could hear a red-faced O'Gara arguing vehemently with Chris White on the ref-mic in the coaches box. We knew then that Ireland had lost the captain of their ship. We dominated the first hour and established an unassailable 29-6 lead. Although the Irish came back at us gutsily in the last 20, they knew they were coming off second best.

By seven o'clock, I'm in 'penguin uniform', with my tux and dicky bow, something I'll probably never wear again, out on the middle of a strangely deserted Millennium Stadium for squad photos. I look at Rhodri Bown's sprawling mass of hair in front of me and chuckle, knowing that he's promised to get it all cut off if we win the Grand Slam. Tomorrow, the barber's, Rhodri.

Eleven o'clock, Mike's strumming his guitar in leisurely fashion back at the hotel; a few of the boys are singing along. That's Mike, quietly strumming his own tune without making a big song and dance about it all. But make no mistake, it is his tune, and he's just orchestrated the first Grand Slam for Wales in 27 years.

7

THINGS FALL APART

'Coming together is a beginning. Keeping together is progress.
Working together is success.'

Henry Ford

The Grand Slam didn't bring happiness. Instead it
brought misery. The level of sheer adulation that members of the
squad and management received created all kinds of little envies and
jealousies. Mike was very good at deflecting the majority of the praise
on to his coaching staff and players, and I don't think he could have
done any more in that respect, but none of it seemed to help. Mike
produced a couple of presentations on leadership during the summer,
and there were some rumblings of discontent among the players about
it: 'I was asked to do a couple of presentations on the back of our Grand
Slam success, and I had a very simple, clear guideline in my mind when
offers like that came along. If they were corporate, I charged a fee;
otherwise, I would do them for nothing, such as the one up at Gethin
Jenkins's old club, Beddau. Wayne Hall, the former Bridgend and
Wales hooker and Wales Under-21 team manager, invited me to do

another at Pencoed Rugby Club. It was a celebration of the return of Bridgend's British Lions – Gareth Cooper, Gavin Henson and Gareth Thomas are all very active Pencoed old boys.'

As Wayne Hall recalls, 'Mike was the only coach available who hadn't gone on his summer holidays. When I asked him if he wanted a fee, he said, "You're joking, aren't you? The price of the taxi and a free plate of sausage and mash will do." He asked for any money generated by the evening to be put into the junior section of the club. But even though Alfie had been over on the other side of the globe with the Lions that summer, somehow he'd got wind of my invitation to Mike and had been told, wrongly, that Mike was charging £3,500 for his appearance that evening. Alfie was incensed. "What's he doing here?" he said, gesturing at Mike and quoting the appearance-money figure at me. I replied, "He's doing it as a favour. I don't know where you got the idea he's charging."' But the incident left a strong impression on Mike as the reality of the new situation after winning a Grand Slam began to dawn on him.

Meanwhile, a very important event on the rugby calendar was occurring on the other side of the globe in June 2005: the British Lions tour to New Zealand. Mike Ruddock was invited out there by Clive Woodward to be an observer and form part of his 'think tank', but after very careful consideration, he refused the offer: 'I was anticipating a reasonably lengthy stay as Wales coach after the Grand Slam so thought it was more important I took a look at the Under-21s than go out to New Zealand with the Lions. I felt I'd missed out on some of their Friday-night games because I'd been meeting referees throughout the Six Nations. I needed to catch up on the domestic game and do some homework on the young players coming through the system.

'I was also conscious that I'd jumped ahead of Gareth Jenkins, who was the media favourite for the Wales job, so when Gareth was picked as one of the Lions coaches I was genuinely pleased for him. The last thing that either he or I needed was for me to turn up on the Lions tour and tread on his toes or encourage the press to develop some kind of story about our so-called rivalry.'

Scott Johnson didn't feel any such inhibitions, and he became the only member of the 2005 management group to join the Lions party, if only as an observer. When I saw the selection of the Lions squad, I didn't feel that Clive Woodward had placed the proper value on what we'd achieved in winning the Grand Slam and running the All Blacks so close in the autumn 2004 match. Andy Robinson had more or less come out and said after the Wales–England game that he thought we were fortunate to win it, and that was manifestly not the case. So, there was quite a lot of resentment in the Wales camp when the squad was announced, because Woodward had so clearly gone back to 'England 2003 vintage' and ignored the claims of Ryan Jones, Brent Cockbain and both of our hookers. Mike had been emailing Clive with regular updates on the form of his players, so Woodward had all the information he needed at his fingertips. Then he rubbed a bit of salt in the wounds by bringing his English-based squad down to the Vale to do their training.

To base the Lions squad so squarely on an England team that had already passed their peak at the World Cup in 2003 was one big mistake. Another was to turn up in New Zealand with effectively two separate squads – two groups of twenty-two – complete with their own coaches and backroom staff. The Worcester and ex-Auckland centre Dale Rasmussen told me that he knew the Lions had no chance as soon as he saw them climbing aboard two coaches during the early stages of the tour. Thousands of other Kiwis thought the same.

The third problem was rather more hidden from view. Steve Hansen knew the England lineout calls and had done since their tour to New Zealand back in the summer of 2003. During our 2005 Six Nations game, I'd verified that nothing had changed, and Andy then implemented those same England calls with the 2005 Lions. He stubbornly refused to change them until the eleventh hour before the first Test, and by then it was too late. The Lions lineout was a mess, and it gave the All Blacks a huge head start in the series. Admittedly, one they probably didn't need.

Ironically, Graham Henry had lost a crucial Test match with the Lions in Australia in 2001 because of Andy's refusal to change lineout calls. In 2005, he was the beneficiary of the same obstinacy. Of course, in 2005 Andy was working underneath Clive Woodward, whose presence on the 2001 tour had been such a big, if invisible, factor. I felt that there was a nice symmetry to the situation and that justice had been done after the insurmountable difficulties faced by the touring party in 2001. When Graham Henry and his wife Raewyn sat down to dinner at the same table as Clive Woodward at a post-match reception in New Zealand with the series win already wrapped up with a crushing 3–0 score, I felt the wheel had indeed come full circle and brought in the appropriate revenges for Woodward's lack of support for Graham on that tour.

The momentum created by the Grand Slam continued over the summer tour to the USA and Canada. The squad was a nice mix of established Test starters and back-ups and youngsters with potential, as most of the top players were out in New Zealand with Clive Woodward's Lions. I asked Rhodri to go on the tour as the analyst to extend the experience he'd had with the squad in Murrayfield and Rome during the Six Nations. We put 60 points on both of our opponents, and Mike turned his attention to his unsatisfactory contractual situation with the WRU. In particular, Mike wanted to resolve the line-manager issue. In the new contract proposal, all assistant coaches were supposed to report to the head coach. However, Mike didn't feel he could sign the document until Scott Johnson had signed his own contract with the union. Mike was hoping that with a successful 2005 behind them the atmosphere within the coaching team would change for the better, and he'd even put up the new structure he envisaged on the whiteboard in his office. He wanted everyone in the same boat, but the problems showed no sign of going away: 'There were three main problems with my new contract. One of the most controversial points was a clause stating that the WRU chief executive, not the head coach, had the final say in selection of the team. In fairness to Steve Lewis, he agreed to get that clause removed.

'The second major issue was the grievance procedure. Any grievances I might have would end up on the table of Steve Lewis. There was no recourse to an independent arbitrator.

'The third was that the contract had to state that all other coaches were to report to me. This was a major problem, as Clive Griffiths didn't have a contract offer and Scott Johnson wouldn't sign one under any circumstances. I explained that until these issues were resolved, it was impossible for me to sign my own contract. So, heading into a new campaign, we were in the ludicrous position of having not one of the three main coaches being tied contractually to the union.'

The union had taken advantage of Wales's Grand Slam status to squeeze in an extra autumn fixture against the southern-hemisphere giants, so we were to play four instead of the usual three high-octane matches in the space of eighteen days, and we had to view Fiji in the second game as a relative breather. It was a big ask, with so many Wales players coming back injured, exhausted or doubtful from the Lions' disastrous tour of New Zealand in June and July. For the first time, the All Blacks and Wallabies were able to spend two weeks in camp preparing for their European tours, while we in the northern hemisphere were beating hell out of each other in the Heineken Cup in the lead-up to the autumn internationals.

We lost heavily to New Zealand, 41–3, and by five tries to nil, and we were well and truly 'potatoed'. We were missing five 2005 stalwarts who'd been wrecked on the Lions tour – Gavin Henson and Tom Shanklin in midfield, Dwayne Peel at 9, Gethin Jenkins at prop and Ryan Jones in the back row – and another, Martyn Williams, who was released on compassionate leave the week before the game. We didn't absorb those losses well, and for the first time since Mike had taken over, we didn't play intelligently. At the very first lineout, with the two tall timber All Black locks Ali Williams and Chris Jack set up to defend the middle and tail of the lineout, we neglected to call the easy throw to Brent Cockbain at the front, marked only by six-feet-two-inch Rodney So'oialo. Rob Sidoli called the throw to himself and was beaten by Williams, and the rest of the game followed much the same mould.

Mark Taylor had to withdraw from the squad after the first match against New Zealand because of a club-versus-country stand-off with Sale Sharks. Tayls is an interesting example of the different view coaches take of the input they have into players who have reached Test standard. Graham Henry, for example, simply accepted Tayls for what he was: a centre who could get you over the gain line quickly from first phase with his outstanding fend off and shiftiness in traffic. Graham never tried to use Mark as a distributor, because he knew that he couldn't pass off his left hand. Steve Hansen and Scott Johnson, on the other hand, would spend hours trying to improve Mark's passing out to the right, trying to manufacture him into the player they thought he could be. Graham and Mike both knew that there wasn't much an international coach could do to work on a player's skill levels once they had made it into the Test squad. They just cut their cloth according to the material they were given and found a way to win with it. Test preparation is all about organising team units in a limited time frame, within an intense environment. For Hansen or Jonno, it often appeared to be more of a training academy.

Mike called me in for a chat after the All Blacks game. There was a concerned look on his face, and I found myself talking to him for the next two hours. After apologising for drawing me into the circle of his own worries, he detailed the problems with the chain of command. Mike was clearly appealing for support, and it didn't take long for some visible signs of a power split in the management group to become apparent. In the debrief after the New Zealand debacle, the first thing I noticed on entering the room was Scott Johnson sitting in the back row among the players, with his arms folded across his chest, instead of sitting up front with Mike and Clive to lead the debrief as usual.

During the meeting, Mike asked a pertinent question about our restarts. We'd planned to use a 7–1 split of the forwards and play the options to both sides, but Stephen Jones had simply banged every kick-off long. When Mike asked Stephen about it, he became quite defensive and irritable. The tone of his response to Mike was off-key and hinted at a deeper problem.

At one lunch during the last week of the autumn campaign, I was sitting with Mike and Clive, and Mike stopped Scott as he walked past, requesting to meet him in the Trecastle Suite in the hotel. Scott made an excuse and said he was committed to a gym session. Mike replied that he'd wait for Scott in the suite after his workout and that he'd be there all afternoon. I was in the room all afternoon preparing information for the game against Australia. Clive Griffiths and Mike were there, but Scott never turned up. There was clearly a growing tension in the camp that had no easy point of resolution.

Inevitably, people started taking one side or the other. To beat Australia in the final match of that autumn series as we did was a very significant achievement in the circumstances. When Andrew Hore left to go back to New Zealand after the Wallaby match, I gave him a copy of Ellen MacArthur's autobiography, with some scribbled comments by me and Rhodri inside it. He received them graciously, and there was an emotional meeting with the players in which he found it hard to hold back the tears. This was the credible emotion of a man not usually moved so easily. Clive also attempted to give Horey a card and a gift of Penderyn Welsh whisky the next day, which was typical of Griff, because he never held a grudge. But I'm not sure how Andrew received it, because there were plenty of other voices telling him that neither the idea of a gift nor the bottle itself in fact belonged to Clive.

Towards the end of the year, attempts at rapprochement continued fitfully. The three-hour debrief at the end of the autumn campaign, with Steve Lewis present, offered little in the way of support or comfort to Mike. I wrote an email to Mike immediately afterwards, reaffirming my support and recording my observations about a rift in the management group and the need to resolve it. But I felt generally that all attempts to address the areas of tension within the management group, at debriefs or in the reports that usually followed from them, were being ignored or suppressed. When Mike called a meeting in December to reaffirm our core values as a management group, I felt there was a great deal of resistance to his lead. Scott gave the impression that he was present by force and not of his own free will. I confronted Scott about his attitude straight after the meeting. He immediately jumped off the deep end and became very emotional. There was obviously a wound there that was still very raw. Apparently, there had been some kind of misunderstanding between Mike's wife and Scott's girlfriend. He could not detach from the hurt that it had caused and continue to work amicably with Mike. After another ten minutes or so, he ended up by talking tearfully about his son, Jarra, who was planning to return to Australia. The conversation was extremely emotional, to the point that I felt bloody exhausted by it. I liked Scott and felt sympathetic towards him, but nevertheless I could see the whole squad fracturing around the issues between him and Mike.

Scott promised to talk to Mike, and they met up at the Barn the following week. As Mike remembers, 'I eventually managed to catch up with Scott just before Christmas, after numerous failed attempts and postponed meetings. I was aware that there were ongoing issues that needed to be discussed. It was time to talk. We had an honest and open exchange about the reasons why our working relationship was floundering. It was very emotional as we faced up to our own frustrations and voiced our criticisms of one another. At the end, Scott became quite tearful, and I gave him a hug. I was hoping that this clear-the-air meeting would help put the past behind us and enable us to move forward together.'

The first match of the 2006 Six Nations was against England at Twickenham. I tried my best to help sew the ragged seams together in a presentation before the game, showing clips from the film *The March of the Penguins*, in which the penguins form a dense circle with the youngest and most vulnerable members in the centre. They create and maintain their own circle of warmth by shuffling almost imperceptibly in and out of the ring, taking turns in the middle and at the extremities, with bodies locked together to retain heat. I hoped it was an image that would inspire players and management alike to bond in a common show of strength.

But when we arrived in London, I noticed that Mike was on edge throughout our stay at the Richmond Gate Hotel, and there seemed to be a prevalent atmosphere of nerviness and apprehension. Moreover, the game itself did not go well. We were missing 13 first-choice players before the start of the match, but were right in it after 50 minutes, with the score at 18–13 to England. However, Martyn Williams was yellow-carded from a restart, and that blew all our momentum. As at the end of Graham's tenure, we subsided embarrassingly in the final quarter, shipping three more quick-fire tries to lose by 47–13.

On the coach journey back to the hotel from Twickenham, Mike reminded the squad to observe some limits in their behaviour socially later that evening. He wanted them to look after themselves and avoid a Saturday-evening binge, with Scotland only seven days away. Gareth Thomas became quite animated about the issue and the players went out on the town anyway. Alfie's own position was quite ironic, given that he cheerfully confesses in his own autobiography that a huge binge after the second Lions Test in New Zealand in 2005 had robbed him of the chance of any meaningful participation in the build-up to the third and final Test. Apparently, lessons like this, even when understood, are not always fully learned. You can even see the contradiction in the manner of the description of the Twickenham incident in Alfie's own book:

> I went to our team manager Alan Phillips and told him that a posse of our players, me included, were planning on heading into London that night, but that even though I was intending to go I did not think it was a particularly good idea.

If he knew it wasn't a good idea, why as captain didn't he repeat Mike's advice to the players and set an example by not going? If he felt it was OK, then why complain that Mike hadn't been firm enough? You can't have your cake and eat it.

The whole episode was an uncomfortable reminder that the players were increasingly taking matters into their own hands. Probably the first occasion on which player power had raised its head in public had occurred back in the autumn of 2004, after the publication of Gavin Henson's book. The book had been quite scathing about certain individuals in the Welsh set-up and about the WRU in general. At first, Gareth Thomas told me that he wasn't bothered by anything Gavin had written, but he must have later changed his mind, because it was he who organised the meeting at which Gavin was asked to explain and justify what he'd written about the other players.

Before the England game, the issue resurfaced. Graham Thomas, the journalist who had ghostwritten Gavin's book for him, wrote an article in the match programme commending Gav's outspokenness and honesty in the age of the meaningless sound bite. The players were in the changing-rooms about an hour and a half before the England game and several started reading Graham's article. There was a lot of agitation about it, which wasn't helpful to our build-up. On Wednesday of the following week, the players were due to give interviews at Glamorgan Cricket Club at Sophia Gardens after training in the lead-up to the Scotland game. Gareth Thomas entered the press conference with Mike Ruddock, then promptly got up and left upon spotting Graham Thomas among the assembled press corps. Graham Thomas's appearance at the press conference might have looked provocative, but, in fact, Graham knew nothing of the players' decision to give him the cold shoulder, so he couldn't be blamed for turning up at the conference expecting to do his job.

Alfie returned to the other members of the Welsh squad, who were having lunch at the time, and they collectively decided to boycott the conference until Graham disappeared – despite Mike chasing him down and repeating his request for Alfie to attend the press conference alongside him. Mike then asked Michael Owen to come into the conference with him and was refused for a second time. He eventually had to go back into the room and face the music without the support of either of his captains. I didn't think it was the right response on Alfie's part, but it did – along with his *Scrum V* interview with Eddie Butler after Mike resigned – accurately reflect his own view of his role as a kind of shop steward for the players at the time. As he says in his book, 'To me, the principle was no different to that of a picket line – you stand together with your colleagues, and you don't cross it just because the boss asks you to.' It is an interesting perception that Mike (as head coach) was already a boss on the other side of the fence, presumably with a different agenda from the players, rather than simply a working colleague of Alfie's . . .

Mike Wadsworth experienced player power at first hand when he descended on the hotel for lunch after a hard morning's massage and physiotherapy. He still had a tight schedule with more players awaiting his attention, but when Wads went to sit down with a plate of food, he was rudely interrupted by Alan Phillips and the dietitian Dan Kings: 'No, Mike, the players have to dine first – that's the protocol.' Wads promptly put down his plate and left the dining-room. As he got to the door, he thought better of it and turned around with the parting shot, 'I think the players are getting a little too much of what they want lately, don't you?'

Wads remembers the incident quite fondly now: 'It was all a bit ironic, as I was rushing down to take a quick snack before hurrying back to massage injured and tired players. So their protocol was really only hurting their chances of recovering properly from their training exertions.'

We won handily against Scotland, scoring a pushover try in the first ten minutes of the match. The lineout produced the best returns of the season – fifteen from seventeen (88 per cent) – and four steals on opposition ball

– four from twenty (20 per cent) – a reflection of the enduring quality of Mike's coaching and better than anything we managed in the post-Ruddock era until Warren Gatland's arrival. However, as in the New Zealand match, the players had ignored some clear instructions. At the lineout, Scotland took a lot of time to prepare for the throw, and we'd worked out where they tended to throw the ball, so we knew where we could pressure them. The forwards were asked to wave their arms about and press the referee to hurry the throw, but on the day it didn't happen. The clear relationship between planning and putting that planning it into practice on the pitch, which had been such a strong feature of our Grand Slam success, had been twisted and broken beyond repair.

Monday, 13 February 2006 was dedicated to recovery, analysis and the debrief from the Scotland match. The next day, we had two sessions planned in the morning: a weights session in the Barn and a lineout meeting for the forwards. After the lineout drill, Mike called me into his office and asked if I'd heard anything more. I'd found out about a clandestine meeting between a group of senior players and Steve Lewis concerning Mike and his coaching. Mike looked gloomy and made a couple of phone calls, and I thought nothing more of it. Later that afternoon, Rhodri came running up to me breathlessly and said that I needed to go and see Mike immediately. As soon as I entered his office, Mike looked straight at me and said, 'This isn't working. There's obviously a split in the camp. People aren't giving me the support I need, and I'm going to stand down at the end of the season.' After the initial shock, I begged him to reconsider, but he'd obviously made up his mind: 'The final detail in my contract with the WRU had not been resolved and all momentum had stopped. In my opinion, all it really needed was one meaningful meeting with Steve Lewis, the WRU's lawyer, Tim Jones – my lawyer – and me to tie up the contractual detail. The substantive terms had been agreed, with the written offer extended and accepted. At this point, the WRU, through Steve Lewis, had even written to my building society to confirm the offer of a new contract for mortgage purposes.

'The backdrop to the start of the 2006 Six Nations had been one of rumblings about player discontent. In my opinion, that must have influenced what happened next. On the Tuesday after the England game in February 2006, I received a letter – via my lawyer – stating that the WRU was withdrawing from our contract negotiation until after the Six Nations. My feeling was that despite the offer of the contract extension, my time in the role would be limited, as I had now become aware that I lacked support on a number of fronts.

'It was against this backdrop that I reluctantly made the decision to resign at the end of the season. I instructed Tim Jones to send a reply to the WRU stating that I would consider stepping down as national coach at the end of the season. I also reserved the right to make comments in the press regarding my future and indicated that I had every intention of fulfilling my responsibilities as head coach until the end of the current Six Nations tournament. This all occurred in the eight days between the England and Scotland games [4–12 February].

'Andy Howell, the *Western Mail* rugby reporter, rang me on the morning of 14 February and asked what the hell was going on, as they'd received an anonymous letter purporting to be from within the playing squad, saying that the players wanted me to go. It was just one hatchet blow after the other. I told Andy that I was planning to step down at the end of the season.

'I rang and then met with Steve Lewis on 14 February and told him I wanted to finish at the end of the season. Steve accepted my decision, and we shook hands. Later that afternoon, I issued a press statement to that effect through Andy Howell and copied it to Steve Lewis. Then, in the evening, I heard that the WRU were calling a press conference. I rang Steve Lewis to ask about the nature of the press conference. Steve said that they – whoever they might be – had discussed the situation and wanted me to step down immediately. I replied, "I expect to come into work tomorrow as normal." Steve Lewis was adamant. He told me not to come in the next day and to stand down immediately. I was totally devastated that it had to end in this manner.'

The very next morning, Steve Lewis called a squad meeting and announced that Scott Johnson would be taking over in a caretaker role from Mike until the end of the season. Amongst the smaller management conclave later that afternoon, Scott asked everyone to pledge their total commitment and support to the cause.

I felt very bitter when Mike left, a bitterness that quite overshadowed the milder forms of grief I'd experienced after Kevin Bowring's departure in 1998 and Gareth Jenkins's gazumping in 2004. I recall going past the physiotherapy room the very next day, only to hear the laughter of the players spilling out nervously into the corridor. I felt sick to the bottom of my stomach. Half an hour of joke-telling and banter before Steve Lewis arrived to tell them they had the morning off while reorganisation was taking place in the wake of Mike's sudden departure. The presentation to the players for the Ireland game was a particularly arduous job for me. Somehow I managed a funny story, telling them that Catherine had left me at the weekend and gone to Bath on a shopping spree instead. There was a sharp intake of breath, and then they fell about laughing, probably more out of nervousness than anything else.

There was certainly a cohesive policy by the media department of the WRU to create their own version of Mike Ruddock's exit and sell it to the media. A WRU memo from Rob Cole to Liz Jones accidentally discovered by the Welsh media at a press conference as the 'Ruddockgate' affair reached its climax showed their determination to in their words 'control the story': 'Perception is everything in this story, and Steve Lewis must be seen to be announcing the news either on his own or in conjunction with Mike Ruddock, rather than reacting to it.' They were clearly aware of the likely reaction to the news of Mike's sudden departure: 'But we are in a situation where Mike is set to go, Scott Johnson is thought to be on the verge of returning to Australia and Clive Griffiths does not have a contract. There is only one interpretation of those facts – chaos and poor management!' The media section of the union clearly understood the key issues and questions the man in the street was going to want answered:

1. How has it come to this after more than six months of negotiating?

2. Why have Steve Lewis, David Pickering and Mike Ruddock consistently said it was only a question of dotting i's and crossing t's?

3. How can you let go a coach that has just delivered a Grand Slam?

4. What are the players going to think about the administration?

The media section came up with the idea of a 'Red Zone' tour of south Wales after the Six Nations, a roadshow in which members of the public could come along and question high-ranking WRU officials about issues of pith and moment. Of course, everyone wanted to ask about Mike and the circumstances surrounding his departure.

Curiously, there was also a positive view of Alfie's notorious *Scrum V* interview with Eddie Butler within the media department. Alfie had clearly lost his temper and his self-control for large swathes of that interview, probably goaded by Butler's evident clarity and refusal to be intimidated while he pursued his line of questioning, but nonetheless his appearance on *Scrum V* was still seen as a significant turning point in public perception.

When this assertion was repeated during the debrief, I burst out laughing. After all, Alfie had just experienced a serious physical breakdown that must have had something to do with his wildness and volatility during that interview. It certainly couldn't have helped restore his equilibrium. Personally, I felt that the media people in the union might have had a pretty good idea of what would happen, but Alfie probably reckoned he owed it to Steve Lewis for agreeing to meet him away from the Barn – up the road at the Castell Mynach Inn – to voice the senior players' concerns about Mike Ruddock. But all the people I've spoken to, Welsh and English, both then and since, were horrified at the way Gareth presented himself in the interview. Whatever righteous content there might have been was simply drowned out by the way in which he delivered the message.

When Scott took charge of the preparations for the third game of the Six Nations, against Ireland, he made a point of keeping both Clive Griffiths and me sweet to begin with. He immediately enlarged Clive's role to include some of the attack coaching, and I was invited to attend all coaches' meetings. Clive made the effort but ultimately found out that nothing had changed: 'I responded to the call when

Scott asked for a renewed commitment, even though I was still hurt and rankling about the manner of Mike's departure. I thought, "Right, I'll give it a go and see what happens." Alan Phillips told Scott, "I think we have underestimated Clive." This comment came after the Italy game in which some of my attacking ideas had been used effectively.

'But although Scott would readily recognise my contribution in private, when he got up in front of the players, he thanked Rob McBryde for his support and didn't mention my name or my contribution. He tried to blag it off, but it was another case of Jonno telling the players what they wanted to hear. He told me afterwards that he was waiting for the right moment to say it in public.'

Smaller changes followed hard on the heels of the larger ones: coaches wore mics at training, and all the sessions were now coded. We were all encouraged to feed back to Scott during and after training, and he introduced evening meetings for the players up at the Barn when they preferred to stay down at the hotel. Rhodri and I were both asked to attend reviews of the day's training over a beer in the evening. The Friday before games was now devoted to a preview of the game plan. There would be films of the moves and ploys to be used in every department of the game – attack, defence, the forwards, the opposition – with cues, moves and visuals from training. All these were positive additions from Scott Johnson and in the spirit of a new adventure with a new coach.

Meanwhile, something curious seemed to have happened to the recent past. Mike Ruddock suddenly seemed to have become the 'great unmentionable'. It is strange how quickly a good man can become a ghost. The new forwards' coach, Rob McBryde, used the same exercises as Mike – in particular, live scrummaging drills and an exercise in which the lifters had to keep the jumper airborne for a solid three seconds – but now the drills were apparently being favourably received by the players whereas they'd been reviled under Mike.

We managed a meagre return of one draw out of our last three games under Jonno, losing heavily to Ireland and unluckily to France, and splitting the points with Italy. We'd all put huge effort into the preparation for all of those games with little to show for it in terms of results. At the end of the tournament, there was the by now customary emotional see-saw from Scott: 'Shall I go or shall I stay?' Even on the Sunday after the France game, Scott was still up in the air and trying to pressure Steve Lewis into offering him the post I believe he wanted – as director of rugby in Wales. All was eventually decided by the departure of Scott's son Jarra from the UK back to Australia. There was still the opportunity for one last emotional farewell to the players in the lounge, with Scott holding back the sobs and promising 'I'll be back'.

So, Scott Johnson returned to Australia. With both Scott and Steve Hansen back in their native lands, I began to consider the impact of the recent line of Antipodean coaches on both Welsh rugby and the Test rugby scene as a whole. Both Steve Hansen and Scott Johnson were products of Super 12 rugby in the southern hemisphere and both believed that they could create a Test team on the Super-rugby model. This was an attractive style of play based on fitness, forward mobility and ball-handling, and with a clear offensive bias. On the positive side of the ledger, it is the style which has proved strong enough to enable New Zealand to become the dominant force in Test rugby over the past three years. On the other hand, it is not a style that has won any of the last five World Cups. All of those competitions have been won by the team with the soundest fundamentals, especially at the set-piece and in defence. Some of those sides, such as Australia in 1991, England in 2003 and South Africa in 2007, have been capable of adding a more expansive element to their game when needed, but in the crucial games all relied on a basic no frills, blue-collar approach. As they say in the world of darts, 'One-eighties for show. Doubles for dough.' Ultimately, defence wins championships, and it wasn't until Mike Ruddock and Clive Griffiths were reunited in 2005 that Wales's fundamentals were sound enough to make the most of our undoubted ball-playing capacity and win some silverware. The same was to apply in the 2008 Six Nations.

Australia and New Zealand do not have the financial resources of their northern-hemisphere counterparts, so they are continually under pressure to produce a spectacle that is more attractive to their paying public than, say, Aussie Rules or rugby league. That is why they are always at the forefront of law changes, trying to drive through amendments that will make rugby union a carnival of fluid movement and ball-handling. Hence the experimental law variations (ELVs). The northern-hemisphere unions and clubs are rich enough to be able to afford to keep the game in touch with its roots. They know that 80,000 plus will turn up to watch Wasps and Leicester smash the hell out of each other in a cup final at Twickenham.

The two Antipodean coaches of Wales who have been most successful over the past ten years – Graham Henry and Warren Gatland – have always had the ability to teach these sound fundamentals. Graham has always coached teams with outstanding scrummages, from Auckland to Wales to the current All Blacks, and he's always favoured a solid citizen and kicker at 10 over more flamboyant rivals – a Grant Fox or a Neil Jenkins or a Stephen Jones. Warren Gatland, meanwhile, has forged a very fruitful working partnership with ex-leaguer Shaun Edwards, who is probably one of the top two defence coaches in the world today. Gatland has spent the better part of his coaching life in the northern hemisphere, and both he and Graham Henry have shown the ability to outgrow their Super-rugby backgrounds as Test coaches. To date, I don't think the same can be said of Steve Hansen and Scott Johnson.

I feel Graham is in an interesting position and in a sense at a coaching crossroads even at this relatively late stage of his career. He too has always had an element of Super-rugby extremism in his make-up. Nick Bishop remembers the first time he was introduced to the extended 'pod' system of attack Graham had devised for the 2001 Lions tour to Australia: 'Graham and I went for lunch in Brisbane a couple of days before the match against the Queensland Reds. I'd done a lot of work on the Australians in the lead-up to the tour, and I was interested to see what plan of attack Graham had come up with. We weren't even into the main course when he started drawing diagram after diagram on the napkins by the side of the table. One by one, the napkins disappeared. My eyes almost popped out of my head and my brain was reeling as he mapped out attacking plans seven, eight phases after the set-piece. Could this really work? Would those opportunities really be there? It was hard to believe that circumstances could be controlled as fully as Graham evidently hoped. I understood that Graham needed a radical method of knitting together the disparate elements of the Lions squad into a single unit in such a short time frame, but I felt it was a product of Super 12 thinking, where the refs automatically "gave" the rucks to the attacking side. That didn't happen at Test level.'

Graham has always been at his best as a coach when he keeps things simple and balanced and pragmatic. As recently as the All Blacks' two back-to-back matches against Australia in the Tri Nations in 2008, there was a see-saw between two different categories of thinking. The All Blacks' decisive 39–10 defeat of the Australians at Eden Park on 2 August 2008 was based on core values, the values which the New Zealand paying public in all probability really want to see from their Test representatives, but it came one week after a heavy defeat in which they looked for all the world like a product of the Super-rugby marketing machine, running the ball from all corners of the park. As one of Graham Henry's old charges, John Drake, put it, 'This victory was built on the basic rugby this country has produced for more than a century. It was won up front by dominant tight forwards. I certainly hope these tactics will become the norm for this All Blacks side. Sure, it's nice to attempt the perfect game of total rugby, but many Kiwis will argue that simple and direct rugby based on forward dominance and territory control beats flashy 80-metre tries. The All Blacks have set a standard which could take them to consistent greatness. Those Aussies will never forget this match, and the home side's performance has gone some way to restoring the Black aura of times past.'

Don't get me wrong, I do feel that Steve Hansen and Scott Johnson really invigorated the national squad in Wales and brought some special qualities with them from the southern hemisphere, but nonetheless we paid a heavy price for their contribution in February 2006. The inability of Steve Hansen to fully let go of the Wales team after he left for New Zealand, the appointment of a Welsh coach in 2004 with powerful elements of the management group outside his control, the emotional 'stormy weather' that Scott Johnson always seemed to attract, and the split between Mike Ruddock and a group of senior players who had established loyalties – none of these made for stability or allowed us to build on the success of the 2005 Grand Slam. To adapt Scott's own story about the Bell Rock, the waves just kept on dashing ships on the hidden reefs of Welsh rugby, lighthouse or no lighthouse.

Mike Ruddock was and is a very good man and an excellent rugby coach. He brings the values of a true man of Gwent to the table, and what I see in Mike is the same set of values I learned to respect and ultimately to love at Pontypool during my own rugby upbringing. But he was also willing to incorporate the more expansive West Walian element in his rugby philosophy because of his time at Swansea, his connection with Clive Griffiths and his experience outside the Welsh goldfish bowl in Leinster with an outstanding generation of young backs. Even with a blue-collar background that put a premium on hard work, effort and humility, Mike never got stuck in the be-all and end-all of forward play. He was absolutely ideal for the time of his appointment and could, I believe, have taken us forward quickly as a rugby nation had he been given the chance over a prolonged period of time with the full support of a united management group. Sadly, that time was brutally cut short, and there would have to be another two-year hiatus and further rugby humiliations before we rediscovered that same diamond-hard ethos and the same balance of virtues thanks to a New Zealander and a northerner: Warren Gatland and Shaun Edwards.

8

THE ART AND SCIENCE OF ANALYSIS

'Chance favours the prepared mind.'

Louis Pasteur

'Everyone wants to win, but not everyone is
willing to prepare to win.'

Bobby Knight, ex–basketball coach

Analysis is becoming an ever more academic process at colleges nowadays, highly refined and ever more distanced from the man in the street. At the same time, it is becoming increasingly influential in the outcomes of professional sporting contests of any kind and has more media exposure than ever before. You only have to look at the amount of detail contained in highly successful sports video games to know how responsive the public are becoming to the analytical side of sport. On TV, I think Channel Four was the first to employ a resident analyst, Simon Hughes, in their ground-breaking cricket presentations, using computer aids such as Hawk-Eye to assist a detailed breakdown of the technical aspects of the game. It's been very stimulating, and the viewing public has been very responsive to the glut of information available. There seems to be a 'thirst to know' in the age of media that can't be quenched easily.

I guess you could call analysis the art of systematic observation expressed in quantitative terms. And by systematic, I mean systematic. As I found out from Steve Hansen after the Wales–All Blacks game in 2004, New Zealand are already at the stage whereby they have at least eight people examining film of their games frame by frame. Each has 'only' a ten-minute segment of the action to investigate, but it still takes eight hours to get through. Such a high-sounding description is a little scary and makes analysis sound like a science, but in reality there are many subjective factors involved. You have to know, for example, what the coaches are trying to achieve, and you have to know the athletes you are dealing with. In other words, you have to know the game you're analysing and have some sense of the relevance of the huge number of different categories in which it's possible to collect data. Data is not an end in itself, and should never become one.

The Americans are ahead of the game in terms of analysis. Games such as basketball and American football have had advanced professional structures in place for much longer than rugby or cricket, for example, so they tend to be world leaders in the field. If you read Vince Lombardi's book *Run to Daylight*, written in 1960, you'll find a level of detailed preparation comparable to most first-class rugby teams of the present day. Each team in the NFL will use a pool of analysts to sieve information, and the coaches all have the tools and the ability to edit game film themselves.

Every nation tends to have its own outlook on analysis. In France, comprehensive analysis is virtually unknown below national squad level, as the French prefer 'conditioned games' for their players to practise decision-making under pressure and then translate that improvisation out on the pitch. Bernard Laporte, with his more methodical and distinctly un-Gallic approach, has been very much the exception to the rule over the past few years. South Africa and to a lesser extent Australia tend to use coaches or ex-players to analyse games, and there's generally a much closer tie between coaching and analysing the game. Jake White had extensive experience as a video analyst before he was offered key coaching roles in the Springbok hierarchy. He worked with Nick Mallett as an analyst before becoming top man in his own right, and Rudy Joubert became Cardiff Blues head coach after filling the analytical role for Kitch Christie at the 1995 World Cup.

Graham Henry says that the new All Black analyst, Alistair Rogers, is actually a Welshman from Gwent: 'He played semi-pro with Ebbw Vale and was a director of rugby at Ballina in Ireland before coming over to New Zealand a few years ago. Then he worked for the Wellington Union and as an analyst for the Hurricanes. I guess you can come from either a rugby background or a background in computing and move into rugby, but having a feel for the game built-in has to give you an advantage.'

In the UK, analysis is more often viewed as a specialised function, and there's less demand for coaching or even any rugby experience whatsoever. There's a preference for people with university experience who know computer systems inside out and can generate a lot of information without having the same cultural background or career aims. In other words, they don't necessarily have rugby blood flowing in their veins, and that can limit their interactions with the players and coaches. Then again, some coaches prefer it this way: they like to keep their distance from the analyst and can find too much rugby knowledge built into that role threatening.

What interests me most is the way in which analysis is redefined by people who do it especially well. They have their own unique approach, which pushes the frontiers and enables the science of analysis as a whole to take a leap forward. First, a little history. One of the first to introduce a system of notational analysis was Wing Commander Charles Reep, a Cornishman born at the turn of the century. Reep was probably the first to look at a football match statistically and analyse elements such as the number of passes that led to a goal and the field positions from which those passes came. Reep reputedly first took a notebook out of his pocket at a game between Swindon Town and Bristol Rovers on 18 March 1950. He used one sheet of foolscap-size paper, divided it into four quarters and used a kind of shorthand notation to track all aspects of the game. Gareth Potter, who received much of Reep's old material six years before he died in 2002, told me that he used to store all his papers in the garden shed.

Reep went on to become the first recognisable performance analyst in football in the second half of his life, and he was well into his late 80s when Egil Olsen, the manager of the Norwegian national football team, began to use him before the 1991 European Championships. He was much revered and treated like royalty in Norway and helped promote Olsen's belief in the long-ball game. Reep believed that three passes – long ball, knockdown and strike – were the path to success, and it was difficult to argue with Olsen's success across the next decade with Norway, however unattractive the football.

Tom Reilly was one of the trendsetters in the 1970s with his pioneering studies on the work rate of professional footballers at Liverpool John Moores University. Ian Franks at the University of British Columbia in Vancouver has also produced a succession of papers on subjects ranging from winning penalty shoot-outs in soccer to 'training coaches to observe and remember' from the early 1980s onwards. One of his protégés, Ian More, went on to work for Clive Woodward's Olympic set-up.

The Welsh structure has been very healthy, with a strong base at UWIC (previously the Cardiff College of Further Education) at Cyncoed. Peter Treadwell, the Mr Fixit of UWIC course structures, brought a couple of ex-Cardiff College students together, Keith Lyons and Gareth Potter, and together they really drove forward analysis in Wales from 1991 to 1998. An ex-UWIC student, Gareth had established his own business by 1989 and was recruited to provide key performance indicators by Brian Thomas at Neath. Keith Lyons attended Borough Road PE college and was by his own admission an abstemious, vegetarian pacifist who would let his own tyres down in order to avoid trouble. He had coached a high-profile university rugby team at Exeter, but his special interest was also analysis, and he had an inner drive that helped make him one of my most stimulating teachers at the college. When Mike Hughes, a student of Tom Reilly's from Liverpool John Moores, joined the group in 1993, he brought with him a programme for analysing football matches, and it was made available to students as a resource within the university. The jigsaw was complete. Analysis started at UWIC in a broom cupboard at the back of the library, so these were modest beginnings, but nonetheless the Centre for Notational Analysis was born.

I joined the department – by then renamed the Centre for Performance Analysis – in 1994, the year before the Rugby World Cup in South Africa. Gareth and I supported Keith Lyons, who was the department director, and we received additional input from Andrew Lewis, who'd been a winger for Treorchy and Newport and could write software. A maverick spirit in ex-referee Corris Thomas also joined the fast-growing department soon afterwards, doubling as an accountant by day and with a special interest in law-making and refereeing performance. I was in touch with Chris Thau at the time, who used to write and edit regularly for *Rugby World* magazine, and he said that he was interested in an objective, statistically based review of the 1995 World Cup. The end product was a magazine called *Kick-off*, and Donal Lenihan told me in 2001 that people globally had sat up and taken notice at both the contents and style of presentation. It had created quite a stir and sparked investment within many unions in the area of analysis.

It was definitely a sign of the times. The department expanded very quickly, attracting contracts with England hockey and badminton and finally with the Wales national soccer team. The soccer contract only really took off when Bobby Gould took over as manager, and we unearthed a chubby Mancunian research student called John Stanhope to work with the players. John was a Manchester City fan who did an excellent impersonation of the 'eternal student' – the guy who seemed to be always doing a masters degree on something or other and stayed on in the student bar on Saturday night until closing time, living off a diet of peanuts and bags of crisps and bottles of Coke. John, or more accurately John's rather lugubrious, laid-back personality, came to the rescue with the soccer contract; within weeks of Mike Hughes reluctantly pushing him forward for the role, he had the likes of Vinnie Jones eating out of his hand. The players loved him. There'd be jaunty late-night calls from Vinnie and other stars in the team: 'C'mon, John, have you got that tape for me yet, you old fuck?'

When the Wales contract ended, John was engaged by the South African football team in 1998 and went to the African Nations Cup held in Burkina Faso, complete with his lilywhite skin and Jack Black figure. At one stage, he was left with his bags out in the middle of nowhere, but that didn't stop him from attending the 1998 World Cup as the South African analyst. The experience with John opened my eyes to the fact that the personality of the analyst had to fit the team. He had to understand the game he was analysing and be able to communicate effectively with the players. He had to be on the right wavelength, and he had to be approachable. One size would definitely not fit all.

Others who passed through the centre all found a specific niche at a high level: Steve Evans with the British Yachting Association, and Stafford Murray, who worked for the England cricket team, is now director of analysis at the English Institute of Sport. People who came to the centre as callow 16-year-old trainees on a work-experience fortnight, such as Naomi Jones and Rhodri Manning, eventually found jobs with the regions when they were created in 2003. Keith Lyons, who started the ball rolling in the first place, is now the director of performance analysis at the Australian Institute of Sport. There are many others, and during the mid-'90s, the Centre for Performance Analysis produced a stream of talent filtering across the whole spectrum of British sport and beyond, in a thriving new world of analysis.

The chief analyst has to have a close relationship with the coach. Sometimes he has to be able to read his intentions without being told directly. That's why you often find that the coach–analyst connection goes back a long way. Mervyn Murphy has been with Eddie O'Sullivan since their days at Connacht together, so there is an unquestionable bond of trust between the two. Clive Woodward first spotted his chief analyst Tony Biscombe filming a player during training at Sunbury while he was a development officer for the RFU back in 1997. He would get the player to perform certain actions, then film those actions and work through the footage with him afterwards. Clive walked over to him, and Tony explained what he was doing. 'Would you like to come and do that for the England squad?' was the response.

That's how Tony Biscombe started, coming more from a coaching background than an IT one. But Woodward obviously saw someone he could trust to decode his needs and intentions, and that was the decisive factor. Their professional link lasted for almost ten years. Coaches with whom I've shared the same kind of professional trust, such as Kevin Bowring, Mike Ruddock and Graham Henry, have gone on to become close personal friends. Nick Bishop could assess the train of Graham's thinking without being told. It's almost symbiotic.

Another example of an analyst fitting and needing to fit the dimensions of his role exactly would be Corris Thomas with the IRB. In 1996, Keith Lyons asked Corris to set up the IRB game analysis project, analysing tournaments worldwide and drawing conclusions about trends in the modern game. The project needed the help of a sturdy researcher, and Corris found his man in West Walian Jason Williams. I think Jason rang Keith Lyons every day for about three months until he was offered the job. Now Corris assists Rhys Jones, who continued his good work when the IRB moved to Dublin, as a consultant. They produce reports on all the major tournaments in world rugby that are well used by the media, lawmakers and laymen alike, and I believe it's principally the work that Corris started that has given the IRB real credibility in their lawmaking exercises, by persuading people that they are aware of the latest trends in professional rugby almost as soon as they occur. Corris Thomas's work has given the IRB a real cutting edge.

To give one example, some of the new laws among the ELVs currently being trialled in the southern hemisphere are very much in line with Corris's distinction between 'material' and 'non-material' transgressions at the breakdown. As an ex-referee, Corris is well aware that every single tackle and post-tackle situation gives the referee an opportunity to penalise either side. The referee needs a guideline or a structure in order to keep play moving, and Corris's philosophy that you should only penalise 'material' offences – flagrant offences that actually affect the outcome of the play directly – fits the bill. It's a little like the soccer ruling that men in an offside position are deemed irrelevant if they're not interfering in the play. Hence, in the ELVs, all transgressions except for offside and deliberate or repeated infringements have now been downgraded to free-kicks rather than full penalties. It simplifies and enhances the ref's control of the game by reintroducing a sense of perspective into the interpretation of the laws, and thus helps build the spectacle for the spectators.

Curiously, Corris Thomas was also involved, this time as a referee, in an early documented instance of analysis having a measurable impact on the outcome of a game of rugby. Tom Kiernan was the coach of Munster when they played the All Blacks at Thomond Park in 1978. Some of the players had never watched a video before when Kiernan took them to a warehouse and had them view footage of their daunting opponents. The effects were extraordinary. The outside-half, Tony Ward, found he had to walk out of the room. Perhaps he thought that the film of the All Blacks' early tour victory over Cardiff might undermine his confidence. Maybe he preferred to simply react to what he saw in front of him on the day, a classic player's response to watching film.

But there was one of Munster's unsung heroes, a small, skinny wing-cum-centre called Seamus Dennison, who saw the value in what Kiernan was doing. He noticed that the All Blacks were scoring tries by bringing one of their wingers, Stu Wilson, into the line between their centres to break Cardiff's man-for-man defence. Dennison decided then and there: 'Stu Wilson's my man. When he appears in the line, I've got to take him.' Footage was shown, Dennison made a decision at the meeting, then fifteen minutes into the match New Zealand had a chance to work the move, and Dennison hit Stu Wilson just as he'd planned. 'I got the ball, and then I got the spot-tackle with it,' Wilson remembers. 'The hole closed on me, and this little fella just blew me back. He just propelled into my ribcage. It was a great tackle.'

Corris couldn't help becoming analyst even as he was trying to referee the game:

> 'It was the most incredible tackle I saw in 17 years as a referee. Stu Wilson came through at a hundred miles an hour on a switch-ball, and it was literally as though he had run into a brick wall and slid down it. He collapsed in a heap. He didn't go backwards, he just crumpled. I looked around and every Munster player had grown 12 inches. You could sense it, you really could. I'm not being romantically reflective. It was a hard-nosed observation I made at the time.'

(From Alan English's excellent book on the match, Stand Up and Fight.*)*

This is perfect continuity for a professional analyst: visual evidence, then player decision and, finally, translation out on the field.

Nobody should be in any doubt how greatly inside information is prized within the community of modern professional rugby. As the Gordon Gekko character said in the film *Wall Street*, 'If you're not inside, you're outside . . . The most valuable commodity I know of is information. I don't throw darts at a board. I bet on sure things. Read Sun Tzu, *The Art of War*. Every battle's won before it's fought.'

As mentioned previously, on both of the last two British and Irish Lions tours of the southern hemisphere, in 2001 and 2005, the home team has made a big effort to decode the Lions' lineout calls. In both instances, their research paid dividends and might even have had a decisive bearing on the outcome of the two series. It is worth exploring this effort in greater detail.

In Australia in 2001, the Wallaby management group employed Scott Johnson – who was unknown to the Lions management at the time – as a water carrier. Beginning with the first tour match in Western Australia, he built up an encyclopaedia of Lions lineout calls over the course of the tour. Scott was there opposite every lineout making notes. When Clive Woodward flew into Coffs Harbour, the Wallabies' main training base, it was not Lions coaches or even his own English players who formed the reception committee. Scott Johnson and Ewen MacKenzie picked him up and went on to acquire more information about the Lions' planning on the ride from the airport to a local hotel. By the time of the third and decisive Test, the Wallabies knew the Lions' lineout code well enough to steal a vital throw on their own goal-line from which the Lions would probably have scored to take the series. They stole seven other throws in the course of the match. Even if the Lions changed or adapted their calls, Scott had worked out that they were using Phil Vickery as a lifter about 80 per cent of the time.

The situation in New Zealand in 2005 was even more extreme. Steve Hansen had picked up a summary of the England lineout calls that had been left behind on a bus, probably during England's tour of the Antipodes in the summer of 2004 – or so the story went. However he'd come by the code, he then transmitted it via Alan Phillips in time for Wales's first match of the 2005 Six Nations versus England. When we looked at the summary and compared it with our own observations of England's autumn matches – their lineout calls were audible over the ref-mic – we found that the summary was definitely for real, so we fed it into the preparation for the game.

Now fast-forward to the preparation for the Lions tour down at the Vale of Glamorgan in May 2005. Michael Owen comes into the office in a state of high excitement: 'You remember those lineout calls you gave us before the England game, Carts? We've just been practising them with the Lions.' Alarm bells immediately started ringing, because I knew that Steve Hansen already knew the code.

So the Lions left for New Zealand with the England lineout calls in place, and it was clear from the games early in the tour that the Kiwi sides knew exactly where the Lions were going to throw the ball. It also took the Lions management far too long to twig that New Zealand knew their codes, and eventually the forwards coach Andy Robinson changed the entire calling system only a few days before the first Test in Christchurch. They swapped over to the Irish system, with the Ireland thrower (Shane Byrne) and the Ireland lineout captain (Paul O'Connell) both in the team for the match. As Steve Hansen proved, ironically enough, during his time with Wales, changing the entire system so close to the game can have only one result – disaster.

The English prop Graham Rowntree pointed out after the game had been lost 21–3, 'We thought the All Blacks had cracked our lineout code, so we changed a few things. In hindsight, that was suicide.' Lifters missed their assignments and jumpers didn't get off the ground, most notably when Ali Williams plucked the ball out of the air at a lineout deep inside the Lions 22 and rambled all the way to the line for the game's opening try. In the driving wind and rain in Christchurch that day, lineout control was going to be everything, and the Lions didn't have any. Arguably, that failure cost them the match, and maybe even the series. The battle really was won and lost before it was ever fought.

As an ex-policeman, Steve Hansen clearly had a taste for undercover detective work, but he would sometimes fail to strike the right balance between digging for inside information and presenting it clearly to players with ample time for digestion, and therefore constructive use;

for example, when he tried to tap into the live radio feeds of the French and Italian coaches who visited the Millennium Stadium during the 2002 Six Nations. We could hear what they were saying clearly enough, but as it was in a foreign language and we didn't have a translator to hand, it was worse than a distraction. Unearthing secrets is one thing, but ensuring that they are translatable is quite another. You have to be careful that the new information doesn't upset your own systems or the players within it. In particular, the information needs to be absorbed well before the game, not at the last minute.

The day before the match against New Zealand in autumn 2003 was too close to allow the players to absorb the changes to our lineout defence that Steve had instigated on the back of Gareth Potter's filming of an All Blacks training session at Sophia Gardens. It created more confusion than it resolved. You might be able to coordinate a new backline move in that kind of time frame, but the modern lineout is the single most complex area of the game, with a huge number of variables. You can't get a group of up to seven players, change their formations and get them lifting and jumping and shuffling up and down the line accurately so close to the game. The most successful lineout in Test rugby is South Africa's, and it has been 'grown' over a number of years with the same components – Smit throwing to Matfield and Botha and Juan Smith – to the point where understanding between the players is intuitive and unit play self-driving.

There are roughly two schools of thought in regard to how information should be presented to the playing group. Coaches such as Graham Henry and Mike Ruddock like to involve the players in strategy sessions for different areas – attack, defence, kicking, lineout, scrum, etc. – so that there is plenty of feedback in these areas. But the key, as Graham points out, is that 'the coach must always do the work himself. He must take responsibility and know his research inside out. You want the players involved but not over-involved, so there is a balance to be kept. You can take a lot out of key individuals doing their own research and maybe even making a presentation on a topic, but ultimately it's the coach's responsibility.'

During Gareth Jenkins's tenure, we probably drifted a little too far into player dependency in terms of both analysis and leadership within the squad, partly because the coaches weren't always totally in control of their own research.

On the Lions tour of Australia in 2001, the English coaches such as Phil Larder came from a different angle. Their attitude was very much that 'we tell 'em what to do', and after an initial effort, Graham abandoned the idea of the feedback meetings. The English mentality probably responds better to a more rigid sense of structure, and they certainly looked lost without it in the initial stages of the 2007 World Cup. As Mike Catt put it, 'I found it baffling we did not seem to have any analysis on our opening Group A opponents, the United States, nor have a game plan of what to do against them.'

Whatever the manner of dispatch, Graham Henry was certainly the best coach I worked under with regard to getting information translated onto the pitch by the players. Graham had the knack of presenting all the research very simply, in easily digestible bites, and that was why we managed to score so many tries from practised first-phase moves during his long run of successful games. He was never satisfied until all the details of a move were right: the positioning before the move and the angles of running after it. You could never quit on a low note or a slipshod mistake.

Under Graham, we worked out that you have – if all goes to plan – about 28 bits of primary possession during a game. You kick away approximately one-third of that, which means that you might have an average of twelve lineouts and eight scrums from which to launch attacking moves. Opportunities are limited, and you need to pick out tactics that stand the clearest chance of working successfully. You try to bet on the sure thing.

One of the peak games in terms of analysis being translated into action on the pitch would have to be the first half of the 2005 game against Scotland. It was as good an example as you are likely to find of blackboard plans being brought to life effortlessly by the players out on the field. One try in particular sticks in my mind: the fourth of that record-breaking first half, scored by Kevin Morgan. As we'd noticed from Nick's report, Scotland tended to use their blindside wing to defend the outside-half channel from lineouts, and we felt we could target Sean Lamont when he appeared in this position. Lamont is a powerful man, but he used to relish planting for the hit so much that he'd forget to wrap with his arms and finish the play off, which would open the space up on either side of him.

At that time, we would run a move called a 'slice', with the centres crossing over as the ball was passed by the halfback. Gavin Henson would drift outside and Tom Shanklin would cut back in on a sharp angle, and we'd have our full-back Kevin Morgan run a tight line of support up through the middle. In the 27th minute, exactly the right situation occurred at a right-sided lineout just outside the Scotland 22. Sure enough, Lamont was standing at fly-half, and the backs called the move. Shanks and Gav did their slice, and Shanks careered on towards Lamont. As Lamont leaned in to punish Tom, I gripped myself and thought, 'Just survive the hit.' Bang! Shanks spun out of the collision like a top, and Kevin – who is a great support runner – picked him up on the outside almost immediately, and we scored right under the sticks. It was all so picture perfect that I almost cried – 31–3.

Things don't always go as well as this. Often you have to trade off the lesser evil against the greater, especially in defence. Against the really good sides, you can't defend everything. You have to make a choice and hope that it's the right one. For example, against Ireland the week after the Scotland match in 2005, there were plenty of headaches in trying to plan for the array of set moves they used to run off Brian O'Driscoll in midfield. The first problem was O'Driscoll himself, who was expert at drifting on to the outside shoulder of his opponent and scuttling through the gap. After much soul-searching, defence coach Clive Griffiths decided on a bold use of blitz principles. Tom Shanklin had been struggling to keep his position in the drift in one of our earlier games versus France, and Griff wanted to give him something simple and direct to do. So he instructed Tom to stay on the outside of O'Driscoll and take him head-on when he started to drift into the gap: 'Before the Irish game, we were well aware of the block plays they ran with O'Driscoll standing at inside centre and running an "overs" line with 12 blocking down hard to disrupt the drift as it shuttled across field. We discussed a slight angle in our backline defence so that we could buy a bit more time to make the tackle if they ran the play well. Line speed was also essential, but it wasn't kamikaze stuff. We looked at them in some detail and pored over the solution for hours.

'In the first half, they cut us with a block inside ball to Denis Hickie, where O'Driscoll went as if to go outside but then passed back in to the blindside wing who was trailing him. Shanks was too far across to help, and the inside defence was blocked out by Kevin Maggs [Ireland's inside centre] and couldn't get to Hickie. At half-time, we told Stephen Jones that he had to hold that inside channel at all costs – which would in turn allow Shanks to really put some heat on O'Driscoll.

'It proved effective, as Shanks hit him man and ball with the tackle of the match midway through the second period. O'Driscoll was bowled over and lost the ball. We forced them into touch, and from the subsequent lineout Kevin Morgan scored the try that took us into a winning lead. It was blitz at its very best. No time. No space. In your face. Shanks listened to me on that occasion, and he read the situation perfectly.'

We told Tom early in the week what we wanted him to do so that he could get used to the change in his mind first. The longer a player has to absorb a change mentally, the more his body will react as if it's second nature during the game itself. What starts as an intellectual process – moves rehearsed in the head – has to become instinctive by the time of the match. Reactions have to be instantaneous. I remember the hours Rob Howley spent in front of a tape I put together of George Gregan's characteristic moves before the 2001 Lions tour of Australia. By the time the Test series swung around, I think Rob knew George better than George knew himself. There was less George could do to surprise or unsettle him, so Rob had more time and Gregan had less. On that tour, Danny Grewcock and Jason Robinson were very much the same, always asking for footage of their next opponents. People probably thought that Grewcock was a bit of brute without a lot upstairs, but believe me he was very active in the department of mental preparation. He did his homework.

Changing Shanks's defensive outlook was a risky ploy, because we knew that with our centres split there was a real danger of Ireland coming back at us with a play underneath O'Driscoll into the large, relatively unguarded space between Gavin and Tom Shanklin. In the event, both scenarios came to pass: one moment O'Driscoll was putting Denis Hickie through the gap, the next he was being smashed man and ball and turned over. Ireland got to within one metre of our goal-line but were held up by some desperate defence, and we made the crucial score from our next attacking play after Shanks's demolition job. The line between winning and losing preparation is incredibly fine. What if Ireland had scored from their opportunity and we hadn't? Griff would have been feather duster rather than rooster. But he was a rooster that day, because he had the guts to make the call.

On the eve of that Grand Slam game in 2005, Clive Griffiths gave one of the best presentations I've ever seen. He showed a video to the players of Ronan O'Gara, the Irish outside-half, no more than six or seven minutes long. The material was mostly culled from a recent Heineken Cup match between Wasps and Munster, in which Paul Volley, the Wasps number 7, really got under O'Gara's skin. He tackled him late, he talked to him, he ran straight at him with the ball and he blocked down one of his kicks.

At the end, O'Gara was substituted and Clive pointed out the demoralising effect it had on the Munster team as a whole. It created an image in the players' minds of what would happen if we could perform the right actions on the field the next day. 'Get a picture in your mind's eye . . .' as Pross would say early in the week before a big match. What happened on that sunny Saturday afternoon had already in a way 'happened' the previous afternoon during that short, intense presentation by Clive. The seed had been planted, and when the boys saw O'Gara arguing red-faced with referee Chris White midway through the second half about a penalty decision that had gone against him, they knew that the image had become reality. O'Gara was replaced by David Humphreys a few minutes later, so that part of Clive's prophecy came true, too.

Preparation is only going to become more involved as computer techniques advance and the pool of available information grows ever larger. The public and the media demand it in the statistically rich sports arena in the USA, and we're still following the Americans in this respect. Rugby is still in its infancy as a professional sport – it's only 12 years old, remember – so trial and error is the order of the day. But analysis is already a huge growth industry, and the pace is only going to increase. Already Keith Lyons, the director of performance analysis at the Australian Institute of Sport, is talking about a kind of digital performance library being made available to the paying public, funding group discussions between people with similar sporting interests: 'What we can now start to do is link a number of people with an interest in performance together, to start to explore ideas, to develop ideas, to push learning, to do all the things that you might not be able to do alone. You might be able to do some things by yourself, but actually this idea now that you're not alone in Australia seems very, very powerful to us.'

You are not alone, whether it's in Australia or Wales. The most important lesson I've learned from my time in charge of the analysis department with the Wales national squad is that however minimal the human input becomes, it's still both the great intangible and the great essential. That close relationship between a Clive Woodward and a Tony Biscombe, between an Eddie O'Sullivan and a Mervyn Murphy, is priceless. The analyst has to have the coach's implicit trust to decode his intentions, spoken or otherwise, or else all the stats in the world won't help you. The human beings and their interactions, not the machines or the processes, are still the key.

9

BACK TO THE DRAWING BOARD

Time for the New Messiah. After a number of swings on the emotional pendulum, it wasn't until 24 March 2006 that Scott Johnson finally decided to leave Wales and go back to Australia. So the hunt was on for a new head coach, and the interviews took place over the next four weeks. Like Mike Ruddock in 2004, Gareth Jenkins didn't apply until fairly late on, and I learned afterwards that he only put his presentation together the day before his interview. Gareth was always a great 11th-hour man, preferring to work with the heat of inspiration upon him.

Gareth wasn't, however, the front-runner as the process started to unfold. Word crept out that Phil Davies, who coached Leeds in the English Premiership, had greatly impressed the five-man interview panel and was leading the field. In fact, the panel had apparently agreed his appointment, but when it went to the committee for rubber-stamping they dug their heels in and insisted on Gareth Jenkins instead. There was some rather theatrical talk of a new Welsh 'Messiah' in the tradition of Carwyn James taking up his appointed role – 'It's his time, it's his destiny' – as Gareth's appointment was duly announced on 27 April. I remember driving up to the Yorkshire Dales on a family holiday when I heard the news on the radio, and I rang Gareth to congratulate him. Curiously, he was heading in the same direction as me, travelling north to join his Scarlets players for a game up in Scotland.

In all honesty, I felt that the backroom staff should have been changed en masse after Gareth's arrival. People such as me, Alan Phillips and Carcass had been in the job for long enough – I had nearly 12 years on the clock and Carcass had over 14, which is quite unusual in top-class sport nowadays – and I think a total clear-out would only have been to Gareth's advantage. At certain points, you simply need to begin with a clean slate, and this was definitely one of those times. I know I felt ready to go, but I allowed my mind to be changed by the results of an independent audit conducted by a company called K2.

K2 was the brainchild of Keith Power, who became the youngest-ever national sports coach in Britain at the age of 23. He has since become a sought-after performance psychologist, working with elite athletes. Amongst rugby players, I know he has helped out Jason Leonard and Will Greenwood. Mostyn Richards was in no doubt about the value of the audit Keith Power conducted: 'Keith led a performance audit for the WRU, the results of which are invaluable to us as an organisation. My gut feeling and experience told me that we were good in some areas and could improve in many others – the audit backed this up. The audit ensured that by benchmarking everything, we knew exactly how good we were and where we need to focus our efforts. This will now allow us to maximise time, energy and resources.'

The audit had been exhaustive and ongoing throughout the last few months of Mike's tenure. The results of the K2 report, which were due towards the end of April, were sidelined for as long as possible. Inevitably, bits of information seeped out at the edges, and it transpired that the analysis department had emerged with flying colours. The players were particularly complimentary in their comments, which persuaded me to stay on if Gareth required my services. But the feedback from the report was never presented publicly, according to the original intention.

It was an unsettling time for Clive Griffiths. At first, he'd been encouraged to apply for the head-coaching role by David Pickering and Tim Burton: 'I knew the score right from the start. I wasn't kidding myself. Gareth was nailed-on to get it, but it was still very useful for me to experience that kind of high-powered interview process, with people such as Dai Pickering and Gerald Davies on the interview panel. So I wasn't too bothered when Gareth got the job. I'd had a chat with Gareth a couple of weeks before the interview, and Gareth told me that if he was appointed, he would want to keep me on as defence coach, with Nigel Davies coaching the attack.

'When Gareth got the job, I rang a couple of times to congratulate him, but he never called back, and I soon realised that something was up. Finally, I managed to avoid his answerphone and got to speak to him. He told me that I no longer formed part of his plans but didn't really give any reasons, other than the need to "freshen things up"! Gareth's U-turn really disappointed me, and I felt that something, or someone, must have changed his mind. The frustrating thing was that I'd been going down to Stradey at Gareth's request to take defence sessions with the Scarlets during their successful Heineken Cup run, so I knew he was comfortable working with me. Twenty-seven years of waiting for a Grand Slam and within eighteen months all the winning coaches are gone. Amazing.'

It turned out that Gareth was canvassing Mike Ford, with whom he'd struck up a friendly relationship on the 2005 Lions tour to New Zealand. But Ford eventually opted for England, and I found myself driving back up to the Barn from the Vale of Glamorgan Hotel with Gareth Jenkins in the passenger seat when he asked my advice on defence coaches. I mentioned Rowland Phillips as one of the promising young Welsh coaches – he was also one of Clive's protégés. I think finance was a mighty factor, and as a result all three of the assistant coaches – Rowland Phillips, Neil Jenkins and Rob McBryde – were taken on part-time, with Nigel Davies above them and Gareth quite a long way above Nigel. Even then there was quite a wrangle over their pay before everything finally settled down.

In June, Wales toured Argentina, and I sent Rhodri Bown with the party as part of his ongoing development. The summer tours provided an ideal learning environment, with a wider scope of tasks to be performed. Rhodri had been part of the summer tour to the USA and Canada the previous year and found it hugely beneficial. I had made plans to accompany him, as it seemed obvious that two analysts would be needed with the bevy of new coaches eager to impress, and this had been agreed and budgeted for by the management group. But after the coaching change, Alan Phillips did some improvised cost-cutting, and the allocation was stripped back to one.

Both younger and older players emerged with reputations enhanced from the first Test in Argentina, a narrow loss in a match that we could easily have stolen. The huge young Ospreys lock Ian Evans scored an interception try from almost 60 metres, and Duncan Jones was a big positive with his energy and enthusiasm both on and off the field. But a problem with the habits within the management group emerged between the two Tests. Standards of discipline off the field were erratic in the group as a whole. Mike Wadsworth remembers that he was often the only member of the group in bed by the wee hours of the morning: 'Every night there was something on. When we got to Buenos Aires and stayed at the Sheraton Hotel, the evenings seldom finished with dinner. A number of the players mentioned to me that they'd bumped into members of the management rolling back at two or three in the morning. It was quite pointed, and it had definitely been noticed. This wasn't something that had happened under Steve Hansen or Mike Ruddock, and it definitely affected the energy level of the coaches.'

I also noticed some unfamiliar regimes when the group returned from Argentina. Gareth and Nigel tended to come into work early, at around eight o'clock in the morning, and leave in the middle of the afternoon. Graham would often analyse games at four or five in the morning; Mike covered every minute of both our own and the opposition's performance on his ever-present A4 lined pad. Even Scott Johnson in his short time in charge would hold informal evening meetings over a beer until nine in the evening. So Gareth and Nigel's more relaxed approach left me walking around the Vale with a large question mark above my head.

Both Nigel and Gareth were very impressed by the quality of the analysis we were producing. I will never forget Nigel's face when he came into my office after reading Nick's report on Argentina. I'd just given it to him in a matter-of-fact sort of way and expectantly sat waiting for him to return. When he came back in, it was obvious he'd been blown away. His eyes were wide open, and all he could say was 'bloody brilliant'. He'd seen nothing like it. I worked hard to complete an audit of the analysis department during June and July, and Gareth Jenkins passed it on to Steve Lewis, praising its content and ideas, many of which were implemented before the sudden end of Gareth's tenure in April 2007.

Gareth had a very strong grasp of the big picture, tending to act more as a director of rugby, while Nigel did most of the on-field coaching and led the meetings and debriefs before and after training. Gareth would confine himself to walking around the perimeter of the pitch in observation mode during training, and in the meetings he would only chip in when he felt it was absolutely necessary. This was clearly the way they'd worked down at Llanelli, and I think it was their long-term expectation that Gareth would be elevated to director of rugby and Nigel Davies become head coach in due course.

Gareth was very keen on monitoring trends in the game and keeping abreast of global developments. When we plunged into analysis of the 2006 Tri Nations, I found that New Zealand were way ahead of the Test-match curve in some key areas, in particular the area of offloading and agility before contact. When they committed to the ruck, their clear-out efficiency was simply outstanding. Nigel also pinpointed other key areas, such as converting line breaks into actual scores – we'd made a lot of chances without converting them into points in Argentina – and 'jackaling' (contesting the breakdown ball) in defence. When Gareth spotted improvements that could be made within the national squad, he also wanted them communicated to and reproduced within the regions – that was the wavelength of his thinking. So there were reports and audits being carried out everywhere. It was the level on which Gareth tended to operate, at least until it became absolutely imperative for him to take control of the coaching after our disastrous defeat at Murrayfield in the second game of the 2007 Six Nations.

With Gareth effectively operating as a director of rugby and a new group chief executive, Roger Lewis, due to take up his post at the end of October, it was really putting the squeeze on Steve Lewis. Gareth was eating into his role from one end, and Roger Lewis was eating into it from the other, and Steve had nowhere to go, or rather, nowhere to stay. Gareth Jenkins was determined to get rid of that strange organisational model that had Alan Phillips and Mark Davies reporting directly to Steve Lewis, the model that had helped make Mike Ruddock's life a total misery. Roger Lewis's arrival gave Gareth the chance to appeal to a higher authority, an opportunity Mike never had, and he lost no time in presenting his views in the strongest possible way.

Steve Lewis must have seen the end coming, because one of his last actions in the latter part of the summer was to try and bring any remaining independent parties in the management group – principally me and Mike Wadsworth – into the fold as employees of the union or dispense with our services entirely. On 25 August 2006, Steve Lewis ambushed me at the Barn, asking if we could discuss the business relationship between Alun Carter Rugby Analysis (ACRA) Ltd and the WRU. He made me aware that the contract between the union and ACRA would probably not be renewed after September 2006. At the time, I didn't have too much of a problem with that, as long as a contingency budget could be made available for consultants such as Gareth Potter and Nick Bishop. I'd learned through experience that the thinking quickly becomes stale if it's all done 'under one roof'.

I didn't hear from Steve Lewis for a few weeks, and the next occasion our paths crossed was at a presentation given by Gareth and Nigel to the newly renamed High Performance Unit on Wednesday, 20 September. The presentation contained a mixture of what they had put in place so far and their vision of the future of Welsh rugby. Prior to this presentation, Steve Lewis put forward a structure for the management group. I watched the projector screen as it scrolled down through the names: 'Mark Bennett – head of conditioning'; 'Mark Davies – head of physiotherapy'; 'A.N. Other – head of performance analysis'. He actually followed this up by saying that the position was vacant – somewhat confusingly, as I was there specifically to help with Gareth Jenkins's presentation, sitting in the room as large as life and only a few yards away from Steve. In the backwash of such a calculated snub, I suddenly felt like the invisible man . . . Fortunately, Gareth and Nigel followed me out of the room as I vented my frustration and helped to calm me down.

Mike Wadsworth's services had already been terminated, and he'd been invited to apply for part-time service to the national squad during the autumn of 2006 and 2007 Six Nations – harsh treatment for somebody who'd worked solidly for the union since 1998 and remained loyal in an expanding market for physiotherapy and sports massage: 'I knew Steve Lewis could on occasion be quite aggressive and dismissive with the players, but he'd always been quite helpful to me personally. When he called me in for a meeting after Gareth had taken over as head coach, he presented it as Gareth's decision to drop the sports massage service I was providing. Obviously, there were three new assistant coaches, so I guessed there was nothing left in the WRU pot. Carcass later told me that the effectiveness of sports massage had no scientific support. They took on Hywel Griffiths as assistant physio to Mark Davies, and I know he didn't believe in sports massage either.'

On 17 September, we had to move from our house in Penarth. Cracks had started to appear in the front of the house, where some large trees had apparently absorbed too much of the moisture in the earth. Temporary accommodation was arranged in Sully to the west of Penarth whilst the building work was completed. Much as I enjoyed walking out in the morning at low tide and hopping across the rock pools and scattering crabs with Henry and Isabelle, it was a very stressful time, with the contract negotiations just beginning. I felt uprooted both personally and professionally, and it took fully three months before we were able to move back into our home, in time for Christmas.

The contract negotiations were by turns tortuous and torturous. I even started to keep a diary so that I could remember everything that had been said and done, offered, considered, agreed or set aside.

SEPTEMBER–OCTOBER 2006

MONDAY, 25 SEPTEMBER

Three regional games are set up and ready to be viewed first thing this morning. The first coach comes in at about 9.45 a.m., the remainder follow by 10.30 a.m.

11 a.m. Team selection meeting. It turns into a planning meeting for November, no warning given. Rhodri and I are trying hard simply to respond to the coaches' demands and concentrate just on that.

TUESDAY, 26 SEPTEMBER

I go to UWIC and interview seven candidates from a masters course on analysis. The intention is to recruit people for age-group analysis within the union. I run this by Mostyn Richards, the head of the technical department. He wants to discuss it further. I receive an email from Steve Lewis later that day asking where the budget is going to come from for this and have I informed the head of the technical department? I reply, reminding him that a contingency budget for the analysis department has already been agreed.

FRIDAY, 29 SEPTEMBER

Steve Lewis asks Caroline Morgan to come and get me. Gareth Jenkins has already asked me not to go in to Steve's office until he has spoken to me first. Steve Lewis comes to the door of my office and begins shouting across the room at me: 'I'm the chief executive. You'll come when I call you. Now get in here.'

Stung, I dig in my heels: 'No, I need to speak to Gareth Jenkins first.' Steve Lewis orders Rhodri Bown to go in instead.

I speak to Gareth Jenkins and Nigel Davies about Steve Lewis. Gareth asks what I have done to upset him so much. Gareth says that he is really hostile toward me. I then relate briefly what happened during Mike Ruddock's tenure and departure. Had a tough weekend after the contract talks thinking about it all.

MONDAY, 2 OCTOBER

Rhodri Bown and I are both formally invited to work for the WRU. We both sign fixed-term contracts to start work for the WRU on 1 November 2006. The contracts are due to end on 30 April 2008.

Gareth Jenkins invites me to take up the role of head of the analysis department, controlling the day-to-day running of the department, overseeing two other members of staff – Rhodri Bown and Andrew Hughes – and acting as the line manager for the consultant Jon Moore.

TUESDAY, 3 OCTOBER

Tim Burton discusses my concerns with the contract being offered to me and Rhodri Bown. Gareth Jenkins also talks to me. They state that these concerns will all be ironed out in due course.

SUNDAY, 8 OCTOBER

Gareth Jenkins meets with Roger Lewis for the first time. I help out with the presentations Gareth gives to the HPU [high performance unit] and the board. Gareth makes Roger Lewis aware of the need for a director of rugby within the WRU. Roger is enthused by what he has seen within the national squad so far.

I have my third contract meeting with Steve Lewis and Tim Burton on Friday afternoon. I agree a figure for my salary. I accept what they have to say reluctantly but call Tim Burton later and voice my displeasure at what they are offering Rhodri. I speak to Gareth Jenkins on Saturday. He assures me that he will talk to Tim and sort everything out. Another stressful weekend with little sleep.

For the first time, I have the opportunity to gauge the players' response to the coaches. Good judo session followed by contact session. The presentations following the two sessions are not well prepared, and there's a mixed response.

THURSDAY, 12 OCTOBER

The WRU (via HR manager Tim Burton) finally send Alun Carter Rugby Analysis Ltd a letter terminating the contract between the union and ACRA, backdated to the end of August 2006. From 2002, ACRA had been responsible for providing the analysis service to the WRU – before that it had been Carter Consulting. No contract was in place between 2002 and 2004, although a service was provided and remuneration given by the WRU. The union also paid the business for two months' extra service – September and October 2006.

FRIDAY, 13 OCTOBER

Roger Lewis, the new CEO, comes in with Gareth. He seems very affable and asks sharp questions. Bright and articulate – looks like he'll be very good for Welsh rugby. He sees the national squad set-up as a model for the union as a whole.

TUESDAY, 17 OCTOBER

I finally sign a formal fixed-term contract with the WRU but still flag up concerns about the contracts offered to me and Rhodri Bown. I send an email confirming that Gareth and Tim Burton have agreed to review the situation in April 2007. I feel utterly fatigued and stressed by this whole process. All this just two weeks before the start of an autumn series rugby campaign.

The build-up to the autumn series of internationals showed all the strengths and weaknesses of the Gareth Jenkins regime, while my own contract negotiations with the union remained up in the air, and painfully so. Gareth Jenkins again demonstrated his grasp of the big picture and ability to connect the national squad with the regions beneath them. With my support, he gave a presentation to the WRU board at the end of September, asking for funding to the tune of £100,000 for a technology proposal from Sportstech. They would regenerate our three-year-old computers and establish a streaming product for footage that would then be accessible throughout the union across the Internet. There would be a database system drawing all WRU information together in an easy-to-use format. The board approved the proposal. Again, success on the broader director-of-rugby level.

Gareth and Nigel made a flying start to the team's preparation for the autumn campaign. They started like a steam train. There were live sessions with the senior team trying out their strategies against the Under-21s and then a review of the film footage afterwards. There was a big emphasis on contact work and physicality, with Rob McBryde bringing in Neil Adams, the world champion judo player, to teach the secrets of leverage and balance in those close-contact grappling matches at the breakdown. All this was good.

But as we progressed through the autumn, the energy levels of the coaches dropped dramatically. As the long, gruelling sessions into the night took their toll, the coaches began to burn out as quickly as they'd flared at the beginning of the autumn. There were some unfortunate omissions and lapses as a result. After Huw Wiltshire had put out the cones for the game against the Under-21s in the week before the New Zealand match, he stood around on the pitch in isolation, waiting in vain for the senior squad to turn up. Someone had forgotten to tell Huw that the game had been cancelled.

A lack of attention to detail became evident. At another game-plan session before the final match against the All Blacks, we neglected to practise any of our attacking plays in the middle third of the field, between our own twenty-two and the opposition ten-metre line. There were crossed wires between Alan Phillips and the coaches so that the daily plan changed almost by the hour, and people didn't know what they were doing. Sometimes Gareth and Nigel would wrap things up quickly by the middle of the afternoon and head back to the hotel without telling Alan their plans. At other times, the day sheet would indicate one activity, while the coaches were anticipating another. It was all a little confusing.

The pattern of the autumn games reflected both the huge energy that had been put into the start of the campaign and the big drop-off towards the tail end. We drew a tremendously exciting six-try game against the Aussies first up, and this after virtually sleepwalking our way through the opening twenty minutes. We were down 17–6 after the opening quarter, and our captain Stephen Jones had already been replaced because of a leg injury. But James Hook came on and showed immediately that he very much belonged at Test level. He kicked perfectly, and we recovered well enough to be leading 26–17 entering the final quarter, though the Wallabies then came back at us with two further tries to retake the lead. Hooky slotted over another penalty to make the final scoreline 29–29.

We followed that with our best performance of the series against the Pacific Islanders and a much patchier win over Canada. Gareth's original idea had been to pick two separate teams for the first two matches and then play the side he expected to face New Zealand in the 'warm-up' fixture against the Canadians, although it didn't work out like that. There was a prevailing sense of uncertainty, and Gareth and Nigel clearly lacked the unshakeable, iron self-belief at Test level that had characterised the likes of Graham Henry and Mike Ruddock. They would regularly ask me how they were doing in comparison with their predecessors. I guess it was no surprise that we received our by-now traditional home stuffing from the All Blacks, 45–10, at the end of the November campaign. Within the coaching group, the tank was already empty.

This sense of uncertainty undoubtedly transmitted itself to the squad, and it extended to the way in which they selected the team. The coaches had perceptions about players that I found hard to share, based on the stats I had to hand and my own observations. Chris Horsman was a good example. Adam Jones wasn't then the player he is now, and Chris was well ahead of him in terms of his effectiveness in the scrum and the clean-out, and he had a very tough attitude to boot, but in the coaching and selection meetings I could never convince Gareth and Nigel, even though I had the stats to prove it. There were other examples: in the choices between Duncan Jones and Gethin Jenkins at loose-head, Ian Evans and Alun Wyn-Jones at lock, and Alix Popham and Michael Owen in the back row. Rob McBryde didn't rate Chris, and we'd fallen back to the Stone Age with Michael Owen, considering him only as a lock. Maybe it was another remnant of the Hansen–Johnson influence. Both had only ever seen Michael as a second row, and Chris Horsman had been brought in by Mike Ruddock, after all.

Another part of the problem was a poor grip of basic psychology. Above all, Gareth and Nigel didn't know how to handle Gavin Henson. Gavin had a thoroughly decent game against Australia, and he was much the most complete inside centre we had in the squad. Both Gareth and Nigel got too hung up on his negative body language at training, and they reacted by giving him a number of dressing-downs. That was completely the wrong way to handle Gavin. Gav is someone who thrives on encouragement and people pumping confidence into him, especially as he'd been injured and out of action virtually since the 2005 Lions tour of New Zealand. Gavin even tried to give them a hint, in his comments about James Hook after the Aussie game: 'I think it could be the start of a really good partnership [between me and Hook], and it would keep opposition defences guessing. He's a natural rugby player. It helps in these sort of arenas, because your instinct takes over. He just looks like he has played international rugby far longer than me.' But Gareth and Nigel kept on pressing him to live up to their behavioural model, and Gavin went from bad to worse, and then to worse still. It would all be so different in 2008, when Gavin would be made captain of the defence by Warren Gatland and Shaun Edwards and even relied upon to give perceptive opinions to the media before matches.

The Stephen Jones–James Hook media controversy was probably born out of the same inability to act decisively on facts you knew to be true. Gareth had decided on Stephen Jones as his captain, and he obviously knew him well from their days together at Stradey Park, but the autumn games had made it abundantly clear that James Hook was a real talent, and his best position was fly-half. There was a moment in the Australia game when both were on the field and we'd been given a penalty. Stephen just tossed the ball to James for the kick and walked away with his head bowed, even though he was the captain and designated goalkicker. It spoke volumes about their situation. The obvious solution, if Gareth wanted both players in the side, was to move Stephen to inside centre, a position for which Graham Henry had always felt he was well qualified and where he thought he'd end up playing at Test level. In practice, the only arrangement under consideration was Stephen playing at 10 and Hooky at 12.

Rowland Phillips also had his own problems as defence coach. Rowland was clearly a talented coach who had put together an outstanding squad at the Gnoll in Neath. But he'd been working at Welsh Premiership level, two hops down from the Test arena. In particular, the hop from regional to Premiership level was a very big jump. Rowland had been mentored by none other than Clive Griffiths at London Welsh before he moved back to Wales, but it looked very much like he was under instructions not to contact him once Clive became *persona non grata* again, which meant that Rowland had lost the mainstay of his intellectual guidance. Trying to manage the distance between Welsh Premiership and Test football without your trusted mentor was not recommended, especially as Rowland wanted to install a version of the blitzing scheme that had come to a nasty end during Mike and Clive's time in charge. Although he was good at creating a relaxed atmosphere among the boys and would always crack a joke with them, he struggled to stamp his authority in an area of the game in which Wales had creaked throughout the first two-thirds of 2006. On occasion, he'd review footage from a training session, but his study of it would be incomplete, and the boys would point out other possibilities he hadn't noticed. Then there'd be an awkward moment. To be fair, Rowland knew he was learning the ropes at this level and would ask for feedback from Rhodri and me, but it wasn't an ideal situation.

The autumn campaign left me feeling shattered, and wondering whether it had been the right decision to stay on under a new coach. The difficult contract negotiations with the WRU also spawned a whole host of second thoughts about the wisdom of giving up my own business to work for the union. The diary that I'd been keeping ever since the contract negotiations began started to take a real battering.

DECEMBER 2006

I go through a stressful month and stay away from work for some days in December. A combination of the stress following the contract talks and the pressure to get back into our house in Penarth finally gets to me.

At the debrief of the autumn campaign, I manage to publicly state how difficult it's been for both Rhodri Bown and me going into these internationals hard on the heels of the contractual talks, which had only just finished.

THURSDAY, 14 DECEMBER

Ashridge College run a training course with national management team, setting up values for the group to adhere to in the lead-up to RWC 2007, led by a sports psychologist, John Neal. I attend. An unwillingness to communicate is identified as a major problem within the group as a whole. The course is refreshing and gets the management group talking more directly. Interestingly for an analyst, I answer a questionnaire and discover that I'm more responsive to people than to data.

Jon Moore has a positive influence on the department, demonstrating to the boys what they can get out of the Mac computers they are using – there's iCal (a diary system) and iChat (a form of communication between users).

JANUARY 2007

In January, we meet up as a management group and discuss what the values that we have chosen mean to each of us. These are incorporated into a 'Welsh Way' document. Jon Neal suggests that the management group deliver their 'picture of performance' (a presentation of the values in a fun format) to the Welsh playing squad. It is decided that we will present this as 'wizards' and in costume!

There is feedback from the K2 audit held in the 2006 season by Keith Power. The analysis department comes out of it really well, with lots of praise. There is a group presentation and individual feedback, too. There are some important messages that coincide with what Ashridge are saying: 1. system processes need to be improved; 2. we need to challenge each other more as a group; 3. mental and emotional areas within the whole group, players included, need attention; 4. there is a need for role clarity; 5. WRU need both a performance director and a sports psychologist.

I point out to Gareth Jenkins that the K2 audit has re-emphasised key areas of concern that Ashridge also identified, even though the contents of that report have been largely ignored. This seems particularly important.

Early on in the build-up to the Six Nations, it is apparent that the coaches prefer Rhodri Bown to attend meetings, but even then his time with the coaches is restricted. This is difficult for us as a department. Much of what we do is coach-driven, and a good working relationship needs to be there between coach and analyst for us to function efficiently.

FRIDAY, 12 JANUARY

I meet with Jon Moore and Gareth Jenkins. After the autumn campaign, I have agreed to go forward with some of Jon's ideas for the Six Nations. I am not altogether happy, as I feel the autumn should be the testing ground for what we do during the Six Nations. We're trying to do too much too quickly. We agree that the real-time analysis live at the game should be done on Sportscode.

The squad for the Six Nations is selected. I am surprised to see two players there who had not been part of the autumn campaign – Chris

Czekaj and Scott Morgan. Normally, the Six Nations squad is the best that can be fielded. There are quality Welsh internationals who I think should be ahead of these two players, in the shape of Dafydd James and Michael Owen. In addition to their Test experience, these players are top of a number of categories by which we measure performance at regional level.

Gareth comes in after watching a Dragons game and isn't complimentary about Michael. I stick up for him and say, 'I thought he played well.' [I phoned Michael a couple of weeks later and asked him if he'd had any feedback from the coaches. He said he'd been told to improve his clean-out efficiency – ironically, one of the categories in which he was in our graded regional top five.]

The server is working, and we are encouraging all departments of the national squad based at the Barn to use this facility. It will help file sharing and file management. In the autumn period, it crashed in the middle of the campaign, causing all sorts of problems. Lots of data was lost. This problem has now been resolved.

THURSDAY, 18 JANUARY

I meet up with Gerald Davies, a member of the WRU board and a confidant of the new chief executive, Roger Lewis. We go to the Vale of Glamorgan Golf Club for a private chat over a coffee. He had quizzed me previously about the Mike Ruddock affair saying that he wanted to know more. I speak to him candidly, giving my interpretation of events. Gerald has already guessed a lot of what I tell him.

THURSDAY, 25 JANUARY

Alan comes into the office while I'm setting up the computer for a coaches' meeting. He says a painter needs to repaint the walls of the analysis room and would I help him choose the colour. I choose magnolia. Alan and Rhodri step into the office and wait for the coaches to arrive. I get the odd feeling in my gut that I've already been replaced somehow and that I'm surplus to requirements. Maybe Gareth is protecting me because I struggled in December. I don't know.

Gareth Jenkins is drawn away on this the first day of the campaign to give media presentations on the Welsh Way: a style of play that is inherent to Welsh players and Welsh rugby and one that he wants to carry through to the World Cup in 2007. I assign Andrew Hughes to work with Gareth on these presentations, freeing me up to run workshops with the players on the use of the server, with Rhodri Bown's help.

SUNDAY, 28 JANUARY

The management present their picture of performance to the players, dressed as wizards! Gareth reads from a big book like Dumbledore in the Harry Potter films. We all have tall pointy hats and home-made costumes, and some of us have beards. I am assigned to talk about Belief. I do this by reinforcing the belief in those who I work with – Rhodri and Andrew Hughes – belief in my own ability within this tournament born of experience and belief we can provide whatever it is that the players need.

I have strong words with Alan Phillips and Gareth Jenkins about the fact that just one analyst will be travelling with the team to away games. They had previously agreed that it was necessary to have two analysts to deal with the many needs of a large coaching team. At the threshold of the tournament, they are now telling me that only one analyst is affordable.

The Ireland game on 5 February 2007 was upon us before we had time to draw breath, what with the audits, the politics and the continuing need to 'sort out' Welsh rugby on a grand scale. It was the first occasion on which we were to try out Jon Moore's new live analysis system, and predictably it was a complete disaster. Six laptops were attached to the server, which had been transported to the Millennium Stadium to allow the computers to be used by coaches during the game and give them access to a live visual review and analysis updates as the match unfolded. We'd performed a dry run on Friday in which everything seemed to go fine. During the game, however, the computers all dropped to 'dead slow', and finally froze only 20 minutes into the match. There was nothing we could do. It was the only time I can recall during my time with Wales that we weren't able to provide any live feedback during the match. Rhodri and I just sat down and watched the game like the other 70,000 fans. Chris Czekaj made a big mistake in defence early on that put us behind, and we lost the game 19–9, despite having the majority of territory and possession.

I felt we'd been trying to accommodate Jon Moore's ideas for improvement far too quickly. It was a ghostly echo of Steve Hansen's demand that we take 32 laptops and a server by air to Italy for the first game of the 2002 Six Nations. I'd prioritised working with the national squad during the 2007 campaign, as it was a new and inexperienced coaching team, and asked Jon Moore to concentrate on the analysis project and communicate with all departments within the union to get them up to speed with the Apple Mac philosophy. Jon disagreed and clearly wanted me involved with the project more than the playing environment. The pressure from him grew steadily as the Six Nations campaign advanced, until he turned up unannounced in the third week of the tournament, just prior to a player-driven group analysis session. There were three groups of players (attack, defence and kicking), each requiring an analyst to lead them through the material in separate rooms. Jon started talking to my junior analyst, Andrew Hughes, who was due to attend one of the sessions. I had to intercede physically to get Andrew out of Jon's clutches and into the room. After that, I asked Jon to stay away for the remainder of the championship, while keeping him updated via my online diary.

So, the pressure on the analysis department was growing all the time. After the Italy match, for example, the stats report was delayed because of the lack of a broadband connection at the Stadio Flaminio, and there were black looks all round. The only two games that ran smoothly from a live analysis viewpoint were those against France and England.

Apart from providing reports on the opposition, I'd also asked Nick Bishop to scout each of our next opponents live and report his findings to the coaches. Nick came in to discuss his observations before the Ireland and Scotland games but was not invited back subsequently. Nigel Davies told me that he had things covered and we could just follow the reports. Nick had, however, noticed a big change in the atmosphere: 'The meeting before the Ireland game was very energetic, even though it occurred late in the afternoon. All the coaches bar Gareth Jenkins were there, and there was a lively question-and-answer session. I came away feeling that it had been a worthwhile exercise. The meeting before the Scotland game was very different. Gareth Jenkins was present and immediately took charge – he did most of the talking and questions from the other coaches dried up almost completely. I got the feeling that he just wanted to get the meeting out of the way as quickly as possible. There was also a noticeable lack of accuracy in some of the thinking: "Oh, so we just want to attack down the 10 channel then." It seemed very woolly. When I left, the sensation was that the meeting hadn't been of much use, and I really wasn't that keen to go back again. I certainly wasn't surprised when they stopped the meetings after that. Alun said that he'd get Nigel to email me with any questions, but I never heard from him.'

Nigel Davies had previously been very complimentary about Nick's material, which had been trusted and used extensively by coaches such as Mike Ruddock, Scott Johnson, Clive Griffiths and Graham Henry. But before the Italy game, Rowland Phillips and Robin McBryde tried to pick holes in the reports, and I could see that there was far too much resistance there to press the issue.

The 2007 Six Nations championship was really a tournament of two halves. The real low point was the second game against Scotland, in which we got smashed up front and hardly fired a shot in anger against a team that really struggled to create any positive attacking opportunities. Rob Sidoli, miscast as a front jumper, hurried into one second-half lineout in only his socks, and we generally played as if we weren't wearing any heads, let alone boots. Gareth was hurried into a press conference only ten minutes after the game had finished for a 'flash' interview, and he had no stats to hand as a result. It was a representative example of both the relationship between the coaches and the analysis department at the time, and communication within the management group as a whole.

In the week leading up to the France game during the second half of the Six Nations, Gareth took the team by the scruff of the neck. He almost literally pushed Nigel to one side and started taking sessions himself and questioning players – it was just the tonic we needed. He'd let Nigel have his head, and it hadn't worked, and by the time of the final game of the championship against England, Gareth was able to produce the kind of one-off performance in which he'd specialised when preparing his Llanelli side to face English teams in the Heineken Cup. However, even the England game exposed the flaws in communication within the management group that had been pointed out by the K2 and Ashridge audits. I'd contacted Kingsley Jones up at Sale to get background information on some of the England players, not knowing that Alan Phillips had been doing exactly the same with the Wasps analyst Rhys Long. Gareth took sustenance from both pools of inside information in his debrief to the players, but I couldn't be happy that the right and left arms of the management group weren't working in concert. Still, we managed to beat a poor England team quite handily, and, coming right at the end of the season, the win put a great deal of gloss on the failings that had preceded it.

Oddly enough, the atmosphere at the Six Nations debrief was very bumptious and upbeat. The sports psychologist John Neal led the meeting, and he asked in turn for positive and negative areas to be highlighted and linked back to the statement of values we'd agreed as a group before the tournament began.

2007 SIX NATIONS DEBRIEF

TUESDAY, 27 MARCH

At the start of the debrief on Monday, it is a case of 'nodding donkeys'. Everyone just wants to say the right thing. No one is challenging each other or saying what they really feel. After the success in the last match against England, everything is OK. Many of the issues and problems from the tournament are not mentioned.

Being unhappy in the current environment, I make a decision to 'let it all hang out'. I probably know the consequences of such an outburst deep down, but I realise I am suffocating slowly anyway. I bring up three areas of concern: 1. energy; 2. day sheets; and 3. the senior player group.

Energy – I start by referring to one of the values we chose as a management group at the start of the year: 'In the first four weeks of the tournament, we had a de-energised environment.' I'm asked to expand further: 'Coaches were turning up to important midweek preparation sessions unprepared. The research wasn't always thorough and timekeeping was poor. It was obvious. On one occasion, we weren't ready for a session while the players were waiting, and it was highly unprofessional.' This causes a strong reaction from Gareth Jenkins. It was only intended to draw attention to the fact that we need to be sharper and more aware of the effect we leave with the players. Gareth Jenkins and Alan Phillips do not perceive that there's a problem.

Day sheets – These are a complete shambles. Nearly every day there are wrong times and venues, and they have to be constantly corrected. This is mainly due to the coaches changing things at the last minute and not conveying that to the team manager.

Senior playing group – Senior players are influencing training plans to give themselves an easy life. If they say, 'We're too tired to do that today,' more often than not you find that the session's been rescheduled. It is also apparent that some of the senior players aren't carrying out their other professional responsibilities, such as completing online diaries. Again, this isn't considered to be an important issue.

This morning, Gareth Jenkins remarks that he hasn't slept well and needs to 'lay to rest' my comments from yesterday. I bring up more comments that were passed to me by Mike Wadsworth and the playing group on the Argentina tour. On my frequent visits to the regions, even the regional coaches have expressed concern about the stories their players brought back from that tour. I'd said nothing at the time and given the benefit of the doubt, but this seems like a better time and place to say something definite.

WEDNESDAY, 28 MARCH

I book a holiday for the family at Easter, because it has been agreed by Gareth and Alan that two analysts will be going to Australia in May. I need to take a holiday with the family now, because there will be no time in the summer whilst preparing for the World Cup.

FRIDAY, 30 MARCH

There are some interesting developments before I leave on holiday:

- I leave comment cards that we had to complete on each member of the management team for Jon Neal. They are 80 per cent positive in emphasis.

- Gareth has a two-hour discussion with Jon Moore and Alan Phillips in Thumper's room. I walk in, but I feel I'm not wanted there. When he emerges, Jon debriefs me on the areas he feels need attention from the Six Nations. Although no one has officially told me as yet, I know already that I am no longer Jon's line manager.

Jon Moore had a meeting with Tim Burton while I was away on leave. He shared a document with them about how he felt the technology project should be moving forward. I was never made aware of this document apart from a brief glance some two and a half weeks later, during a meeting on Tuesday, 17 April with Gareth Jenkins.

My major disagreement with Gareth Jenkins, which I aired during the debrief, was that we weren't creating a harsh enough environment for the players. They were still well within their comfort zone. It was contrary to everything I'd learned in my rugby education at Pontypool. The atmosphere felt lax and undemanding, and it aggravated me no end.

On my first day back in the office, Gareth Jenkins called me in with a very solemn look on his face: 'Jon Moore has indicated that he doesn't think you're the right man to take this project forward.' I reminded him that he picked me as head of analysis only six months ago and asked him where he stood. He replied, 'I don't know whether he's right or wrong, do I? He's the expert.' It was hardly a ringing endorsement, and at that moment images of Mike Wadsworth and Clive Griffiths flickered across my mind. I began to squirm uncomfortably, recalling how quickly they'd been cut adrift by Gareth. I remembered how Gareth had allowed senior players to control training sessions, or even have them changed to suit their needs, and how slow he'd been to insist on a high standard of time-keeping and preparation during meetings and sessions. I realised on the spot that he wouldn't support me. Within three weeks, I was history. Events must have been running in parallel, because in that same period two people whom I was close to died – Margaret Davies, our cleaner and a close personal friend for the better part of the previous eight years, and Aunty Aude, my father's sister. Margaret had a heart attack suddenly, and it all just amplified the atmosphere of instability.

MAY 2007

FRIDAY, 11 MAY

I receive a letter from Tim Burton stating that the head of analysis role has changed and that the union feel I do not have the ability or technical expertise to fulfil it.

MONDAY, 14 MAY

I meet with Tim Burton and present my qualifications to do the job. I list a number of things in my favour, and he appears to be both sympathetic and impressed, and I certainly come away feeling that I've made a good impression. On my return, Gareth and Alan Phillips looked surprised to see me back at the Barn.

TUESDAY, 15 MAY

With Alan present, Gareth and I have a discussion at 2 p.m. He opens by saying that the head of analysis role has changed from the one that I had originally been given. He speaks for both himself and Alan Phillips, saying that it is nothing personal against me. I was not perceived as having the ability and technical expertise to fill that role: 'The decision was made a number of weeks ago, and it has been difficult for us working with you in that knowledge.' Again, he repeats that it's nothing personal, but I'm less convinced with each repetition. He asks to shake my hand before hopping on the bus to the airport.

The squad leave for Australia this afternoon. None of the players will know I've left until they come back from the other side of the world – and some not even then! Gareth Jenkins tells Rhodri Bown and Andrew Hughes while they're waiting to depart at Birmingham Airport, but there is no formal announcement of my leaving and even some of the management don't know I've gone! I have not had the opportunity to say my goodbyes properly. I've become the invisible man. That is my reward for 12 years of honest slog.

WEDNESDAY, 16 MAY

I have a phone conversation with Robert Appleyard (a WRU skills coach). He has spoken to Jon Moore this evening, indicating that the Wasps analyst Rhys Long would be taking over my role within the union. Gareth Potter would certainly have been well qualified for the role if he had been given the opportunity to apply for it. Gareth worked at Llanelli under Gareth for four years.

My relationships with Alan Phillips and Jon Moore had poor history. By spring 2007, too much water had passed under the bridge for us to resolve disagreements and bitterness dating back at least five years. I certainly felt that our collective history would colour any judgements they made about me and my ability to fulfil the head analyst's role. There was definitely a clash of personalities at work. And throughout this sad ending to my career with the Welsh national rugby squad, I was aware of just how much the tumult of the previous 11 years had been informing my own personal situation in the 12th. In one sense, I had only myself to blame. I'd known I was probably ready to leave when Scott Johnson finished and Gareth Jenkins took over, so I guess it was inevitable that I would end up another plaything of Welsh rugby politics as soon as I made the decision to stay on. Just like Mike Ruddock, Clive Griffiths and Mike Wadsworth over the course of the previous 15 months . . .

10

PROPHETS FALSE AND TRUE

Mike Ruddock was my saviour over the next few weeks. Having endured much the same experience with the union in 2006, albeit on a much larger scale, he was in a good position to give me practical help and support. When I first talked to Mike after being sacked, he cut through all the crap immediately. 'How are you sleeping?' he asked. I hadn't been sleeping at all well, getting up regularly in the middle of the night to pace the corridors, with thoughts buzzing in my head, replaying the course of events endlessly and wondering if there was something I could have done differently. I was short of money, so that was a big part of the problem. At more than one point, I even considered selling the family home, which I had always looked on as a 'keeper' and intended to hand on to my own kids. My mum and dad were pillars of strength during an uncertain period of negotiation with the WRU. They offered Catherine and me the support we needed to cover our mortgage and living costs while I was negotiating with the union: 'This is our gift to you to help you through the next few months.' They'd always been as strong as iron for me, and here they were again, my solid bedrock.

Mum, Dad and I all travelled down to Devon to celebrate 'Founder's Day', the last day of school at Kelly College in Tavistock, where my daughter Emma had been schooled and was now head girl. There was a chapel service on Saturday in which Emma read from Ecclesiastes and a reception in a marquee in which she gave an address wearing a blue pin-striped suit and a red carnation. The headmaster, Mr Steed, explained to me later how well she'd done. I was so full of fatherly pride I thought I was going to burst. With Mum and Dad there to share the moment, there was nothing that could have been added to the day that could have made it any better. Emma reciprocated one month later, by travelling up to help celebrate Mum and Dad's 50th wedding anniversary at Brynich, with a wonderful spread courtesy of Steve and Cath Maggs. Meeting up with my sisters – Sara, Rachel, Elizabeth and Hannah – after a long absence was another special moment. I really appreciated the time I had been given, having had hardly a moment to look up from my computer during the previous 12 years.

Of course, I hadn't lost contact with my friends and colleagues who were still working within the union, and I'd spoken to two senior players. They all persuaded me that I was still considered part of the 'inner sanctum', so I had a pretty good picture of the chain of events in Australia over the summer. The grapevine was positively tingling with information, and many of the goings-on in the national squad were something of an open secret. All the points of observation I'd made during the 2007 Six Nations debrief seemed to have been exacerbated. The Wales squad had returned licking their wounds after losing the first Test narrowly to a last-gasp try, 29–23, then getting rolled over 31–0 the following Saturday in a humiliating rout.

According to my sources, for the first few days the players had been given their heads and were allowed to do whatever they wanted. This was unfortunately typical of my experience of the Gareth Jenkins era, and it could not have assisted the process of bringing the squad together before the World Cup and providing a leadership model the players would respect. I believe it was unprofessional, but the seeds had already been sown while I was still in place.

The lack of professionalism and the lax attitude towards drinking were a consistent theme all the way through to the World Cup in September 2007. According to one member of the 2007 World Cup squad, even as late as five days before the crucial group game against Fiji on 29 September, players were encouraged to enjoy a nice night out in Paris. The night duly turned into a morning, which then turned into an all-day affair. Not all the players were involved, but the majority were. They must have been experiencing the effects of the alcohol in training and the build-up to the game, if not during the game itself. The reaction to defeat in that final pool game was very much along the same lines.

If you want to find one difference in the way the culture of the national squad has changed after the handover from Gareth Jenkins to Warren Gatland, it is there in the players' response to defeat. After they had been heavily beaten by the Springboks in the first Test at Bloemfontein on 7 June 2008, Gatland was unhappy about the manner of defeat but pleased with their reaction to the loss: 'You want to see how they react to a disappointing performance, and it started on Saturday night. We went out for a meal after the match, and the players made a call themselves that they weren't going to have a beer. They went back to the hotel, had an early night and prepared themselves for Monday. When you see that sort of response from players you have been working with and you see that sort of maturity, you have got to be proud of that. From a coaching point of view, that's a very mature response from a group of players. They obviously believed they had let themselves down and let the country down, and a number of individuals who were disappointed with their performance were desperate to improve.'

I think Gareth Jenkins also made the same error of underestimating the importance of the World Cup warm-ups as had Steve Hansen. As in 2003, there was a big emphasis on conditioning programmes, and the importance of winning the games themselves receded correspondingly. It was as if an unhealthily large group of people had the opinion that it might actually be beneficial if we lost the warm-ups and kept our powder dry for the World Cup itself. Mark Taylor drew a comparison between the preparation for the 1999 and 2003 tournaments: 'In 1999, we came into the tournament on a high after winning a lot of matches, but we struggled with performances, whereas in 2003 we played much better rugby in Australia having lost to England by 40 points in the warm-up, which was a real low and affected the confidence of the boys.' This superstition about the 2003 World Cup was hard to shake. Everything, as they say, would be all right on the night. Except that it wasn't.

Far more appropriate was the comment offered by Rob Howley, later a successful part of the 2008 Grand Slam coaching team: 'The psychology of the warm-up games is you want to win the games and make sure that the things you have done in training, the policies in defence and attack that you have put in place, are effective. The only way you can do that is in the warm-up games, because training doesn't actually match the intensity of the games. So it's really important that things that have worked well are transferred from the training pitch against the likes of England, Argentina and France. Momentum will start with selection, and Gareth and his management team will be looking to pick their starting XVs against Argentina and France to give the team extra experience of playing together prior to the opening game.'

Our defence policy certainly wasn't effective after the Six Nations in the spring. We'd only conceded nine tries in five games in the tournament and achieved the best ratio of possession to score. Teams had needed more than 11 minutes of possession to score a try against us. That all changed, starting with the Australia tour. The low point was a nine-try defeat to England at Twickenham on 6 August, in which England made a succession of simple scores off the back of scrums and lineouts that they hardly had to work for. It could scarcely even be called a World Cup warm-up, because the only thing warming those heavy English forwards on such a bright and sunny day was the weather itself. Effort-wise, they never had to break out of a gentle trot. It was embarrassing.

Gareth made it worse afterwards with some misguided comments about how they weren't prepared for an England onslaught up front and had expected a wider focus of attack – despite the fact that England had picked a heavy pack, with three men of six feet four inches and over, weighing more than seventeen stone each, in the back row . . . In the course of the August to September period, our average of tries-per-game conceded ballooned from 1.8 to almost 4. The opposition in three of those seven games was provided by Fiji, Canada and Japan, so the average against the top-tier nations was really closer to five tries per game. That is nowhere near Test-match standard.

And so to that fateful afternoon: Saturday, 15 September 2007. When I sat down to watch the key Wales v. Australia group match on TV, I was hoping for the best but fearing the worst. Although the Wallabies had been forced into making a late change at outside-half, with young, untested Berrick Barnes replacing Stephen Larkham, I didn't honestly believe that our coaching group would be going that extra mile to find footage of Barnes and find something they could use, making the same extra-curriculum effort that Graham had made before the 1999 Springbok game with van Straaten. The first 25 minutes said it all. Wales used the same attacking ploys from set-piece that Nigel always used, attacking wide and not once asking questions of Australia's late replacement. The best we could offer in that crucial first half was a crude late challenge by Alfie Thomas after Barnes had just delivered a scoring pass for the Wallabies' opening try. It was a fitting epitaph for the manner in which we prepared for the tournament.

What has thrown Gareth and Nigel's failings into sharper relief has been Wales's unbroken run of success since they left, with roughly the same bunch of players under a new coach in New Zealander Warren Gatland. I know Mike Ruddock sent Warren a message of congratulation after he was appointed, and it's become evident that Gatland has sought out and trusted good counsel. I don't think Warren and Shaun Edwards have put a foot wrong in their handling of the squad, and they've certainly addressed all of the problems that seeped out of the Gareth Jenkins era.

As Graham Henry says, 'I think Warren has started with a huge advantage, because he knows the players and the opposition so well from his time in Ireland and with Wasps. When I first came to Wales, I didn't know anyone, and I was thrown completely out of my comfort zone. When I asked for advice about players, I didn't know whose opinion to trust, because I learned that opinions often varied with the geography. But both Warren and Shaun Edwards have that other huge advantage, that they're above the "villageism" of it all. They're not from

Wales, so they don't have any regional axes to grind. People are selected on merit.'

Warren Gatland started by creating a level playing field in which no player or group of players was seen to be more favoured or influential than any other. He was greatly helped by the fact that the cabal of senior players established during Steve Hansen's time – the trio of Gareth Thomas, Stephen Jones and Martyn Williams – had already dissolved. Alfie had just retired from international rugby so wasn't a factor, and Martyn had also briefly retired after the 2007 World Cup so was in no position to dictate to Gatland the terms of his return. Stephen Jones, meanwhile, was generally considered to be playing second fiddle to James Hook in the fly-half stakes. Personally, I wouldn't mind betting that Stephen and Martyn were actually quite relieved to have a character as strong as Gatland in charge, relieving them of the 'political' responsibilities they appeared to carry around as a burden throughout the previous regime.

Others who had wielded a certain amount of influence under Gareth, such as Tom Shanklin, were given the blowtorch treatment. Shanks didn't start against England when he was clearly expecting to. As Shanks put it in his BBC online diary:

> I've never had a coach screaming in my face before, but do you know something? It's great. That's part of life under the new Wales coaching regime. Warren Gatland and Shaun Edwards are blunt, direct and say it as it is. They do not beat about the bush – they say it straight away. I could repeat some of the choice words Shaun has used, but perhaps swearing is not the way to go in this column . . . People should have seen the effect he, Warren and the other coaches had on the team at Twickenham. It is a no-nonsense approach, and all the boys respect it.

Respect. It's all there in that one word. Suddenly, there was no doubt about who was in charge and who was taking the orders. A clear boundary was established. Gavin Henson, always an outsider in the Gareth Jenkins era, immediately noticed a difference when he spoke on *Scrum V*: 'They [the coaches] are pretty strict, and they command respect. We are all living on the edge. Everyone knows that they are one bad training session away from not being picked. We had a poor session the other day, and Warren Gatland was speaking his mind at lunch, saying that perhaps we should change the side . . . Everyone can see who the coaches are and who the players are. Before, we had senior players who would voice up a lot, and you did not know whether to listen to them or the coaches. Sometimes, the senior players would overrule the coaches, and it did not quite work, I felt. It has totally turned around now. You know where you stand with these coaches, and that is when you react the best.'

Gatland reinforced his own position by rotating the squad throughout the Six Nations in 2008. He wasn't afraid to make gutsy calls and change apparently key players before big matches, swapping Stephen Jones in for James Hook after Hook's virtuoso kicking performance at Twickenham, and swapping Steve out again after he'd played well against Ireland for the finale against France. Any player who thought he might not have a challenger for his place, was challenged – Adam Jones was replaced by Rhys Thomas for the Italy game, and even the captain Ryan Jones came under pressure for his spot prior to the match in Dublin.

In view of the past, I felt it was a highly symbolic moment when Wales finally adopted a blitzing scheme of defence under Gatland and Edwards. Of course, when Clive had tried to introduce the blitz in 2004, it had been rejected by both Scott Johnson and the players with whom the Australian had such a close relationship. It compromised Mike Ruddock's authority and gave the players the inch that eventually persuaded them that they could go the whole mile during the events of February 2006. That compromise was encapsulated in the word Clive coined for the mongrel form of defence that he was forced to evolve to keep all parties happy – the dritz. But there were no ifs or buts about the style of defence in 2008. The likes of Shanks and Gethin Jenkins and Stephen Jones were dumped temporarily, 13 Ospreys (who were used to the blitz) were picked and the players were simply told, 'This is what you will be doing.' It was an astute political manoeuvre by Gatland. Moreover, Shaun Edwards went on to prove what Clive Griffiths already knew in 2004: that the blitz could be a match-winner at international level. Wales conceded a meagre two tries in five matches in the 2008 Six Nations.

Another positive aspect of the selection and preparation of players was that it demonstrated the common sense that on occasion went missing under the likes of Steve Hansen. Gone was the sense of the national squad as a kind of advanced training academy. Gatland and Edwards had players doing what they did best, and doing it repeatedly. Ian Gough, for example, was told by the coaches to concentrate on hitting rucks and to forget about the fancier parts of the game, such as handling and passing. And Gethin Jenkins was asked to scrummage, hit rucks and make tackles, taking advantage of his prodigious work rate. This wasn't Test fairyland any more. It was about the consistent repetition of established strengths built over the course of a career in professional rugby. Ian Gough came off the field against Italy having hit a monumental forty-seven rucks, which had resulted in him losing five kilos in bodyweight during the course of the game.

Psychologically, Warren and Shaun have also proved a lot shrewder than Gareth and Nigel. Gatland clearly recognised that he had a major talent on his hands in Gavin Henson and was determined to find a way to get the best out of him: 'Shaun and I specialise in this kind of player. We had a joke about it at Wasps and called ourselves "The Home for Wayward Players".' They pumped confidence into Gav and made him a defensive captain. Although quick to administer kicks up the backside for breaking team rules, Warren Gatland was just as quick to forgive Henson when he showed the desire to get back on the rails. Although Gavin's rowdy gaffe on the train back from an Ospreys game in London counted against him, it did not do so terminally.

With Gatland's experience in Ireland and Shaun Edwards' experience of Welsh players from rugby league, there was also a shrewd assessment of the Celtic temperament. The ex-Connacht prop Peter Bracken, one of Edwards' charges at Wasps, remembers Shaun Edwards saying that as Celts tend to burn on a shorter fuse, they generally need to be psyched down rather than up: 'He would be trying to gee up other guys by shouting and roaring, and then whisper to me, "That does not apply to you."' So Warren and Shaun immediately came to the same conclusion that Graham Henry reached after two Six Nations losses in

1999: that the top three inches needed to be kept ice-cool within that burning Celtic brain. Coolness and clear thinking under pressure were among the salient features of the 2008 Grand Slam side, especially during Mike Phillips's sin-binning in the Ireland game when Wales kept the ball for almost the whole of those ten short-handed minutes and quenched the fire of the home crowd at Croke Park.

The 2008 training regime is clearly a harsh, unforgiving one in the best Pontypool style. Gatland and Edwards have been striving hard to create a training environment that has some of the intensity of an actual Test match. Sessions are short but brutal and represent the amount of ball-in-play time during a real international – about 30 to 40 minutes – so the mental aspect has to be spot-on. They set up sessions that addressed both individual and area weaknesses from Gareth Jenkins's side, such as defence. As Shane Williams said, 'The World Cup showed that . . . our defence was not good enough, and Shaun has really put us through our paces . . . [He] is very intense and emotional, and he has given me special defence sessions. He has had me working with the back row and the centres. We battered hell out of each other, and Shaun joined in.' Live drills, in real time and on a clock. Pressure forcing you to the physical limit. It's very much the same formula used by Pross and Graham Henry, allowing for the difference in rugby generations.

I'm sure it's no accident that Shaun Edwards is a northerner with blue-collar values. There's an emphasis on work ethic, on producing results through sheer hard work and bloody-mindedness when the going gets tough, that comes straight out of the mines and the steelworks. You do your job and you do it as hard as you can, then you can relax, as Rob Howley remembers from his time at Wasps: 'Shaun would get the backs in early one morning and have them work incredibly hard on one aspect of their play. At the end of the session, he would invite them to a diner in Ealing for breakfast and pay the bill.'

One of Mike Ruddock's big aims was to empower the players and encourage them to behave as a community. Graham Henry always used to emphasise the need to act with a degree of poise and good humour, and above all to act socially, with a sense of responsibility to your mates and the people around you. It was enshrined in his code of conduct. However, this was something that went missing under Gareth Jenkins's stewardship. There was one incident in particular, a visit to a restaurant in Pontypridd between the Scotland and France games during the 2007 Six Nations, that demonstrated this. The whole squad was there, but the boys became a little disgruntled when the food took a long time to emerge. The one and only waitress was looking more than a little harassed with so many customers, and with all the running around she slipped and took a fierce tumble to the floor. As she lay there, clearly in some distress, a remarkable thing happened. Absolutely nothing. Not one of the boys raised a finger to help her – they just stared at her rather indifferently while she struggled on the floor.

It's a small point but one you couldn't have imagined happening with a Shaun Edwards or a Graham Henry in the vicinity. With characters like that, a team remains a team in all circumstances, and the sense of community and comradeship steadily moves out beyond its immediate circle . . . That's part of the Welsh Way, it's part of the Gwent rugby communities I grew up with and it's part of the working-class traditions of south Wales generally. You look after your mates, whatever the circumstances. Trust, loyalty and sometimes harsh honesty: these are the values that I feel are important. They are the values that have underpinned all the successful national squads over the past 12 years, with Graham Henry, Mike Ruddock and Warren Gatland at the helm.

For that matter, I don't think that incident would have occurred with Steve Hansen and Scott Johnson in charge either. Steve Hansen would never have let a little thing like that go unquestioned. However, for all their good work in creating a comradely spirit within the squad itself, I never felt Scott and Steve extended the hand of trust as definitely to other members of the management group, or to the coaches that followed them, as they did to the players. It was as if the wagons were drawn in too tightly and the players had invested too heavily in Steve and Scott, and it was almost impossible for anyone else to enter that charmed circle. When Mike took over in 2004, he didn't have the chance to penetrate the players' hearts and minds, even if he was able to improve several aspects of their performance as a team. The end result was a cataclysm in February 2006, only ten months after the first Grand Slam for Wales in twenty-seven years. Gareth Jenkins was still experiencing the fallout at the World Cup in September 2007 and wasn't strong enough to reverse the trend. It took a new coach and a very strong character in Warren Gatland to create a fresh start and build on the playing foundations that were still very much in place from 2005 to 2006. At least he has been strong enough and concerned enough to help the old lady of Welsh rugby back to her feet and get her walking the town again.